The world's largest collection of visual travel guides

Corsica

This edition updated by Alphons Schauseil

Editorial Director: Brian Bell

Part of the Langenscheidt Publishing Group

INSIGHT GUIDES

Corsica

CONTACTING THE EDITORS: Although every effort is made to provide accurate information in this publication, we live in a fast-changing world and would appreciate it if readers would call our attention to any errors or outdated information that may occur by writing to us at Apa Publications,
P.O. Box 7910, London SE1 1WE, England.
Fax: (44) 171-403 0290.
e-mail: insight@apaguide.demon.co.uk.

First Edition 1990
Third Edition (updated) 1999

Distributed in the United States by
Langenscheidt Publishers Inc.
46–35 54th Road
Maspeth, NY 11378
Fax: (718) 784 0640

Distributed in the UK & Ireland by
GeoCenter International Ltd
The Viables Centre, Harrow Way
Basingstoke, Hampshire RG22 4BJ
Fax: (44) 1256-817988

Distributed in Australia & New Zealand by
Hema Maps Pty. Ltd
24 Allgas Street, Slacks Creek 4127
Brisbane, Australia
Tel: (61) 7 3290 0322
Fax: (61) 7 3290 0478

Worldwide distribution enquiries:
APA Publications GmbH & Co. Verlag KG
(Singapore branch)
38 Joo Koon Road, Singapore 628990
Tel: 65-8651600
Fax: 65-8616438

Printed in Singapore by
Insight Print Services (Pte) Ltd
38 Joo Koon Road
Singapore 628990
Fax: 65-8616438

This guidebook combines the interests and enthusiasms of two of the world's best known information providers: Insight Guides, whose range of titles has set the standard for visual travel guides since 1970, and Discovery Channel, the world's premier source of nonfiction television programming.

The editors of Insight Guides provide both practical advice and general understanding about a destination's history, culture, institutions and people. Discovery Channel and its Web site, www.discovery.com, help millions of viewers explore their world from the comfort of their own home and also encourage them to explore it firsthand.

To capture all the diverse richness of an island such as Corsica takes a guide book which can reflect its beauty and describe all its idiosyncrasies and charms. Why, ever since antiquity, has Corsica been regarded as "the island of beauty" and rough and wild at the same time? And the Corsicans? Are they really the taciturn, gloomy, melancholic and choleric individuals as portrayed by the German Ferdinand Gregorovius (1852), whose tempers are unleashed in acts of blood revenge, here called *vendetta*? Or is their character better epitomised by their proud love of freedom and limitless hospitality, for which they have been admired and respected since time immemorial?

These are just some of the questions examined by this book, which provides a vivid picture of the island's stunning landscape and reveals the enduring culture of a people who were so close to James Boswell's heart when, in a letter to Samuel Johnson, he wrote: "Empty my head of Corsica! Empty it of honour, empty it of humanity, empty it of friendship, empty it of piety."

Insight Guides are famous for their photojournalism and their incisive texts, which ensures that *Insight Guide: Corsica* is an ideal introduction to the island. After background features on history and culture, *Insight Guide: Corsica* presents a Places section describing the island in detail, backed up by a Travel

Moulijin

Schültz

Schauseil

Lücke

Geiss

Tips section containing all the practical information a visitor needs.

Jutta Schütz, a writer and journalist from Darmstadt in Germany, took charge of assembling a team of expert writers and photographers who could provide a true insight into the island. Schütz, a regular visitor to Corsica, contributed generously to both text and photography.

For an authoritative view of various aspects of life on the island, Schütz turned first to two Corsican journalists. **Dominique Ettori** works in Corsica for *Radio Monte Carlo* and **Antoine Gannac** is a producer at *Radio Corse Frecuenza Mora*. These articles were translated from French by **Christine Hallacker**.

However, Schütz thought it best to leave the description of the Corsicans themselves not to a Corsican, but to someone from the outside who has an intimate knowledge of their ways. The task was assigned to **Dr Alphons Schauseil**, an experienced German journalist who has lived on the island since 1982, working as a freelance writer and photographer. He has settled in a village in the Balagne and, with a weather eye on the island's comings and goings, he has kept the book up to date, supplying the updated text for this new 1999 edition.

Richard S. Moulijn studied politics and law and has lived in Switzerland as a freelance journalist and author since 1971. His first trip to Corsica was in 1965, since when he has returned many times. For this book, he described the east coast and the scenic mountain route from Corte to Sartène; he also pieced together the practical information for the original Travel Tips section.

Dr Hartmut Lücke is the geographer in the team. He has been concentrating his research on the island since 1966, and has a string of publications to his name. He provides this book with a summary of the island's geographical make-up, examines the various landscape features, and explores the realm of present-day politics.

Ruth Merten and **Ilse Tubbesing** are experienced travel writers for whom the "Ile de Beauté" has long been close to the heart, a fact reflected in their articles on the west coast and the southern tip.

Heidemarie Karin Geiss was sailing in the Mediterranean when she was driven on to Corsican shores by a storm. She immediately fell in love with the island and it wasn't long before she returned to consolidate those first impressions. For this book, she anchored out in the harbour at Bastia and made trips ashore to sample the local cuisine; she also contributed to the history section.

But the ups and downs of Corsican history were primarily the preserve of **Dr Gerhard H. Oberzill** from Vienna. For more than three decades, he has worked all over the world as a travel guide and writer and he was a contributor to *Insight Guide: Madeira*.

The journalist **Anita Back** deals with Corsica as seen through the eyes of the poets and reports on what she saw at the Festival of the Virgin Mary in the Niolu. This glorious mountain region and the hiking trails in Corsica's national park are described by **Gert Hirner**, who has published a number of books for hikers, including one about Corsica.

Particular attention was paid to picking the most stunning photographs of the destination. Many pictures in this book are the work of the Hungarian photographer **János Stekovics**, who has lived in Germany since 1989. He has taken part in several exhibitions of artistic photography and has won a number of prizes. **Guido Mangold** and **Werner Stuhler** also provided some memorable shots. The pictorial palette was completed by **Jutta Schütz**, **Patricia Bonnin**, **Hartmut Lücke**, **Neill Menneer**, **Ken Wright** and **Christine Osborne**. Thanks go to **Lyle Lawson** for her assistance with the photo edit.

Thanks are also due to the **Maison de la France** in Frankfurt, the **Comité Regional de Tourisme** in Ajaccio (especially the ever-helpful **Michèle Narducci**), **Karin** and **Rolf Köllges**, and **Air France** for their generous support and assistance. The book was translated into English by **Jane Michael-Rushmer** and **David Ingram**. This edition was supervised in Insight Guides' London office by **Tom Le Bas**.

CONTENTS

Maps

TRAVEL TIPS

AN ISLAND OF SURPRISES

Corsica has many faces and many names. Geographers tend to refer to it simply as *"Ile des Contrastes"*, while writers have fondly called it the *"Ile de Beauté"* and the tourist brochures often sing its praises as the "Queen of the Mediterranean islands". But no single phrase can provide sufficient description of an island with such a varied landscape and temperament as Corsica.

Approaching Corsica by ship, a visitor will at first have the impression of a single majestic mountain range jutting straight out of the sea. Although its topography is considerably more complicated than that, Corsica is indeed the most mountainous island in the Mediterranean; within only a few kilometres of the shore are landscapes of soaring peaks, dramatic gorges, rushing torrents and magnificent pine forests. The island extends from Cap Corse in the north to Capo Pertusato in the south, a distance of 183 km (114 miles), and from Capo Rosso to Alistro, its widest point, at 83 km (52 miles).

Mountainous backbone: Closer examination will reveal that the topography of Corsica resembles a skeleton. The backbone of the island is linked by more than 20 mountains over 2,000 metres (6,562 ft), including the impressive Monte Cinto (2,710 metres/8,891 ft), the island's highest peak. As the main watershed, this great ridge of mountains, often as little as 30 km (18 miles) from the coast, runs from the northwest to the southeast, dividing the island into two halves of approximately the same size: the western half called by the locals *"Au delà des monts"* (beyond the mountains, when looked at from the direction of the Italian peninsula) and the eastern half which they refer to as *"En deçà des monts"* (this side of the mountains).

The high mountains, which make up no less than 47 percent of the island's total area, are broken by only four passes: the Col de Vergio, Col de Vizzavona, Col de Verde and Col de Bavella. This geographical divide has always had a decisive role to play in the

fortunes of the island and its inhabitants; all down the centuries, when barely a road existed and the only means of transport was on foot or by mule, Corsica was virtually split into two separate entities. La Haute Corse and La Corse du Sud, the two French *départements* which make up the island today, roughly follow this ancient *En deçà* and *Au delà* partition.

Corsica's mountain landscape is characterised by rugged peaks, jagged ridges, steep slopes and deep valleys – a paradise for

mountaineers, hikers and skiers, rock-climbers and pony-trekkers. High corries and the rock formations left behind by moving glaciers are unmistakable evidence that the higher elevations of the island were subjected to the rigours of the Ice Age. Even in summer, patches of snow are still to be found at altitude. A number of mountain lakes, such as Lac Cinto, Lac Bellebone, Lac de Nino or Lac de Creno are further evidence of the glaciation that took place during the Pleistocene era.

Forests and gorges: Glacial activity ended at the milder altitudes of today's canyon-like river valleys. Classic examples of such

Preceding pages: Napoleon statue; chalk cliffs near Bonifacio; the Calanche near Piana; Solacaro is steeped in history. **Left**, Restonica Valley. **Above**, a climber's paradise.

ravines are the much-visited Scala di Santa Regina as well as the gorges of Restonica, Asco and Spelunca. This is also the level at which the forest begins, and Corsica possesses some of the most beautiful forests of any Mediterranean island, indeed of anywhere in Southern Europe. A particularly characteristic tree is the Laricio pine, which can grow to heights of more than 40 metres (130 ft). Large stands occur in the forests of Valdu Niellu, Barocaggia, Tartagine, Aitone and Vizzavona.

Streams cascade between the trees. There are deep pools and waterfalls. And when the stone hut (*bergerie*) of a shepherd appears in a clearing, then the scenery of the mountain

tain massif primarily consists of granite formed during the late Palaeozoic era about 350 million years ago. Since then the granite has been weathered into bizarre formations which can be seen up to a height of around 2,000 metres (6,500 ft). Rock cavities are the most common feature, created by weathering of the lines of weakness in the rock structure which gradually gouged out the core of the crags. "Windows" to these caves were subsequently created when the elements broke through the rock faces.

Then there are rocky summits which rise steeply for several hundred metres above the level of the main mountain ridge. Because of their shape they are called "bell" mountains

forest is complete. During the summer months the shepherds make their delicious curd cheese called *brocciu*.

Cul-de-sac valleys: From the main ridge of the island, countless subsidiary ridges descend like ribs down to the coast to the east and west. They are separated by long valleys, such as the Filosorma, Sorru, Cinarca, Ornano and Tallona. Each of these is a cul-de-sac with no easy access to the neighbouring valleys. This inaccessibility has for centuries made them ideal sanctuaries for the local inhabitants, seeking refuge from conquerors or pirates from across the sea.

The geological make-up of the main moun-

or "helmet" mountains. An impressive example can be found on Monte Tritorre near Guagno.

A further natural wonder of a very special kind can be seen in the gigantic "rocking stones". Only the tips of these huge boulders actually rest on solid rock; they are balanced in perfect equilibrium despite the efforts of nature to topple them from their pedestals. A spectacular example is the Uomo di Cagna (Man of Cagna) near Sartène. The locals maintain that the outlines of the boulders resemble animal and human figures, and many of them are named accordingly. The granite crags of Les Calanques above the

Gulf of Porto have also been worn into bizarre forms resembling fabulous animals.

Chestnut country: The mountains in the north-eastern part of the island are generally much less rugged than those of the main central massif. The contours are more gentle and rounded and much of the area is covered in forest. The highest mountain in the area is Mont San Petrone (1,800 metres/5,905 ft)). Most of the passes do not go any higher than about 550 metres (1,800 ft).

Geologically speaking, this area is younger than central and western Corsica and is composed of different rock types. Its base consists of a mantle of schist, a metamorphic crystalline rock. During the course of the

Springs bubble forth from the limestone in abundance, a fact which has had a great influence on the settlement and cultivation of the area: this is the most densely populated part of the entire island.

A varied coast: Many tourists to Corsica come here for its fantastic beaches. In fact there are three types of coast along the island's 1,000 km (over 600 miles) of shore: straight coast, gulf coast and cliffed coast.

In the east, the mountains rise from a flat coastal belt of up to 12 km (7½ miles) in width which drops in a series of shallow terraces into the Tyrrhenian Sea. In the north, in the regions of Marana and Casinca, this is known as the Plain of Biguglia; in the south

alpine orogenesis – the Tertiary period of mountain building – this was submerged by a layer of Triassic and cretaceous formations consisting of limestone and conglomerates advancing from the east.

It used to be said that the inhabitants of this area nourished themselves from the "bread of the forest" and drank the "wine from the rocks". One only needs to take a stroll in the forest to understand why: edible chestnuts as far as the eye can see. Even in the height of summer the region looks fresh and green.

Left, there is more rock than beach along the West Coast. **Above**, lush vegetation near Aullène.

as the Plain of Aléria. In between, in the Tavagna and the Compoloro, the belt is narrower because the hills of the Castagniccia Massif reach to within only 3 km (2 miles) of the shore. In a broad curve between Bastia and the Solenzara estuary 90 km (56 miles) to the south, this stretch of coast is characterised by its fine, sandy beaches.

In the course of time, the two longest rivers on the island, the Golo and the Tavignano have transported vast amounts of material from the interior of the island. Arriving at the sea, the alluvium gets washed along the coast by the current and the waves. The sand bars and marshy lagoons so typical of this stretch of coast have been created from the resultant deposits. The sand bar to the north of the Golo estuary is more than 10 km (6 miles) long and forms a barrier between the sea and the Etang de Biguglia, the largest lagoon in Corsica, which is rich in fish. Such lagoons are also to be found along the southern coastal belt which begins around Alesani: Etang de Diane, Etang d'Urbino and Etang de Palo.

At one time, the coastal strip was virtually uninhabitable and deserted, not only because of the constant invasions from across the sea, but also because the marshlands provided excellent breeding grounds for the anopheles mosquito, a character that plagued the region right across the centuries, until its

final irradication by DDT after World War II. Since then, drainage and irrigation systems, which were first established here by the Romans, have been put in place and the area transformed into the largest intensively irrigated area of cultivation on Corsica, a development repeated in the rapid expansion of tourism on this side of the island.

While tourism booms along the sandy beaches of the east coast, those with a taste for the dramatic should explore the north and west, where the coastline looks very different. The mostly granite formations provide for a constant fluctuation between sandy and rocky shore. Here, the subsidiary ridges of

the west Corsican mountains often reach right down to the coast, where they then drop, often for hundreds of metres, straight into the sea. The gulfs of Porto, Sagone, Ajaccio and Valinco are separated from one another by broad peninsulas, with exposed rocky capes and outlying islands. These gulfs were created by tectonic forces when the land sank and submerged whole valleys, producing this typical indented coastline of *rias*. Apart from the larger sandy bays, the occasional sandy beach can also be found in amongst the rocky headlands. But because of the steep and therefore inaccessible nature of much of the terrain, many of them can only be reached from the sea.

Spectacular cliffs: A very special wonder of nature is to be found along the stretch of coast around Bonifacio in the far south of the island. Gleaming white cliffs rise for up to 60 metres (200 ft) out of the sea, providing a magnificent contrast with the azure-blue waters of the Straits of Bonifacio. The cliffs are composed of thin layers of Miocene chalk, which during the course of the millennia have been eroded into the spectacular cliff forms that we see today. And the waves continue to loosen the rock, carry off the debris and gouge out caves along the lines of weakness. The constant undercutting has resulted in massive blocks of rock breaking away from the cliffs and landing in the water at their base, where the process of erosion is continued by the relentless pounding of the waves. The erosive force of the sea has not only endowed this stretch of coast with these marvellous cliffs, but also with underwater grottos that provide an absolute paradise for divers and snorkellers.

So, from the jagged summits and deep ravines of the high mountains, to the thick forests of the lower hills, to the beaches and rocky inlets of the coast, Corsica offers such an incredible diversity of scenery that it is very much an "*Ile des Contrastes*". But the fact that visitors will, on their journeys round the island, unavoidably stumble across some extraordinary wonders of nature, may also give them the feeling of having come to an "*Ile des Surprises*", an island of unending surprises which even gives geographers cause to marvel.

<u>Left</u>, Laricio pine on the Col de Bavella. <u>Right</u>, the Eagle Cliff in the Calanche.

Vast expanses of trees and shrubs, covering hills and valleys as far as the eye can see; the sight is a familiar one to the traveller who has visited other regions surrounding the Mediterranean. But nowhere else does the evergreen undergrowth characterise so completely the landscape; nowhere else is the botanical palette so varied – and nowhere else is the vegetation so luxuriant and impenetrable as here on Corsica.

More than half the island's surface area is covered by this scrubland. The islanders call

it *macchia*, derived from the Corsican name for the rockrose (*mucchiu*). The French name is *maquis*. Many species of plant growing in the scrubland of Corsica are only to be found here; since they are endemic, their generic name includes the epithet *corsicus*.

An impenetrable refuge: During World War II, French partisans hid from Italian and German troops in the thick undergrowth of the *macchia*. The scrubland gave them their name: the *maquisards*. During the war, the term Maquis was applied to any resistance organisation, but it clearly originated in Corsica where it took one Axis soldier to control two Corsicans, including women and chil-

dren. Even in historic times the *macchia* was used as a refuge from Roman, Saracen and Genoan invaders. Last but not least, it offered many a Corsican protection when he needed to escape from his pursuers because he had perpetrated an act of *vendetta*, blood revenge.

The *macchia* consists of a dense undergrowth up to three metres (10 ft) high, of sclerophyllous shrubs; in general it is the result of the over-use and over-grazing of the island's holm-oak forests. On Corsica the scrubland consists of 12 main shrub types, the most typical of which are brier, arbutus (strawberry tree), myrtle, mastic and broom. Its composition varies on the island according to altitude, site, rainfall, soil conditions and degree of depredation. The various types of *macchia* are labelled according to the dominant species or combination of species. There are three main levels: the myrtle level (up to 200 metres/640 ft), the mastic level (200–600 metres/640–2,000 ft) and the arbutus-brier level (600–1,000 metres/2,000–3,200 ft).

Many-sided uses: The scrubland of Corsica is seen at its most magnificent in spring. The shrubs are still bright green from the winter rains, and across the hillsides and valleys their blossoms extend in a sea of colours. Spring is also the best time of year to walk through this unique botanical garden. The brilliant golden yellow of the gorse gleams between the characteristic rockroses, filling the air with a sweet smell of honey. It attracts countless numbers of bees from the brightly-coloured hives dotted throughout the scrubland, in which is produced the much-praised local honey with its characteristic taste. The brier may grow taller than a man in places, its shoots adorned with tiny, white, bell-shaped flowers. Known in Corsican as *scopa*, the brier's twisted stems are used to carve the famous *bruyère* pipes.

In shady spots grows the myrtle, whose scent carries over long distances. The stamens glisten decoratively against the white petals. The branches produce a fine aroma when burned; for this reason, they are often used to grill fish and tender meat. The leaves yield an aromatic oil which is used as a seasoning for sauces; from the resiny-tasting fruits is distilled *myrte*, the famous Corsican liqueur.

Not far away can be seen the bell-shaped blossoms of the arbutus, which produces tempting-looking bright red fruits in autumn. Although they are inedible when raw, they can be made into a delicious jelly, *gelée d'arbouses*. *Erbiglie* is the islanders' collective name for the herbs used to give their cuisine its unique flavour. Rosemary and marjoram both grow wild in the *macchia*,

the dew falls and the dawn breaks, ethereal oils are exuded by the thorns, twigs, stems and sclerophyllous leaves, most of which are small to prevent excessive transpiration. Only in this manner can many plants survive the drought of the summer months.

From earliest times the *macchia* has served the Corsicans as a hunting ground, where they pursue wild boar, partridge, birds and – until recently – the mouflon. Scarcely a Sunday goes by on which one does not hear the cracking of rifles in the undergrowth. Today,

whilst lemon balm can be found along the wayside and various types of mint in the damper spots.

The many flowers blossoming under the thicket of shrubs help to round out the characteristic scent of the *macchia*. In the dry, hot summer months, when the shrubs are no longer in flower, the scent still lingers unforgettably. It explains why Napoleon, the island's most famous native son, always maintained: "I would recognise Corsica with my eyes closed, from the scent alone." Before

the huntsmen mostly return without prey, for despite restrictions, poaching and shooting at anything which moves have sadly decimated the game stocks. Nowadays, many regions of *macchia* have become a silent scrubland, where scarcely a bird can be heard singing. Of even greater ecological significance are the effects of the seasonal grazing by migrant flocks. In many places the continuous depredations of sheep and goats have resulted in the replacement of the typically lofty shrubs by semi-high and low-growing bushes.

The monstrous match: The magnificent blossoms and aromatic scents of the *macchia*,

Left, the strawberry tree is one of the most typical shrubs. **Above**, a natural rockery.

together with the many-faceted usefulness of a number of the plants, represent the sunny side of the situation. When the scrubland catches fire, however, tragedy strikes. Large areas are completely destroyed, villages temporarily cut off from the outside world, and even holiday complexes must sometimes be evacuated.

Why is the island so frequently plagued by fires of this kind? Corsican farmers maintain that shepherds are responsible for the vast infernos, by which they gain new pastures for their flocks of sheep and goats. The police and fire brigade, however, insist that, in most cases, political extremists use this method to draw attention to Corsican de-

mands for independence. Also under suspicion are careless holidaymakers; during a dry summer, a cigarette stub which is still burning when it is tossed away, or an incompletely extinguished camp fire, can set an entire region ablaze.

It is seldom possible to pinpoint the culprit with certainty. What remains is a frightening record of destruction: during the past 20 years, an average of 5,000 hectares (120 acres) of shrubland went up in flames each year – almost half the total area of *macchia* on the island.

Even decades later, the damage caused by fire can be seen like a scar across the country-

side. Across the hillside, against a background ranging from light brown to deep black, charred remains of shrubs and tree stumps, like black skeletons, rise up towards the blue sky. There is no more vegetation, so during the next winter the rain will be able to erode the soil unhindered. Thus it is by no means certain that the dense undergrowth of the *macchia* will ever be able to re-establish itself here again. It is usually replaced by a degenerated form of scrubland, the so-called *garigue*, which establishes itself on Corsica above all on steep slopes where there have been repeated fires. One representative of this adaptation which is widely found on Corsica is the poisonous asphodill, which has large numbers of flower-bearing stems growing up to one metre high.

Fire-proof fauna: The typical vegetation of the *macchia* has developed a certain resistance to fire. Many species seem to possess an almost inexhaustible capacity for regeneration. Some are even largely resistant to fire: as soon as the autumn rains begin to fall, new shoots develop from buds at or near ground level which remained undamaged by the fire. In some cases, the roots send up new shoots. Unfortunately such tender young greenery is likely to provide a welcome source of nourishment for goats and sheep.

Many islanders are strangely indifferent to the ravages of fire, as if they were unavoidable. And yet, the Corsicans themselves should demonstrate the greatest interest in helping to preserve the *macchia*, for it is their lifestyle which is most closely linked with this habitat. It would be a tragedy if one day this irreplaceable natural resource were to be completely destroyed and replaced by a sterile wilderness.

Until the local administration succeeds in improving measures against the catastrophic fires and over-grazing, there is little chance of conservation laws for the preservation of the unique Corsican scrubland providing effective protection, for example by means of the creation of a national park. The nearby Mediterranean coastal regions of Italy and Spain provide plenty of examples of the tragic fate awaiting the *macchia* if they fail. But on Corsica it is – so far, at least – not yet too late.

Left, a garland of anemones. **Right**, rocks in bloom, harbingers of spring.

MEGALITHIC CULTURE AND THE TORRÉENS

Arriving on Corsica, the visitor is greeted by the blank gaze of the menhirs, the enigmatic stelae populating the island landscape either singly or in groups. They bear secret, almost eerie witness to the passage of the millennia, so that the observer wonders why it took so long for archaeologists to start their investigations into these early witnesses of a past civilisation.

The first reference in the western world to these man-made monuments will be found in Prosper Mérimée's *Notes d'un Voyage en Corse*, published in 1840. The celebrated author, who was the Inspector General of Historic Monuments in France at the time, confessed that "the island's early history is veiled in a dense cloak of mystery".

This state of ignorance was to continue for more than a century, for until a few decades ago archaeologists expected little joy from a serious investigation of Corsica, an island notorious for the inhospitableness of both its terrain and inhabitants. It was not until 1954 that the French archaeologist Roger Grosjean, inspired by his teacher, Abbé Breuil, began to shed a very different light on the island's early history.

Stone-Age culture: Even during the centuries before Greek invaders brought their civilisation to these shores, Corsica was hardly a refuge of primitive goatherds. It was the home of a sophisticated culture able to construct monuments with a clear religious purpose. In this respect, Corsica can match its Mediterranean neighbour Sardinia as well as Sicily, Malta and the Balearic Islands of Mallorca and Menorca. Many of these ancient stones were appropriated across the intervening millennia to build houses or walls surrounding the fields, or were weathered away or overgrown by the *macchia*. Nonetheless, Grosjean was successful in shedding considerable light on their origins.

The first settlers, who were "primitive" hunters, fishermen and collectors, probably reached the island during the 7th millennium BC, towards the end of the Mesolithic era. They arrived via Elba from Liguria, the North

Italian region surrounding Genoa. A second wave of immigrants with a knowledge of agriculture and cattle farming descended about one thousand years later, at the beginning of the Neolithic era.

The original inhabitants of Corsica knew how to make simple clay pots, which have been demonstrated by radiocarbon dating to be some 7,500 years old. Cardium ceramics of this type, named after the mollusc used to create the dominant dot-like pattern, can be found all over the Mediterranean area, sug-

gesting that trade and cultural exchange across the sea was already taking place.

Early village life: As far as we can tell, living conditions during these early years of Corsican history must have been almost idyllic. Those of the inhabitants who no longer dwelt in caves or sought shelter under overhanging cliffs lived in open, unfortified villages. During the winter months their sheep grazed the lower plains; in summer they were driven up to the higher mountain pastures, a custom maintained to this day with the practice of transhumance. The women wove cloth on simple looms. The hard materials required to make arrowheads and tools did not occur

Left, the blank gaze of a statue-menhir. **Right**, the Central Monument at Filitosa.

naturally on the island: it is thought that the early settlers brought in flint and obsidian from neighbouring Sardinia, which was as yet uninhabited.

And yet, man shall not live by bread alone. He fears the powers of nature, sees them as the manifestation of a superior being, questions his own origins and the purpose of his existence and speculates over the possibility of life after death. Such preoccupations lead to ancestor worship and reverence for the dead, including the construction of burial places and temples. The ancient Corsicans were no exception in this respect. From about 3500 BC the erection of megaliths became more widespread. The word, derived from more likely that the practice developed independently within the continent. But that doesn't exclude the possibility that it had its origins in the worship of the great Earth Mother and other deities, which had been practised in the Aegean and Asia Minor for thousands of years.

Stone coffin cult: Archaeologists distinguish three periods of megalithic culture in Corsica. Previously, the placing of modest burial gifts in the grave beside the deceased had been customary. During the middle of the 4th millennium BC, under the influence of new trends (possibly a new wave of immigrants), the new practice of burying the dead in stone chambers came to be widely ac-

the Greek for "big" and "stone", defines this characteristic practice of the early island inhabitants.

For many years it was believed that the origins of these monumental constructions, which seem to embody their builders' longing for permanence, were to be found in the Eastern Mediterranean. However, research has shown that the megaliths of Brittany are at least a thousand years older than the earliest pyramids of Egypt. Moreover, the largest concentration of "big stones" is to be found in the Western Mediterranean and along the European Atlantic coast (Carnac, Stonehenge, Jutland, etc). For this reason it seems cepted. The sarcophagi were constructed of single, precisely hewn stone slabs, which were set into the ground and covered by a mound of earth (tumulus). Entire cemeteries or necropolises containing stone tombs of this kind are to be found near Porto Vecchio and in the Sartenais.

Standing sentinel over the graves would be found one or two so-called menhirs or druid stones. These are simple upright monuments, almost always of granite, which, because of their frequent occurrence in Brittany, take their name, which means "long stones", from the Breton words *men* ("stone") and *hir* ("long").

The second period of megalithic culture on Corsica is characterised by a change in burial customs. From about the middle of the third millennium the stone coffins were no longer buried but simply placed directly on the ground, although they continued to be covered by a tumulus. After the mound of earth had been eroded by wind and weather over a period of time, the constructions thus exposed came to resemble stone tables. They were also given a Breton name: *dolmen*, or "stone table". The finest example, discovered by the 19th-century French novelist Prosper Mérimée, is the dolmen at Fontanaccia in the Cauria region.

During the earliest period of megalithic

ever, this does not rule out the possibility that mystic cult concepts existed here as well.

Stelae with faces: The third phase of megalithic culture can be distinguished from about 2000 BC. The phallus-shaped menhir of earlier times, looking for all the world like a fertility symbol, slowly started to take on human features. A head and shoulders gradually emerged from the stone column, later developing a mask-like face with eyes, ears, a nose and a mouth. Then ribs and clothing became discernible; later still, the figures were depicted with weapons and occasionally with arms. In order to make them more lifelike, the statues were probably originally painted with blood-coloured haematite or

culture the druid stones were scarcely more than 1–2 metres (3–6 ft) high, and were unadorned. During this later phase, however, they doubled in size. They continued to flank single tumuli or were positioned in rows known as *alignements*, or parallel avenues of stones.

In contrast to the discoveries in Brittany, where the rows of menhirs were clearly aligned in accordance with various astronomic criteria, virtually all such rows on Corsica follow a north-south direction. How-

Left, the dolmen at Fontanaccia. **Above**, stone coffins were placed above ground.

ochre. These anthropomorphic stelae were positioned facing eastwards, towards the rising sun. Maybe it was hoped that the resurrection of the dead would also come from that direction.

Do these stone images we see today actually portray the deceased in person? Perhaps they represent some glorified ancestors, or possibly the swords and daggers indicate some protective function. Perhaps they are even enemies conquered by the deceased, who have thus been banished or forced into obedience beyond the grave? One riddle gives way to another, each as insoluble as the last. What cannot be disputed, however, is that these Corsican monuments represent the first large-sized sculptures in the Western hemisphere, constructed centuries before analogous works were created by the Greeks or the Etruscans. Most of these expressive, humanoid menhirs are to be found in Filitosa in the southwest of the island.

The legend of the Torréens: By the middle of the second millenium this early culture had reached its climax. After that, it fell into an abrupt decline. Until the late 1980s scientists believed that this collapse was caused by an invasion of a belligerent foreign people whose arrival marked the beginning of the end of the Stone Age. Unlike

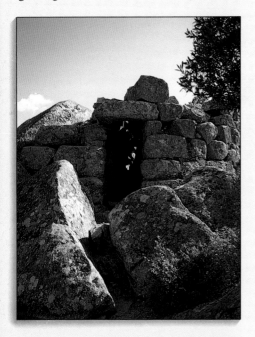

the existing inhabitants, the new arrivals had the advantage of bronze weapons. It is still uncertain where these new immigrants came from and what they were called in their own language. The archaeologist Roger Grosjean called them Torreani – Torréens in French – after the *torre* or towers which they were thought to have introduced to the island.

Historians believed the first Torréens landed about 1500-1200 BC on the Gulf of Porto Vecchio in the south of the island. Some of the tower-like constructions in the surrounding plain, such as those found at Torre and Tappa, were considered to be

among their earliest constructions. Their architecture and traces of ashes and fire suggested that the place-name Torre was used for sites that served as crematoria, and possibly for human burnt offerings as well.

Only later, according to this theory, did the Torréens advance towards the interior where they inevitably came into conflict with the Corsi. These original inhabitants defended their positions determinedly, but ultimately their stone weapons proved no match for the bronze swords and daggers of the newcomers. The Torréens completely destroyed the Stone-Age settlers' villages and the defeated Corsi withdrew to the northernmost regions of the island.

The latest theory: Current research now suggests that there were probably no such representatives of a foreign superior culture as the Torréens at all. The long-running theory was based on a belief that the Torréens brought to the island the metallic weapons that are shown on the Paladini, the armed menhir-statues, and that it was these same foreigners who constructed Cyclopean citadels such as Araghju on a rock ledge near Porto Vecchio. They also apparently transformed the peaceful peasant village of Filitosa into a *Castellu*, using demolished menhirs to reinforce their walls.

All those rather convincing theories broke down in the 1980s when archaeologists made new discoveries. In Terrina, close to the area later inhabited by Etruscans, Greeks and Romans on the plateau of Alalia (now Aleria), they detected not only a copper pit but also moulds for shaping metals to produce exactly the kind of daggers and swords that can be seen on the Paladini menhirs.

With help of the Carbon 14 dating method this early civilisation can be traced to around 3500-3000 BC. That is at least 1,500 years before the Toréens are supposed to have arrived. These dating tests showed conclusively that the so-called Torréen fortresses were built during this period.

The Corsican word *torre* is still used to describe both smaller constructions and part of the bigger *castelli*, however, so the term Torréen is still thought to be appropriate and it continues to be widely used to describe this later period.

Left and right, the entrance and stairs to the Torréen place of worship at Torre.

Which reader has never seen the famous Moor who, sporting a jaunty headband, adorns a large number of cars and recalls the fact that the occupants have spent their holidays on Corsica? On the island itself the Moor has a deeper significance: for centuries he has been the symbol of the island's independence after long years of foreign rule. That the Corsicans should have been faced with a perpetual struggle throughout their turbulent history was due in no small part to their island's attractive location as a trading post in the Mediterranean.

The arrival of the Phocaeans: The Greek colonisation of Corsica began in the 6th century before Christ, as Herodotus, the celebrated historian, relates. When Harpagus, the King of the Medes, besieged the town of Phocaea in Asia Minor, its citizens were faced with the alternatives of surrender or flight. They chose the latter. Since the Greeks living in Phocaea were a seafaring nation, their escape route was also clear: the sea. After a long voyage they finally landed on the east coast of Corsica (Greek: *Kyrnos*), where they were welcomed by the Greek colony already on the island. In 565 BC they founded together the town of Alalia, later known to the Romans as Aléria. Legend has it that their choice of a new home was determined by an oracle.

Since the Greeks were canny and experienced merchants, they were able to make a living from a flourishing trade in copper, lead, silver and iron. They extracted the raw materials from the island interior, especially from Mercuri, Conca and Venaco, transporting the ores to Alalia for smelting. The resulting highly-prized metals were then exported by ship. The Greeks built most of their sailing vessels themselves, from materials found in the forests of Corsica: wood, wax and resin. A nation of experienced mariners, they brought the requisite skills with them from their homeland.

Alalia as a trading centre: The processing of metals was not the only avenue to prosperity open to the commercially-minded Greeks.

Left, the excavations at Aléria. Right, a fine example of Attic pottery (5th century BC).

On the fertile coastal plains in the east of the island, formed by the alluvial deposits from the River Tavignano, they grew grapes for wine, as well as olive trees and cereals. A small proportion of the harvest served the citizens' own needs and the remainder was exported. A further source of income was provided by the bounty of the sea: salted fish, prepared with salt from the salt marshes along the coast.

Within a short space of time Alalia had become an important commercial centre and

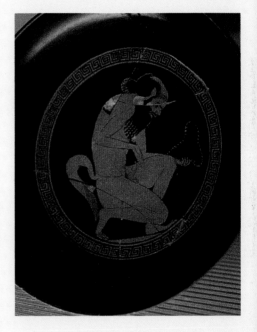

staging post on the way to the Greek settlement on the mainland at Massilia (Marseille). Archaeological finds such as the fine Greek vases, today on view in the Jérôme Carcopino Museum in Aléria, provide evidence of the lively trading activity which must have gone on here as well as the high standard of living at the time. The clay used for the domestic utensils came from the Casabianda Plateau.

But the Phocaeans, whose ambition it was to gain control over the entire Tyrrhenian Sea, were not permitted to enjoy their wealth for long. Not only did they fail to establish good relationships with the native population, the Corsi, who had retreated to the island interior; they also attacked and robbed their neighbours, the Etruscans and Carthaginians, who retaliated in 535 BC by sending over a combined invasion fleet.

Although the Phocaeans carried the day in the ensuing naval battle of Alalia, it was really only a Pyrrhic victory. Having lost most of their ships and sustained heavy casualties, they decided to transfer their capital to Massalia, retaining Alalia solely as a mercantile link with their new colonies in southern Italy, as well as with Greece, Carthage, Gaul, Sicily and Spain. A sample of what the Greeks left behind them can be seen today in the museum in Aléria. They also bequeathed

nised its favourable location as a trading post in the Mediterranean.

It was in that year, during the course of the First Punic War waged by the Romans against the Carthaginians (264–241 BC), that Scipio conquered Alalia. From this point onwards the town was known by its present name, Aléria. By 230 BC the entire east coast of the island was firmly under Roman rule. The Romans took over their predecessors' profitable sources of income, but on a much larger scale than before. The agricultural hinterland was extended, and everything was better organised – to match the dimensions of the Roman Empire. They also established oyster farms which soon became a highly

the island its most popular and enduring epithet: *Kalliste* – "The Beautiful".

A Roman colony: Invaders of Corsica always arrived on the east coast, not only because landings here were much easier than on the rocky western shores, but also because of the relative proximity of the long Italian shore. In successive waves of settlement the Etruscans and Carthaginians now took advantage of the island's rich resources. Before long, however, Corsica was to become a bone of contention once more. The next significant date was 259 BC, when Corsica attracted the attention of the Roman consul, Lucius Cornelius Scipio. He recog-

profitable business. The wealthy Romans on the mainland were fond of banquets at which it was considered fashionable to serve one's guests molluscs from the coast of the island colony. The oysters were packed in jars of brine and transported to the cities of the mainland.

The enslavement of the Corsi: The Romans had more difficulty bringing the island interior under their sway, for here they encountered the obstinate resistance of the native Corsi, who lived in a state of perpetual rebellion against their oppressors. After a series of successful military campaigns against the indigenous population, the Romans finally forced them to pay high tribute. Corsican prisoners were compelled to work for their new masters in the quarries, mines and fields. Corsican slaves were also popular on the mainland, on account of their tough constitution and strong physique which made them suitable for arduous manual work. In view of the continuous building projects throughout the length and breadth of the vast empire, they were in constant demand.

In 221 BC Corsica and Sardinia were amalgamated to form a single Roman province. On Corsica itself the only towns the Romans colonised were Aléria and Mariana, named after its founder Marius, an uncle of Julius Caesar and lying to the south of what is now again throughout the island's turbulent history: they withdrew to the interior, where they went into hiding in the forests. They lived simply, relying on the resources nature had to offer them.

Urban luxury: Now known as "Colonia Julia", Aléria became the Romans' capital on the island, with a population of some 30,000. The town acquired an urban countenance as a result of the construction of a triumphal arch and forum as well as an aqueduct, baths and a harbour for civilian and naval vessels.

On a walk around the archaeological site of Aléria, the prosperity of the Romans can best be appreciated by a study of the *Balneum,*

Bastia. Between 181 and 172 BC, when the forces of occupation overdid yet again their exploitation of the Corsi, repeatedly raising taxes and the tribute due in cork, honey and wax as well as the customs duties payable on the rivers and harbours, the local inhabitants revolted. But they had no chance against the legions sent from Rome; over half the island's native population perished. The remainder, totalling some 30,000 souls, did what their descendants were to do time and

Left, Early-Christian reliefs on the church of Santa Maria Assunta in Canari. Above, the grave of a prisoner in the Musée Jérôme Carcopino.

a vast bathing complex. It included changing cabins, several swimming pools and tanks for cold, warm and hot water. The ground was warmed by underfloor heating; the boilers were fuelled with wood from the island interior. Nor were economies made when it came to the fittings and decorations of the houses, which included a number of fine mosaics.

Many of the consumer goods the Romans used, such as their fine glazed ceramics, were locally produced. Aléria developed into a centre of light industry. There were, for example, cloth dyers' and craftsmen's studios and firms specialising in the preservation of fish. The Romans acquired most of the agricultural produce they required from their colony at Mariana, which formed the centre of the Roman territory in the north of the island until the 6th century.

The early church complex at Mariana testifies to Rome's first attempts at converting the island to Christianity during the 3rd century; in the first instance this, like the Roman colonisation, was restricted primarily to the coastal areas. The first five bishoprics on Corsica apart from Mariana were at Nebbio, Aléria, Sagone and Ajaccio. The earliest Christian engravings found on the island – in Aléria – date from this period: the symbolic *olla* and the fish. When the Western Roman

Empire collapsed during the 4th and 5th centuries, the Church took over the administrative tasks of the Roman governors. The administrative boundaries were redrawn, later forming the parishes (*pieve*).

The Moor with the headband: Aléria's fate was sealed in the 5th century AD. From AD 410 to 430 the town was stricken by a raging fire followed by malaria epidemics. In AD 456 the Vandals invaded the island and destroyed the town completely. This Germanic tribe had left their home in the Danube valley to invade Gaul and subsequently crossed into Spain and conquered Roman Africa before sacking Rome itself in AD 455. They

restored Carthage and made it the capital of their empire. But the reputation of the Vandals is not based on what they did, but how they did it: they laid waste practically everything they came across. Such was their cruelty that in the 18th century a French bishop coined the term "Vandalism" to mean wanton destruction.

During the following centuries the island was plagued by a succession of fresh invasions by the Goths, the Byzantines and the Langobards. The 9th century saw the beginning of the conquest of Corsica by the Saracens or Moors – a reign of terror which was to last for more than two hundred years. The Saracens proved to be even crueller masters than the Vandals. They conquered the coastal regions, expelling or killing the inhabitants of Aléria and Mariana and preventing the continued spread of Christianity. As during the Roman occupation, the Corsicans retreated to the forests of the interior. The legacy of the years of Moorish rule can be found today in Campo dei Mori, Morosaglia and Campomoro.

Corsican folk history has kept alive the memory of a Roman nobleman, Ugo della Colonna, as a popular resistance leader. He had fallen out of favour with Pope Stephen IV and was able to save his honour by winning Aléria back from the Moors in a knightly duel, by finally routing the Saracen king Nugalon in the Battle of Mariana after a 20-year military campaign, and by forcing all pagan Corsicans to be baptised.

The Moor's head with the white headband, chosen as the island's official symbol on 24 November 1762, recalls to this day the final expulsion of the Saracens during the 11th century. No one seems to know, however, whether the Moor's head, portrayed on a white background, was depicted from the beginning with the headband as a symbol of the liberation of the fatherland, or whether the bandage originally covered one eye to symbolise slavery. It is claimed that the great Corsican patriot Pasquale Paoli was responsible for placing the headband in its present position on the Moor's brow. Whatever its origin, the pirate-like Moor epitomises even today the stubborn resistance to foreign rule which fills the heart of every Corsican.

Left, a Roman beauty who has seen better days. **Right**, mosaic floor of the baptistry in Mariana.

In 754, in what became known as the Donation of Pépin, Pépin the Younger – whom later historians adorned with the less-than-flattering title of "The Short" – had vowed to hand over the land to Pope Stephen II. This promise of a gift of territory was to form the basis of the Papal States which still exist in rudimentary form today. In doing so Pépin wanted to return the favour of the curia, which had acknowledged him as King of the Franks. Amongst the lands which fell to the Holy See as part of this barter was the island of Corsica.

But Rome was far away, and so by and large the island was left to its own devices. It was not until the rival naval powers of Pisa and Genoa had formed an alliance, to drive out the marauding pirate fleet of the Saracens in order to protect their own trading interests, that noblemen from Tuscany and Liguria appeared on the scene to appropriate parts of the island for themselves.

The new feudal lords paid lip service to the authority of the Malaspinas, who had settled on Corsica some time previously from Tuscany, but to all intents and purposes they were able to do exactly as they thought fit. In any case, the rival clans lived in a state of perpetual feud, which they carried on amidst much bloodshed and suffering on the part of the ordinary people.

The island's chronicles record in favourable terms the deeds of only one of these local lords, Count Arrigo Bel Messer, who ruled round about AD 1000. However, his attempt to replace the intolerable anarchy with law and order came to an abrupt end under the dagger thrusts of hired assassins; his seven young sons were also all put to death by drowning. After the death of the "Good Count" the island inhabitants lamented: "Lord Bel Messer was killed by a murderer's curse: And the state of Corsica goes from bad to worse."

The Pope intervenes: The seeds of new strife were sown when some of the Ligurian noblemen acknowledged the suzerainty of the bishops of Genoa, whereupon the Tuscan

lords swore their allegiance to their fellow-countryman, Pope Gregory VII. In him they acquired a belligerent henchman who at the time was embroiled in the Investiture Dispute with the German king, Henry IV. The quarrel concerned whether the right to appoint bishops lay with the Papal mitre or the Crown, and ended in Henry's famous submission as a humble penitent in Canossa. Gregory VII, a native of Tuscany, made use of his territorial advantage and in 1077 awarded Corsica in feoff to Bishop Landolfe of Pisa. It was a sinecure which was subsequently to slip out of the hands of the Church once more.

Eastern influence: Thanks to its favourable location on a broad, fertile plain near the place where the River Arno flows into the Ligurian Sea, by the early Middle Ages Pisa had already grown into a prosperous port and trading centre. Its ensuing rivalry with Genoa and Venice for the dominance of the Mediterranean area was inevitable. In 1099 the citizens of Pisa took part in the First Crusade to liberate the Holy City of Jerusalem from the rule of the "infidel" Moslems, taking ample advantage of the opportunity to gather up a vast hoard of oriental treasures. But in the Levant they were also exposed to new artistic influences, which they combined with the architectural tradition of Lombardy in the construction of magnificent buildings which have earned a special chapter in the history of art under the rubric "Pisan style".

The wealth acquired by fair means or foul by the soldiers, ship owners and traders strengthened the political influence of the middle classes. Full of self-confidence, the Pisans (like the citizens of other northern Italian cities) were no longer prepared to permit decisions to be made for them from the pulpit. They gradually took over responsibility for their own fate. The aristocracy (of wealth) elected from its midst councillors (*signori*) and invested them, under the direction of a *podestà* or leader, with political authority within the state. The role of the bishop was restricted to spiritual affairs. And so Corsica acquired a secular government.

"The Pisans ruled wisely, justly and peacefully," wrote the chronicler Giovanni della

Left, nowadays the Pisan tower at Porto only has to stand up to the waves.

Grossa, admittedly some 200 years later. He described them as "by and large beloved of the populace". In any case, the rule of law and order returned to the island; under Pisan protection the Corsicans summoned up the courage to return to the coastal plains, which had been depopulated by pirates and marauding knights.

An economic boom was set into motion, accompanied by the construction of more than 300 churches to ensure the eternal salvation of the citizens. By contrast, the Pisans left behind relatively few secular buildings. In the past some historians have attributed to them the square watchtowers, claiming that only the round ones are Genoese. But the

theory never found much support and is nowadays regarded as obsolete.

Romanesque simplicity: Today many of the churches on Corsica dating from the Pisan era, built in a style corresponding to the Romanesque, lie in ruins or have completely disappeared. The visitor should not expect architectural wonders of those buildings which have survived. If you associate Pisa with the Piazza dei Miracoli, bordered by masterly examples of western architecture, from the Baptistry and the Cathedral to the famous Leaning Tower, you are bound to be disappointed if you expect to find something similar on Corsica. It is important to remember that Corsica has always been regarded as the back of beyond. Even though artists from the mainland were called in to assist the local stonemasons, masons and painters the result was always relatively modest.

And yet, Pisa's influence is still unmistakable today, especially on the north of the island, in the regions around Nebbio, the Castagniccia and the Balagne. As in the parent city, the Corsican churches of this era are characterised by careful craftsmanship of the fine building materials and polychrome masonry: in Sisco and Brando on Cap Corse they quarried marble blocks which were placed in alternate narrow and wide layers in the church of La Canonica, which stands on the site of the Roman settlement of Mariana near the present airport at Bastia. Santa Maria Assunta, which is modelled in both style and material on La Canonica, stands sentinel above Saint-Florent on the north coast of the island. In the Bevinco Valley, the master builders who created San Michele de Murato (in the mountains southwest of Bastia) discovered dark-green serpentine and whitish limestone, which they combined with pink and yellow slabs to produce what Prosper Mérimée described as the "most elegant church on the island".

Only exceptionally does one find – as in the examples cited above – that the Corsican churches built during the Pisan era take the form of substantial triple-naved basilicas. Most are unadorned small churches or chapels with a single nave; despite their harmonious proportions they are more rustic than elegant, and blend perfectly with the bucolic landscape.

In many cases the roofs of the Pisan-style churches on Corsica consisted merely of wood or *teghie*, slabs of natural stone. At first the ornamentation was very simple, consisting of nothing more elaborate than geometric patterns. Representation of figures only came later; the finest examples of these, too, will be found in the places of worship listed above. Lions and fabulous creatures gaze down from the facades and capitals, alongside rams' heads and serpents, lambs bearing crosses and wolves baring their teeth. Here and there you will also spot mysterious "manikins", like those on the Church of the Holy Trinity in Aregno. In Murato there is an unusual portrayal of the Temptation of Eve.

Half-and-half is no answer: The period during which Pisa was able to enjoy undisturbed its island colony was to last for less than 50 years. Genoa was prepared to go to any lengths to wrest the prize from its strongest competitor, even resorting to bribing the Roman curia. In fact, all six dioceses on Corsica were transferred to the Ligurian Republic, an act which provoked open hostility – even on the island itself – between the rival maritime powers. Innocent II saw the solution to the dispute in terms of a Solomonic judgment; in 1133 he divided Corsica, permitting the northern dioceses of Accia, Mariana and Nebbio to remain under Genoese control whilst transferring those in the south

the Corse du Sud area, which used to be Pisan. In fact, however, the "two Corsicas" existed long before that, for the differences have their foundations in the geology of the island. The main watershed runs in a north-west-southeasterly direction along the central mountain ridge.

In the 13th century, however, half the island remained under the jurisdiction of Pisa until, on 6 August 1284, a decisive battle was fought off the island of Meloria (near Livorno), during which the Genoese won a resounding victory. The Corsicans resisted their new masters – or at least, the supporters of Pisa did so – and the island produced its first freedom fighter: the rebel

– Ajaccio, Aléria and Sagone – back to Pisa. It was an unhappy solution which brought no joy to any of the parties concerned.

The general consensus is that this decision by the "innocent" pope created a division on the island, the after-effects of which can be seen in some spheres to this day – for example, in the modern administrative districts within the Département Haute-Corse, which more or less corresponds to the boundaries laid down by the former Genoese region, and

Left, simple decoration above the door of the 9th-century chapel of Santa Reparata near Bonifacio. **Above,** the church of La Canonica at Mariana.

Sinucello della Rocca. In his capacity as the *Giudice* – the Judge – of Cinarca, he succeeded in making himself master of all Corsica, firstly in the name of Pisa, and then, having swapped sides, in the name of the Genoese. But when the latter finally defeated Pisa, he was captured through the treachery of one of his own men and had to spend the last seven years of his life festering in a Genoese dungeon.

The demise of this legendary *condottiere* put at least a symbolic end to the resistance, and the new power over the Western Mediterranean began its rule over Corsica, which was to last for almost 500 years.

Pisa was thus defeated and in 1288 formally abandoned its claims to Corsica. Not only the islanders rose up against Genoa, however; for financial as well as political reasons the Pope was not in favour of the new constellation. In 1297 Boniface VIII gave the King of Aragón, James II, both Corsica and Sardinia in feoff. The Ligurian Republic was not prepared to accept this; however, as it was involved in a dispute with Venice at the time, it was in no position to defend its colony properly. And so a sort of war by proxy came to pass: the belligerent feudal rulers of Corsica took up the cause of first one side and then the other, depending on which of them offered the better deal. In between times, they settled old scores.

Once again the island was plunged into civil war and anarchy: epidemics of plague, malaria and famine also took their toll of the population. The unrest did not even stop short of the churches and monasteries, and many of the ruins in evidence today can be traced back to this turbulent era.

Revolts against the aristocracy: From 1358, rebellious peasants, tired of the perpetual family feuds, laid siege to the castles of their feudal lords throughout Northern Corsica. Since most of the latter were Aragón sympathisers, Genoa felt obliged to support the revolt, which was led by a certain Sambucuccio d'Alando. He conquered large sections of the island; however, only in the northeast, *en decà des monts* – in the "land on this side of the mountains" – did he succeed in putting the noblemen to flight. Their estates were handed over to the communities in return for the guarantee of free grazing rights for the herds of all villagers. That is why the land in question is known as *terra di commune/terre du commun*, whereas in the southwest the *terra dei signori/terre des seigneurs* remained the property of the nobles until the French Revolution in 1789.

These "free" communities established a form of self-administration based on organisational structures (*paese* and *pieve* - commune and parish) introduced under the Pisans. The "mayor" was theoretically chosen by election, but in practice the *caporali*, the heads of the leading families, were able to assert their will. It was not long before they, too, were drawn into alliances and feuds just like those they had witnessed amongst the nobility. And yet, the effects of this early democratisation are in evidence to this day. Whilst the *terra di commune* tends to think and vote on the left, the land beyond the mountains is regarded as right-wing and conservative.

Genoa was obliged to accept the liberties for which the citizens in the north had fought; its governor urgently needed allies against

BONIFACIVS·VIII·PAPA

Aragón. For almost two centuries the Spanish refused to give up their official title to the island. They appear to have been helped in their claims by Arrigo della Rocca, a great-grandson of the same *Guidice* de Cinarca who had fought for Pisa against the Genoese. But no sooner had he landed on the island in 1376 than he forgot his orders and took possession of the disputed territory – not for Aragón, but for himself, subsequently having himself proclaimed Count of Corsica.

At the beginning of the 15th century King Alfonso V of Aragón tried to conquer Corsica once more, sending Arrigo's nephew Vincentello d'Istria. The latter ruled as viceroy in the name of the Spanish, building in the heart of the island the citadel at Corte. But when, in 1434, the Genoese managed to track down Vincentello, Aragonese intervention on the island came to an abrupt and bitter end. The viceroy was captured on the high seas whilst attempting to escape and publicly beheaded on the staircase in front of the Palace of Government in Genoa.

A bank as peacemaker: It goes without saying that such an occurrence did not put an end to the inglorious feuds between the island

nobility. On the contrary: each and every minor princeling laid claim to the office and title of a Count of Corsica, and Genoa remained too weak to restore law and order. This was the unfortunate situation in 1453, when the city state let out the island to the Genoese Bank of Saint George, with which the miniature republic had run up massive debts over the past 50 years. What was even more remarkable, within a short space of time the financial authorities were successful in achieving what neither governor nor

Left, Pope Boniface VIII, who gave Corsica to Aragón. **Above**, the distinctive Genoese style.

viceroy had managed so far: they brought peace to the island. The governor sent by the bank, Antonio Spinola, used the stick-and-carrot method of overcoming the islanders' resistance. His methods were based on a canny mixture of threats, promises, blackmail and force. His task was made easier by the fact that by this stage the nobility had largely destroyed itself.

The atmosphere of security prevailing during the reign of "Saint George" encouraged economic development, and especially building. Along the coastline, within sight of each other, the bank had erected a chain of turretted watchtowers, the system of defence known as the *torregiana*. Within the towers a permanent watch was kept with the aim of preventing the perpetual pirate raids with which the island had been plagued for as long as anyone could remember. At the time there were several hundred of these vaguely conical constructions, between 12 and 17 metres (38–54 feet) high, with a diameter of some 7 metres (22 feet) and tapering slightly towards the top. Today, only about half a dozen remain intact.

As soon as the sail of a pirate ship appeared on the horizon, the sentinels on the watchtower platforms would light a bonfire and the citizens would flee into the hinterland. Even so, it was not possible to prevent the *turchi*, as the predominantly North African Muslim pirates – Saracens or buccaneers from the Barbary coast – were called, from landing. They set fire to farmsteads, drove away the cattle, raping the women and killing those inhabitants whom they did not carry off into slavery. In the middle of the 16th century, in Algeria alone, no fewer than 6,000 Corsican prisoners were sold on the slave markets or were already languishing in the homes of their various masters.

In some places on the island, the city of Genoa had begun a building programme even before it handed over the territory to San Giorgio. In contrast to their former rivals, the Pisans, who had constructed churches and chapels to the greater glory of God, the Genoese showed a more practical talent. Their main activity lay in the fortification of existing or newly founded towns around the coast. As early as 1195 the citadel of Bonifacio was completed; it was followed by that of Calvi in 1268, Bastia in 1380, and later by Saint-Florent, Ajaccio and Porto Vecchio. A further example of the down-to-earth architectural approach of the Genoese merchants will be found on the island: their elegantly arched bridges. Although they, like the watchtowers, are also decaying rapidly, Corsican conservationists have so far shown few signs that they intend to preserve them. It is a pity, for their design – usually incorporating a single, or more rarely a triple arch, with a characteristic central angled bend and widely spaced steps – are not only typical of the era, but also make an essential contribu-

Corso, who was obsessed by the idea of rescuing his native island from the Genoese yoke. The military campaign was led by the French Marshal de Thermes, and supported by Muslim corsairs from Algeria under the command of the notorious mercenary Torghud Ali Pasha, alias Dragut, with whom the "Grande Nation" had formed an alliance.

Apart from the fortified towns of Calvi and Bastia, the entire island was conquered by the new invaders; most of the resident Genoese were expelled. In 1557, Giordano Orsini, the French king's representative, declared at a public assembly in the mountain village of Vescovato that Corsica had been "assimilated under the throne of France".

tion to the charm of the island's landscape. Nowadays they are seldom used by anyone except riders on mules or, more recently, tourists on foot.

A French intermezzo: The relatively peaceful years during which Corsica was ruled by the Bank of Saint George came to an end in 1553, after the French king, Henri II, had taken a liking to the island. At the time he was engaged in a war against the Habsburg emperor, Charles V, whose allies included Genoa. Thus it was that the military campaign acquired to all intents and purposes a moral justification. The advice to invade Corsica came from Henri's general Sampiero

Most of the local inhabitants cheered. However, two years later, to the boundless disappointment of Sampiero and his supporters, Henri II returned Corsica to the Genoese as part of the Treaty of Cateau-Cambrésis. In order to maintain the balance of power in Europe, the French king abandoned all claim to his Italian territories.

Since the search for other allies proved fruitless, Corsica then rose up under Sampiero without foreign assistance. In order to quash the popular revolt more effectively, the city of Genoa bought the island back from the Bank of Saint George in 1652, simultaneously involving an entire armada of ships.

Nonetheless, the powerful city republic was unable to conquer the badly equipped but intensely patriotic freedom fighters in a fair fight. Once again, the fate of Corsica was to be decided by treason and murder.

The island must suffer: Following the violent death of his father, Sampiero's eldest son, Alfonso, continued the underground struggle for two more years. He finally abandoned the cause, retreating to exile in France. The last pockets of resistance were gradually exterminated. What was left of this once-prosperous country? In what condition was the island in the midst of these trials and tribulations? "By the end of Sampiero's rebellion the full extent of Corsica's misery

respecting Corsican without a gun felt he had been deprived of his manliness, he gritted his teeth and paid up, thus helping to swell the state coffers by a tidy sum of money. It was some years later, during each of which up to 1,000 murders were registered, before the authorities banned the general carrying of weapons, having come to the conclusion that it might be counter-productive to the maintenance of public order. The inland revenue promptly found another taxable item to compensate for the loss of income: 12 soldi were levied annually on each and every Corsican hearth.

In order to put an end to at least the political quarrels, in 1571 Genoa granted Sampiero's

was evident. The island had become a desert, its people decimated by war, enforced emigration – impoverished and run wild" (Ferdinand Gregorovius, 1852).

In spite of this, Genoa's sole interest in its newly repossessed colony lay in exploiting it to the full. The capital invested in the repurchase of the island had to be shown to produce returns. One example of the endless ingenuity of the Genoese tax inspectors can be seen in the "weapons tax", payable by everyone bearing a firearm. Since any self-

Left and above, defiant watchtowers and elegantly arched bridges are both legacies of the Genoese.

followers a general amnesty. The *Statuti civili e criminali di Corsica* were passed – a series of binding clauses which formed the basis of a code of civil and criminal law. A tightly structured administration was to forge closer links between the island and the parent city. Corsica was divided into ten provinces and a total of 66 parishes (*pievi*), each of which including up to 50 villages (*paesi*) entitled to hold public assemblies (*consultas*). A governor appointed by Genoa took up residence in Bastia; he in turn was represented by a deputy. Ajaccio, Bonifacio and Calvi were ruled by commissioners; commandants took over the island fortresses and administrators were appointed for the rural areas. A Council of Twelve, consisting of local residents, advised the governor and was entitled, with his permission, to present petitions to the Genoese senate on behalf of the *magistrato di Corsica.*

Corsica's "Golden Age": To be fair to the Genoese it should be pointed out that they also built a handful of churches, but they were few in number. Between 1270 and 1350 St Dominique's, the island's only Gothic church, was built in Bonifacio. Nor did the Renaissance ever establish a hold on Corsica – one of the few examples of the style will be found in the Cathedral of Ajaccio. Nonetheless, once the fortresses were secure

ostentatious architecture, damask-lined walls with a wealth of pictures, turn them into an overwhelming experience. Some of the best-known examples are St Mary's Church and the chapels of the Conception and the Holy Cross in Bastia. Local artists were mostly responsible for the wood carving (statues of saints, pulpits, choir stalls and scenes of the Cross); the paintings were mainly the work of Italians. In a number of instances entire altars and choir screens of polychrome marble were imported in their entirety from Liguria and merely assembled in situ by local craftsmen.

The beginning of the 18th century saw the rapid eclipse of Genoa's star. The maritime

and the opposition had been crushed, Corsica lived through some 150 years of virtual peace. The economy recovered, and even the building industry experienced a unique boom. It was during the baroque era that almost every village – at least in the more prosperous regions – received an appropriate place of worship. The most prominent example is undoubtedly the Church of St John the Baptist in La Porta, a hamlet with fewer than 500 inhabitants.

The external facades of the churches of Corsica's "Golden Age" often appear unadorned. Inside, however, they are all the more magnificent. Gilt stucco, pompously

republic sank further and further into political and economic difficulties, trying as it did so to extract even higher taxes from Corsica. This pressure, combined with other unpopular measures such as allowing Greek refugees who had fled from Turkish invaders to settle in Cargèse, led to still greater discontent. This finally resulted in a war of independence which was to last for 40 years, and which was fought under a single watchword which was to prove impossible to ignore: Corsica for the Corsicans!

Above, Sampiero Corso was convinced that his young wife, Vannina d'Ornano, was a traitor.

SAMPIERO CORSO

Barely 50 km (30 miles) northeast of Ajaccio, perched above the Prunelli Valley, lies the scattered village of Bastelica. The little community's main claim to fame is "the most Corsican of Corsicans": in front of the church belonging to the Santo district is a martial bronze monument dedicated to the freedom fighter Sampiero Corso. With a battle-cry on his lips, he stands on his pedestal brandishing his dagger in the air with his right hand whilst his left rests on a shield bearing the family coat of arms complete with lion. At his feet, relief pictures depict scenes from the hero's struggle against Genoa.

The son of a peasant family, Sampiero was born on 8 May 1498 in the hamlet of Dominicacci. An intelligent boy, he strove for higher things – an ambition always easier to achieve through a career in the army. Entering the pay of the Medici family as a *condottiere*, he led a band of mercenaries known as the "Black Band", and his reputation soon spread. He arrived at the French court in the retinue of Catherine of Medici, the wife of the Dauphin Henri de Perpignan, where he distinguished himself as brilliantly on the dance floor as on the battlefield. Always to be found in the front line, Sampiero was reputed to be "worth 10,000 soldiers".

In 1547, King Henri II promoted the distinguished warrior, who had even saved his monarch's life in battle, to the rank of General of the Corsican infantry. Cloaked in glory, Sampiero returned to his native island and, at the age of almost 50, married the 15-year-old Vannina d'Ornano, the daughter of Corsican rural aristocracy. Genoa, having followed the general's career with extreme suspicion, took advantage of the elderly warhorse's moment of weakness to clap him in prison under a pretext. Only the intercession of King Henri brought about his release. Sampiero, offended that the Genoese should have ruined his honeymoon, took up the bitter fight to expel them from the island.

The general persuaded Henri II of France that it was strategically necessary to annex Corsica. The king responded by sending an expeditionary force under Marshal de Thermes; the fleet of the notorious buccaneer Dragut provided cover on the flank. Sampiero incited his people to rebellion, and within a short time they had driven the

Genoese from the island. In 1557 Corsica was declared to be part of France. But the hero's jubilation was premature: two years later, for political reasons, Henri II returned his newly acquired province to Italy. From this point onwards, Sampiero fought for his island's independence without outside support.

But his ultimate downfall did not come in battle. Rightly or wrongly, Sampiero was convinced of the infidelity of his young wife. But hers was not a crime of passion: she had made a journey to Genoa and he accused her of establishing political contact with the enemy.

Beside himself with rage, the Corsican Othello set off in pursuit of the fleeing Vannina. Having caught up with her in Aix-en-Provence, he

strangled her. The deed provided the scenario for a dramatic vendetta. Genoa offered a reward of 2,000 gold ducats, soon attracting the attention of members of the d'Ornano family who could well use the blood money. On 17 January 1567 Sampiero wandered into the ambush laid by Vannina's brothers near Eccia, not far from his birthplace.

For a century now a monument has marked the place where the Genoese cavalry surrounded the warrior and hacked him to pieces. His son Alfonso managed to escape with a handful of followers. Sampiero's head was put on a spear and exhibited by the town gate of Ajaccio as a warning to the people. Corsica had acquired a martyr. ∎

Right, the monument to Sampiero in Bastelica.

For many years Genoa had shamelessly exploited its island colony to the utmost. The poverty of the Corsicans and their hatred of their rulers grew ever greater, to the extent that in 1729 it only took a trivial cause of annoyance for armed resistance to break out. An old woman or an old man – the event is recorded differently by the various historical sources – reputedly owed the Genoese tax collector "half a sou" (a few pence). The Genoese official had no pity on the desperate poverty of the debtor and threatened punishment, possibly even execution.

Ferdinand Gregorovius describes how the old man ran around his village, "deliberating on this act of cruelty and talking to himself, as old men are wont to do. Other inhabitants met him, listening and forming a crowd by the wayside. The old man started to lament, then, passing over from his situation to that of the whole country, he roused his listeners to anger, describing to them the plight of the people and the tyranny of the Genoese, finally uttering the cry, 'Now it is time to put an end to our oppressors!'" The appeal spread like wildfire across the island as trumpets and alarm bells summoned the people to revolt against the forces of occupation.

Two Corsican noblemen were chosen by plebiscite to serve as generals at the head of the revolution. They tried initially to patch up the family feuds in order to be able to lead a united Corsican army into battle against the Genoese. In 1731 the rebellion was given official recognition by the legal assembly in Corte; even the Church began to see it as self-defence and released the islanders from their duties as subjects of Genoa.

Imperial intervention: By the time the Corsicans had already conquered a number of towns and were laying siege to the coastal fortresses of Bastia, Ajaccio and Calvi, the city state of Genoa, by no means as powerful as it once had been, requested Emperor Charles VI to send them reinforcements. Within a short space of time, Austrian troops

under the command of General Wachtendonck landed on the island. In desperation the Corsicans appealed to their countrymen living on the mainland to return to join the fight. Many of them did so.

The Corsicans fought so bravely that the Emperor was forced to send additional forces: a second army under the leadership of Prince Louis of Württemberg. But the Corsicans retreated to the mountains and embarked upon a guerilla warfare campaign against the invading troops, who had no knowledge of

Kaiser Karl VI. Ansicht in Rüstung mit Mantel).
Gemalt und gestochen von Antonius Vierhart.

local conditions. In 1732 a peace was negotiated in which the Corsicans were promised an amnesty, tax exemption and the right to apply for public office.

Scarcely had the foreign troops withdrawn when Genoa violated the treaty and the fighting resumed. In 1735 the Corsicans proclaimed the island's independence from Genoa during an assembly in Corte, granting themselves a democratic constitution. Since their emissaries to the courts of Europe found no allies, they placed their little nation under the protective care of the Virgin Mary.

A German baron becomes king: Genoa now resorted to a sea blockade. As the Corsicans'

Preceding pages: Soldier of the regiment "Royal Corse" (Bandera Museum in Ajaccio). **Left**, a map of Corsica by Monath of Nuremberg, 1736. **Above**, Emperor Charles VI sent troops to Corsica.

supplies dwindled to a desperately low level, help suddenly appeared from a most remarkable quarter. On 12 March 1736, Baron Theodor von Neuhoff of Westphalia anchored before the coast of Aléria with a ship full of weapons, ammunition and other supplies. An adventurer and knight of fortune, he had not been entirely neglecting his own interests when, in searching for financiers to support his rescue plan, he used his connections not only to wealthy merchants, but to the royal courts of Europe. He wanted the throne of Corsica.

Having no alternative means of gaining their independence from Genoa, the Corsican leaders agreed to the deal. And so Corsica

Nonetheless, after eight months it was plain that his extravagant promises were lacking in substance. The allied navy he had announced failed to arrive, and the Corsicans' situation once more became acute. Theodore realised it was time for him to abandon his island. He claimed he had to visit the mainland in person to summon the tardy assistance. And indeed, Theodore did succeed in raising funds from all kinds of Corsica sympathisers, sending from time to time a relief ship with aid and instructions to stand firm.

Paris sends troops: Having observed the comings and goings initially with an air of amusement and scorn, Genoa gradually be-

was actually declared a kingdom and the German nobleman was proclaimed king. However, the authority of Theodore I was limited by a council of 24 men chosen by the people and by the Corsican parliament, which continued to retain legislative powers. King Theodore held court in the episcopal palace of Cervione in the Castagniccia. However, he did not merely enjoy the trappings of monarchy, but appears to have campaigned energetically on behalf of his island kingdom. Internally, he restored law and order, tried to revive trade and led a newly created Corsican army in a series of successful battles against the Genoese.

gan to feel uneasy. Already heavily in debt, the city state raised further loans in order to buy in Swiss regiments. When even this failed to produce the longed-for breakthrough against the unruly Corsicans, the Genoese finally asked the French for support. In 1738 King Louis XV sent five regiments to bring the rebels under Italian sway.

At first the French commander, Count Boissieur, followed his instructions to negotiate with the Corsicans. But even after six months the latter were not prepared to surrender and to submit to the authority of the Genoese Republic. King Theodore next reentered the scene with three fully-laden ships flying the colours of the Netherlands. This time he had been able to convince a number of Dutch merchants of the attractiveness of supporting Corsica. Now it was the turn of the Corsican aristocracy, however, whom he had generously adorned with the titles of count and baron, to refuse him their obedience, since they laid greater store by negotiations with France. The Dutch ships turned back when they found the situation too precarious; for Theodore the only alternative was to leave the island once more.

The negotiations with France and Genoa collapsed when the Corsicans were called upon again to put away their weapons and accept Genoan rule. Then they were de-

with three English ships laden with military supplies. But the Corsicans would have no more truck with their monarch. He was forced to accept that his efforts had been in vain, and that his dream of a kingdom had vanished for ever. Disappointed, he retreated to England.

From Gaffori to Paoli: The Corsicans found their next tragic hero in Giampietro Gaffori. His storming of the citadel in Corte has become a legend. In his distress, the Genoese military commander had Gaffori's young son kidnapped and held him over the fortress wall in order to stop the Corsican attack. Another version of the story claims that it was Gaffori's wife who begged him to continue the siege regardless. In any case, Gaffori

feated in battle by the French troops, who had received additional reinforcements, and their leader was sent into exile. Almost before the French had left the island, hostilities again flared up between the Corsicans and the Genoese. This was the scenario in January 1743, when King Theodore made his third and final entrance in the Corsican theatre of war. Once more he had managed to find financiers for the Corsican cause, this time in England. And so on this occasion he arrived

Left, Corsican clergy approved the declaration of war against Genoa. Above, sails before the Corsican coast rarely bode well.

refused to allow himself to be intimidated by the fact that his son had been taken hostage, and went on to take the citadel. As if by a miracle, his son survived.

In 1746 a public assembly proclaimed Corsica's independence once more. Gaffori was elected the sole leader of the country. He succeeded in winning back almost the entire island; the Genoese governor finally had to instigate a conspiracy to get rid of him; Gaffori was murdered in 1753.

The Corsicans had one more trump card to play. In 1755 they entrusted Pasquale Paoli with the task of bringing their struggle for independence to a successful conclusion.

KING THEODORE I

On 12 March 1736 a hoarse horn-like sound, repeated on a shell trumpet from village to village, announced the arrival of a ship flying the British flag off the coast of Aléria. Fishermen, shepherds and peasants thronged together, even bringing their wives riding on mules to observe the island's leaders going on board to negotiate with a mysterious stranger. They were finally permitted to see the new arrival. "He was dressed in a long caftan of scarlet silk, with Mauresque breeches and yellow shoes. A Spanish hat with a feather covered his head; tucked into his yellow silk belt were a pair of

richly ornamented pistols; a long sabre hung at his side, and in his right hand he held a long sceptre." Thus he was described by Ferdinand Gregorovius in his history of Corsica in 1852.

The theatrical entrée was not that of some oriental sultan; the gentleman clad as for an appearance in an operetta was in fact Baron Theodor von Neuhoff from Westphalia, who had just arrived from Tunis, where he had completed the preparations for his Corsica expedition. A few days later he was to be crowned King Theodore I of Corsica. Whether the idea was his own, or whether it was the reward for his efforts to secure the release of four leading Corsicans from a Genoese prison is a moot point.

What is certain, however, is that the local citizenry was confident that this outsider, free from involvement in the local family feuds, would be able to free them from the yoke of Genoese rule. The hereditary royal title was certain to give him the necessary authority, despite the fact that a wreath of bay and oak leaves had to serve instead of the unavailable gold crown. Alas, the Corsicans' hopes were not fulfilled; does that mean that they were the victims of a confidence trickster, a false baron? Who was this amazing character, whose bizarre fate served not only as the subject for novels and an opera, but who is also mentioned by Theodor Heuss, amongst others, who sees him as a "marginal figure in history" in his book *The Shadow Conspiracy*?

"King" Theodore was born in 1694 as the son of a Westphalian nobleman in Metz. His father had quarrelled with his family following his marriage to a member of the bourgeoisie, and had subsequently enlisted in the French army. After his premature death his relatives showed their desire for reconciliation by providing a home for his widow and the two children, Theodor and Elisabeth. Amélie von Neuhoff later moved to Paris with her adolescent children, taking up a post as lady-in-waiting to Liselotte von der Pfalz. Theodor acquired the manners of court by serving her as page, and she subsequently arranged for him to undergo officers' training.

Theodor was, however, also attracted by the frivolous life at court. He had soon run up his first gambling debts and fell out of favour with Liselotte. For the rest of his life he was always on the move – at the court of Spain or England as a political agent in the service of Sweden, or fleeing from his creditors or from a marriage he had contracted in Spain with an Irish lady-in-waiting upon the insistence of influential patrons.

Theodor's involvement with Corsica revealed him to be a skilled negotiator with considerable powers of endurance. "He must have had a remarkable talent for gaining access to the most impossible funds, and for presenting himself to the world's leaders in such a way that they saw their own real interests reflected in his," wrote Theodor Heuss. Others describe him as a "brilliant tactician without fortune".

Living in exile in England, Theodor spent seven years in a debtors' prison and died shortly after his release in 1756. A memorial plaque in St Anne's Church in London, in whose cemetery he was buried in a pauper's grave, reads: "Fate gave him a kingdom, but it refused him bread". ∎

Paoli had grown up in exile in Naples, whither he had gone in the company of his father, the Corsican general Hyacinto Paoli. The young Paoli had received an excellent humanistic education in Naples. And so his first measures were not the continuation of the war, but the alleviation of the deplorable state of affairs amongst the Corsicans themselves. He found his people "run wild, unused to the rule of law and order, and torn apart by parties and blood feuds" – to quote Gregorovius again. For this reason, agriculture and industry as well as educational establishments were all in a parlous state.

A democratic constitution: Whilst attempting in the first instance to reconcile warring

by the construction of schools and the foundation of the university in Corte. Paoli was distrustful of professional soldiers and reduced the full-time army to a small force enlarged by the introduction of conscription.

The improvements in Corsica were noted with amazement and admiration throughout Europe. "If we take into account their progressive ideas, the self-government by the people, the freedom of the citizens laid down on all sides by the law, their participation in national life, the public nature and simplicity of the administrative system, the people's courts, then we must admit that the state of Corsica was more humanely structured than any other of its century," commented

families, Paoli also ordered *vendetta* murderers to be pilloried and hanged. The restoration of peace within the island's frontiers was, however, only the first phase in the development of a comprehensive national infrastructure. Paoli organised the administration, creating – even before the French Revolution – a democratic system of government based on the traditional Corsican community principle of the *Terra del Commune*. He was also responsible for a progressive, liberal legal code and encouraged education

Above, The only crown "king" Theodore ever wore was the one on the coins he had minted.

Ferdinand Gregorovius. Famous intellectuals and rulers of the time also expressed their respect, including Jean-Jacques Rousseau and Frederick the Great of Prussia.

This did not mean that the conflict with what had once been the mighty sea power of Genoa was over once and for all. Assisted by French troops, the Genoese continued to occupy a number of coastal fortresses. However, they were forced to concede that they were no longer a match for the freedom-loving and by now well-organised Corsicans. And so in 1768 they decided upon a tactical move: as part of the Treaty of Versailles they allowed their claims to the island to be purchased by the French. The latter showed absolutely no scruples when it came to agreeing to the deal, thus securing for themselves a strategically important outpost in the Mediterranean.

Sold and conquered: The Corsicans were not asked for their opinion; they simply formed part of the island's "inventory" and were thus included in the sale agreement. Thus it came about that France was forced to put an end to the islanders' autonomy. A French fleet set sail, and the Corsicans summoned up all their reserves of strength to resist. In any case, the French victory was not won without considerable effort. In the battle of Borgo the Corsicans showed once more

battle took place at Ponte Nuovo on 9 May 1769. The Corsican forces were driven from the Golo Bridge into the defile and annihilated. Paoli abandoned the struggle and fled into exile in England. France took over control of the island. By an ironic stroke of fate, Napoleon Bonaparte was born in Ajaccio during the same year – a man destined to be crowned emperor, but who would not be prepared to give his native island its freedom once more.

In 1790, one year after the French Revolution broke out, Paoli again returned to Corsica. He was nominated as President by the National Assembly, an election acknowledged by Paris. When the French Revolution

that their militia, despite being inferior in numbers, was able to put to flight the well-trained French army. Even Corsican women, armed with swords and shotguns, took part in the fighting.

But how should the Corsicans assert themselves against a world power which could send unlimited troop reinforcements, whilst their own reserves – despite active support from English, German and Italian sympathisers – were bound to be exhausted some time? The Corsicans' only chance would have been official intervention by England, but the British government decided to maintain its position of neutrality. The decisive

assumed violent proportions of which he did not approve, he asked England for protection. Between 1794 and 1796 Corsica was ruled by a British viceroy. In the final instance, however, the English abandoned the field in favour of the French. Paoli died in exile in England in 1807. His death did not, however, mark the end of the Corsican dream of self-determination and freedom. Today, after 200 years of belonging to France, the desire for autonomy is as much alive as it ever was.

Above, Ajaccio in the 19th century, as depicted by Edward Lear.

PASQUALE PAOLI

Pasquale Paoli, revered by Corsicans as the "Father of the Fatherland", was born on 5 April 1724 in Morosaglia as the son of General Hyacinto Paoli. At the age of fifteen he followed his father into exile in Naples, where he soon joined the local Corsican regiment. In 1745 he became a Freemason, thereby coming into contact with the train of thought underlying the European Enlightenment. The ideas were reinforced by his attendance at lectures in philosophy and national economy at the Academy of Naples. From 1752 he conducted a lively correspondence with residents of his native island, in the course of which he urged them to continue the struggle for freedom from Genoan rule. In 1755 he responded to the appeals of his compatriots to return to Corsica in order to serve as their leader.

His main service to his country was his achievement in transforming the "slovenly band of rebels", as the rest of Europe saw the Corsicans, into a state with an exemplary national structure. The Scottish travel writer James Boswell, who visited Corsica in 1765, regarded the Corsican government of the day as "the best model... ever to exist in the democratic tradition". In his book about the island, *Account of Corsica* (1769), Boswell reports on his first meeting with Paoli: "He is tall, strong and well-built; his features are handsome, with a free, open expression and a manly, noble bearing. He was in his fortieth year at the time, and was dressed in green and gold. He generally wore simple Corsican attire; only when appearing before the French did he believe that a little superficial glamour might help to give the government a more glittering appearance." Although relaxed and self-controlled, Paoli must have possessed a lively temperament. Boswell relates that he was never still and that he only sat down to eat. The Scottish traveller reports that his conversations at table were instructive and entertaining.

The restless statesman felt little inclination to marry. Boswell comments that he was "married to his native land, and the Corsicans are his children". Indeed, he seems to have been the object of a real personality cult. Boswell experienced the thronging of a vast crowd whom Paoli's guards could not prevent from forcing its way into his room. But Paoli had only to tell them that he was not at that moment holding audience, and his supporters respectfully withdrew.

In a burst of self-criticism, Paoli later explained his own flight into exile in England after the defeat in the battle of Ponte Nuovo as a lack of boldness in the way the war was conducted. Only the French Revolution some twenty years later summoned him back to Corsica. During the journey, he arrived in Paris for the first time on 3 April 1790. The French government had put a violent end to the liberal constitution of his people; now, on his entry into the capital, he was greeted as the George Washington of Europe.

In Marseilles he was met by a Corsican delegation including the two Bonaparte brothers, Joseph and Napoleon. Once again, Paoli was able to take up the cause of his native land as the president of the National Assembly. But the

bloodthirsty excesses of the French Revolution repelled him. He broke with France once more, joining forces with England, the country which had given him asylum. Corsica spent a period of two years under the rule of an English viceroy. One might have expected this to be Paoli, but King George II decided to send Gilbert Elliot.

The king requested the elderly Paoli to return to England, which he did for the last time in October 1795. Like Neuhoff, he died in London, at the age of 82. But 82 years later he was brought home again by his fellow Corsicans. He was finally laid to rest in the house in Morosaglia in which he had been born; today, it serves as a memorial to the Corsicans' patriotic struggle. ∎

On a number of occasions during the course of Corsican history, the interests of the major European nations in the island's strategic position prompted them to conquer it by force. Until the 19th century the attempts of the various occupying powers to develop Corsica's economy failed due to a permanent lack of funds, the apathy of the native population towards economic matters and the island's mountainous topography.

A life of self-determination: The remoteness of most of the mountainous and upland communities favoured their economic autonomy and political self-determination. This was evident even during the Middle Ages in the inhabitants' resistance not only to exploitation by the various invaders but also to outside attempts at political influence. Every scheme aiming at the economic, political or religious subordination of the reputedly barbaric populace introduced by the missionaries of civilisation from the mainland, was interpreted by the island's leaders to their own advantage and virtually never accepted by Corsican society as a whole. Thus, the largely autonomous Corsican regional culture was able to survive until well into the 19th century.

Only during the course of the industrial revolution was the island opened up as an export market for continental Europe. Initially, only the more densely populated coastal regions were encouraged to give up their economic independence and to face up to the unpredictability of economic crises in return for the chance of economic expansion. The island interior, however, was able to preserve during this period its stable symbiosis between agriculture and cattle farming until this was disrupted by entry into the world market and finally superseded after World War I. The destruction of the rural social milieu caused by heavy losses in that war, and the temptations offered by the culture of continental France, set in motion a pattern of

Preceding pages: The Moor's head remains a symbol of the independence struggle. **Left,** no shortage of headlines for the island's newspapers. **Above,** Monument at Ponte Nuovo, site of the French victory over Pasquale Paoli.

development whose implications, both social and ecological, reach far beyond the control of those affected.

The winds of change: When, in 1909, the French president Georges Clemenceau drew public attention to the misery and deprivation on Corsica, his aim was not merely to reveal economic defects, but also to point to the steadily rising numbers of young Corsicans who were choosing to emigrate. Only pensioners and the elderly remained behind; the villages were decaying, the fields and hill

terraces lay fallow and the island's industry was also in decline. In principle, the situation is unchanged to this day. The Corsicans' main complaint, however, is that virtually no one seems to take their problems seriously, despite the fact that they have always fought with both word and deed for autonomy and independence.

After World War II, two striking political innovations did much to encourage the formation of regional movements in France. Firstly, in the Treaty of Evian (1962), Algeria was granted its independence. The treaty symbolised the victory of the right of self-determination over and above the principle of the indivisibility of the French Republic. Furthermore, the end of France's colonial policy marked the beginning of a new era, that of so-called internal colonisation. It aimed at an increased mobilisation of resources by means of a specific regional policy, and was intended to balance the very real damage suffered by the French economy as a result of the loss of Algeria. This new concept of "economic regionalism" required not only a reform of the functions of the central bureaucracy on a national level, but also a political decentralisation.

Moderate demands: In recent times, new trends of this nature have accelerated the formation of regionalist tendencies on Cor-

island, which ran parallel to the immigration of foreigners, and against the centralised administration. It appealed to the population not to leave the concern for their well-being to technocrats and profit-conscious business-men, and voiced protests at the increasing land speculation on the east coast of the island. The union's cultural demands included the application of the so-called "Loi Deixonne", which lays down the compulsory teaching of the Corsican language and Corsican history in all schools.

The following year, the Corsican doctor Max Simeoni – with his brother Edmond the best-known propagandist of the Corsican people – founded the *Comité d'Etudes et de*

sica as well. In the initial phase, which lasted from 1962 to 1973, Corsican regionalism was marked above all by demands for economic and administrative privileges. At the beginning, they were voiced only by an élite class of intellectuals and led to the establishment of various action groups.

In 1963, Corsican students on the mainland founded the *Union Corse l'Avenir*, whose name was soon transformed into the *Union Nationale des Etudiants Corses*. Amongst its decidedly left-wing aims was the establishment of an independent university for Corsica. The union's newspaper campaigned against the growing exodus from the

Défense des Intérêts de la Corse, a committee whose aim was the protection of Corsican interests. Simeoni maintained that "Our opponents are the State and its regime – not France, and not the French people, but colonialism in all its forms." The members of his association were traders and lower middle-class town dwellers, who demanded tax concessions to compensate for the cost of living on the island, which was higher than that on the mainland, as well as the repair of the roads and bridges damaged during World War II, subsidies for the costs of sea transport and the maintenance of the island's narrow-gauge railway.

In 1967 there was a split within the regionalist movement to form the *Front régionaliste Corse* (FRC) and the *Azzione per la Rinascita Corsa* (ARC). The latter founded the now-famous publication *Arritti* ("Upright"), which gained a respectable circulation amongst minor industrialists, artists and manual workers. After the division, whilst the FRC went into a decline with relatively few activities, the ARC was able to create a stable, tightly organised association. Since it saw Corsica's problems as institutional in origin, its initial reaction was to reject any idea of political affiliation. Its demands for an autonomous administration led to the creation of an elected Corsican national assembly with its own

opening of the university in Corte and the foundation of institutes of agriculture and tourism. The programme was obviously fed by the illusion that by means of state protection the island would gain sufficient freedom to develop its own economy. This idea corresponded in certain points with the intentions of the French government, but was only put into practice by the latter in a limited manner and at a remarkably slow rate.

And so, in this first phase, a radical minority within the ARC began to voice its demands for complete self-determination, *Autodétermination*, on behalf of the Corsican people. At first little notice was taken, but later the first illegal moves on the part of the

executive, and legislative, administrative and financial powers under the control of the French government.

The ARC's programme for the development of the island included the creation of a tourist infrastructure by means of the construction of new roads, ports, airports and sports stadiums, reforestation after forest fires, the maintenance of extensive grazing areas, the production of quality wines and the prevention of emigration by the retention of existing schools. It campaigned for the re-

Left, demonstration for a "global solution".
Above, the FLNC, which is itself divided.

Comité pour la Corse Indépendante and the *Front Paysan Corse de la Libération* began to attract public attention. Within this category belonged the *Ghjustizia Paolina*, formed on the occasion of the visit to Corsica by the French Prime Minister. Acts of "democratic terrorism" against banks, travel agencies, police stations, estate agents and public buildings were proclaimed.

Radical trends: During the second phase, which lasted from 1974 until 1980, the legal wing of the Corsican regionalist movement was successful in abandoning its intellectual isolation and winning over the support of the majority of islanders for its demands for autonomy. This change of political affiliation was provoked in the first instance by means of protests at the pollution of Corsican coastal waters by thousands of tons of highly toxic industrial waste. Montedison, an Italian firm, deposited the refuse out at sea, but a proportion of it drifted onto the Corsican coast in the form of red sludge.

Since the central French government provided no diplomatic support for the justifiable Corsican environmental protests which ensued, the campaign culminated in a spectacular attack on a ship belonging to the Italian firm concerned. Whilst a number of militant members of the group subsequently landed in various mainland prisons, the ir-

revocable step from moderate regionalism to demands for radical autonomy was taken.

Lethal waste and legionnaires: The environmental scandal had been preceded by a massive wave of protest at the proposed construction of an underground atomic testing station on the island, and at the plan to sink atomic waste in the sea between the French mainland and Corsica. Further adding to the tension was the stationing of French Foreign Legionnaires on the island following their withdrawal from Algeria. The troops were generally viewed as an army of occupation.

Moreover, there was growing resistance to the sale of the Corsican coast to financial consortia from the French mainland, which went on to line their pockets with the vast proportion of the island's income from tourism. As far as the new holiday villages were concerned, virtually everything was imported from the mainland, from the building materials to the food supplies: even the staff was almost exclusively non-Corsican.

Thus Simeoni was speaking for many when he said: "The loveliest areas of Corsica were handed over to real estate speculators and industrial tourist agents, who now destroy the local hotel business, commandeer the beaches and mutilate the countryside without producing any real profit for the inhabitants."

In radical circles it was claimed that "if the speculators carry on with their construction projects, they will find they have built upon sand, for we shall blow it all sky-high."

Wine scandal: In 1975, public indignation reached its climax when the ARC uncovered a wine scandal, in which a mainland firm that marketed Corsican wine had apparently gone bankrupt, thereby causing the financial ruin of a large number of Corsican wine growers. The protest resulted in the violent occupation of the wine cellar of one of the fraudulent bankrupts by supporters of the ARC near Aléria, with the aim of withdrawing after holding a press conference to bring the matter to public notice.

It appears that the French Ministry of the Interior took advantage of the occurrence to frighten its subjects by means of a demonstration of public power; they had heavily armed "Gardes mobiles" flown into the island. During the course of the subsequent siege two policemen were shot dead and several of those occupying the building were injured. After they had been arrested the ARC was officially banned. Since the affair, Aleria has become the symbol for the continuing struggle for freedom. It is in many respects the "Wounded Knee" of Corsica; today, most radical supporters of autonomy maintain that they merely represent the latest generation in the centuries-old tradition of Corsican freedom fighters.

The event itself unleashed a wave of terrorist attacks by the *Front de Libération Nationale de la Corse* (FLNC), under whose banner all existing underground organisations had amalgamated in 1976. Since then its members have continued to wage an illegal war to liberate Corsica. Their hero is Pasquale Paoli, who for 40 years fought bitterly against first the Genoese and then the French. They are spurred on by the romantic dream of an independent island where there are no property sharks, crooked businessmen, clan-dominated politics or drug pushers, and the least they ask for is the right of self-determination for Corsicans within the framework of the French Republic.

Internal colonialism: Since no real concessions to those demands were made by a succession of governments, the underground militia intensified the battle against what it describe as "internal colonialism" by dynamiting illegally constructed villas or holiday

personal pride in being an Corsican, to a matriarchal family tradition and strong village ties, which are still felt by the 95,000 Corsicans who live on the mainland as well as those in distant countries. All of them have a strong desire to cling to their roots.

A strong common insular identity mixed with a tendency to adopt opposing opinions – especially where internal politics are concerned – is deeply rooted in the Corsican character, so it was inevitable that the nationalist movement should split. Within the underground militia the more moderate part which condemned "unnecessary" violence, took on the name of FLNC "*canal authentique*" (authentic route), while the hardliners added

villages and attacking such symbols of the state as tax administrations and Gendarmerie stations. Whenever supposed bombers land up in prison, even moderate islanders join the demand to release these self-styled patriots. Corsicans demonstrate a certain understanding for the terrorist actions, maintaining that, although the nationalists do not represent a significant percentage of the population, "for a few minutes each day every Corsican feels himself to be one of them".

Explanations for this attitude range from

Left, FLNC graffiti can be seen everywhere.
Above, the male-dominated Corsican Assembly.

"*storicu*" (historical). Both claimed to represent the original organisation.

A similar development took place in the legally constituted parties. The first to distance itself from any form of destruction and armed actions was the Unione di u Populu Corsu (UPC) which was founded in 1977 by Edmond and Max Simeoni, both doctors who had been imprisoned because of their participation in the Aleria disaster. Edmond became an independent symbol of national unity accepted by hardliners, autonomists, independence seekers and even by part of the traditional "French" parties, while his brother Max was elected deputy of Les Verts, the ecologists, in the Strasbourg parliament where he could fight for the island on the European platform.

Both FLNC militias showed signs of reflection and declared themselves open to negotiate a political solution, but part of their adherents continued the "armed combat" under the slogans of "Resistenza" or "Fronte Ribellu". The Paris government obviously was interested in – and perhaps even pushed – this process of self-destruction. In the mid-nineties the split had turned into a lethal feud. Supposed top-figures of the underground were killed in an outburst of fratricidal violence. This tragic chapter was only brought to a close by spontaneous demonstrations of

a non-political movement called "Women against violence".

A limited truce: A period of stocktaking followed. There were secret contacts between government agents and the underground which then declared, as so often before, a limited truce. It would have been helpful to ease the situation if an enlarged Regional Statute for Corsica would have been adopted with the preamble of the *"peuple corse partie intégrante du peuple francais"* ("the Corsican people as integral part of the French people"). Both the Regional and National Parliament voted for it, but the Constitutional Council rejected it as "not compatible with the principles of the French Republic". Then in February 1998 the "governor" of this Republic, the Préfet Claude Érignac, was shot on his way to a concert in Ajaccio. The indignation was unanimous. All politicians and even the known underground groups condemned the killing and distanced themselves from the unknown murderers. The event changed the political context completely.

Missing millions: Préfet Érignac had stirred a nest of vipers. He had started to investigate the whereabouts of millions of subsidies that had been granted by the state, mostly just to calm down Corsican demands, but whose appropriation had never been effectively controlled. In a far-reaching action a considerable number of people in executive positions in both agricultural and financial institutions were put under arrest, as well as former and active nationalists.

In September 1998 a parliamentary fact-finding committee established a double complicity of both the Regional Assembly and the French State in the misleading and squandering of public money. This official report was received with satisfaction by all political groups. But the suspects were arrested in the presence of the Parisian media, sparking racist anti-Corsican insults. They were then held for a long time pending trial, without the right to meet a lawyer or relatives. This was not what Corsicans had expected from the government declaration to re-establish a legal status on the island.

As a reaction, one of the FLNA militia groups, A Cuncolta, added *"indipendentista"* to its name, leading to the dismissal of hundreds of members and a complete reshuffle of the nationalist scene. From his prison Francois Santoni, a former high-ranking militant of the Cuncolta, declared that the assassins of Préfet Érignac might be former extremist nationalists, "but they acted as instruments of other interests".

By now there were about a dozen nationalist groups, both old and new and the killers have not been brought to justice. Meanwhile Corsica was still waiting for the government to ratify the European Convention on minority languages, so Corsican could be a compulsory subject in island schools.

**Left, the voice of the people – Edmond Simeoni.
Right, the mask of an outlawed organisation.**

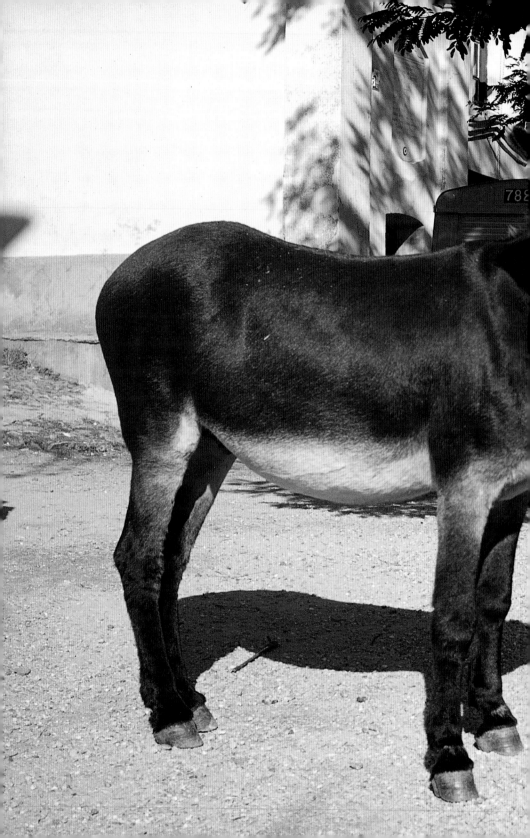

THE CORSICANS

The *paesanu*, his back bent double, tends his beans. Although he may be only a stone's throw away from the road, the passer-by will see little more than his straw hat, bobbing up and down. But peering out from under the rim, and without interrupting his work for even a moment, his keen eye has already made out who is behind the wheel. Local or stranger. The former will just be able to catch the greeting gesture of his hand, the latter probably won't even realise that their passing has also been registered.

Day in, day out, they're always watching: the shepherd on the hillside, the road worker resting under the shade of a tree, the old man on the bench in front of his house, his wife airing the sheets at the window, the *boule* player next to the war memorial. They hardly move their heads but they see everything. It is an involuntary action, this scrutinisation; a survival instinct moulded out of two thousand years of dangers coming from across the sea, of foreign sails drawing ever closer. Today it is simply a question of recognising those who belong, "us", and those whose purpose on the island is unclear, "them". Are they just speeding through the countryside, or will they stop and maybe even venture to the bar and enquire about some refreshment?

Corsican hospitality: That is something that the *paesanu* definitely hopes. Like so many islanders he needs several strings to his bow: he is shepherd, gardener and innkeeper rolled into one, and he likes uniting all these little jobs under the honourable title "farmer". He will serve his guest with a calm dignity that might seem almost cool; but then, even if the stranger has only stopped for a quick drink, he will always nod his farewell before getting down to another task. But maybe he wants a snack. In this case the *paesanu* will take the ham from its hook on the ceiling, carve some generous slices, then some sausage, and the crusty bread. He'll slice up a couple of tomatoes and produce a handful of olives, fill a large jug with water, and a smaller one with wine.

<u>Preceding pages</u>: looking to an emancipated future; the *paesanu* in his mountain village; life in the fast lane. <u>Right</u>, home with the catch.

The stranger has become a guest, and as soon as he has banished that initial hunger, the *paesanu* will strike up conversation. How does it taste? Well yes, the ham was smoked by a cousin, the bread baked by a friend in the next valley; he himself marinated the olives and he buys his wine next door. Depending on the response, the *paesanu* will soon know if it's worth carrying on the conversation. If the guest is a tourist who has to get on, then it probably won't get beyond the small talk, about the weather and suchlike. But if it's an islander, even from the other side of the mountains where the *paesanu* hasn't been for ages, if ever, then the gossip will continue; after a lifetime of peeking from under

the mainland who has lived here for decades will find it hard. Whether or not he will, eventually, become one of "us", whether he can ever consider himself to be *parmi nous*, will sometimes even be decided at that first *spuntinu*, the first glass of wine with bread and ham. In the meantime, every newcomer to this tightly knit community remains a potential intruder.

It wasn't so long ago, maybe two decades at most, that village children would repel the evil eye of a stranger by pointing their outstretched index and little fingers towards him, as he passed through. But just as the Greek *xenos* denotes a stranger as well as a guest, so on Corsica can someone whose

the rim of his straw hat, of picking up snippets from countless conversations at the bar, he'll know all about where the stranger comes from. So he lives in X on the other coast. Isn't there a valley with five mills there? Doesn't family A own property in those parts? Didn't the eldest of three brothers die recently? Why, of course, there are relatives of that clan on this side of the island as well, just two valleys away.

Anybody from the mainland, whether Frenchman or total foreigner, will find it completely impossible to latch on to the system by which the Corsican navigates with such amazing certainty. Even someone from

initial reception was cool quickly become a friend. But Corsican hospitality will only ever be extended to the individual; it will never be applied to a group, let alone an anonymous group of tourists. And hospitality always has to be earned, through openness towards the locals, accepting their ways and respecting their pride and their highly sensitive sense of honour. Then it doesn't really matter where the stranger comes from.

Contradictions in character: A social psychologist doing research on the island asked the Corsicans what they considered to be their most important virtues. A clear first place was invariably occupied by hospitality, then came emotionalism, solidarity and honour. However, on the list of their self-admitted character deficiencies, inhospitality also occupied third place, after aggressiveness and unfriendliness, before power-mongering and vindictiveness. This inconsistency in the local character has always determined the image of the Corsicans in works of history and literature. As Edward Lear wrote in 1868: "The people are unlike what I expected, having read of 'revenge' etc; they have the intelligence of the Italians but not their vivacity: shrewd as Scotch, but slow and lazy and quiet generally. It must be added that a more thoroughly kindly and obliging set of people so far as I have gone, cannot easily be found…"

But there is also a constant factor which serves to explain the contradictions of the Corsican soul. That is the solidarity of the Corsicans among themselves, which has developed over hundreds of years and proven itself time and again. While on the one side "them" might be taken by the foreigner as some kind of threat, it is only a feeling of "us" that gives the Corsicans their real strength and security. Family, relatives, clan and people are the natural bonds that make the Corsican identity so strong.

The sense of belonging to an extended family provides the individual with a safety net of relative security that will accompany him from the cradle to the grave. From babysitter to teacher to employer, whether in Bastia or Paris, down to the pall bearers who have spontaneously leapt out of the crowd during someone's funeral, there is always a helping hand from some near or distant branch of the family; one doesn't expect to have to depend on anyone else. But these intimate elements of solidarity can also provide the seed-bed of passionate conflicts. Altercations often begin over matters of honour or when the meticulously heeded system of *quid pro quo* is not correctly observed. When this is applied beyond an individual family to a whole clan, interpretations tend to be rather over-sensitive.

The power of the clans: The clans, whose origins are lost in the mists of time, and whose existence is often denied, especially by those at the head who pull the invisible

strings, continue to play a prominent role in the life of a Corsican. Only when he leaves the island can he escape traditional constraints. But even then, this requires a conscious act of emancipation, which will cease to be valid should he ever return.

If the ministry official Colombani returns on holiday from Paris, where he probably helps to cultivate the Corsican phobia of central government, then he can be sure that the people of his home village will be full of admiration for his social status. But at the *fucone*, his own hearth and home, his word counts for no more than that of the *zia*, the grandmother, or of his brother, who is "only" a shepherd – and often it counts for less. That

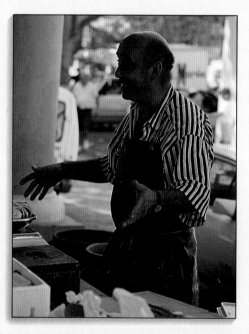

he is a man of great influence in Paris, and that he may also have secured his nephew a nice little job over there, will cause some envy in the community at large, although not amongst his immediate family.

Whether or not such envy erupts into a dispute really depends on which larger community such families are attached to. If they belong to the same clan, the flames will probably be quenched by a respected elder. Between two different clans, however, an event that induces jealousy, however trivial, can easily decide the outcome of the election of the next mayor. The power of the clans reaches beyond party divisions, a fact

Left, boules is a popular pastime amongst the men. **Right**, keeping the customers happy.

that explains why a basically conservative electorate can vote for a communist. Whatever his political orientation may be, the main thing is that he is their man, who can be relied upon to represent their interests.

Corsicans readily state their position, even if this defies all possible logic. It seldom has anything to do with party membership cards. The fact that they tend to get easily worked up over issues is the result of a history that has never let them get a word in edgeways. Planting bombs is a more extreme means of articulating what they feel. Indifference has never been part of the Corsican spirit. Neutrality in dealings both among and with Corsicans is just about impossible. The main-

some lively conversation about world or local events. Their dazzling white shirts with impeccably ironed collars provide clear evidence of where the womenfolk spend most of their day.

A French women's magazine once described the sacrifices Corsican women have to make in a traditional, male world. But despite her disadvantages, the Corsican woman enjoys a high social status. From time immemorial she has played out her role as matriarch and may sometimes be happy to stand apart from the imperious men, the noisy hotheads and all the swaggering at the bar. While this involves her being tied to the home and doing all the housework, it is also

land French, however sympathetic they may be to the struggles of minorities elsewhere, often consider their Corsican compatriots irresponsible trouble-makers, their actions inexplicable.

Male honour, female honour: Another cliché with which the Corsicans are so often branded is that they are arrogant machos who oppress their women. Visitors may feel there is some justification for this, as they watch the daily comings and goings from the chair of a street café. From sunrise till sunset, the vast majority of people he sees will be men; men strolling under the plane trees, drinking espresso or pastis at the bar, often involved in

a position from which she exerts a great deal of authority.

The first megalithic sculptures on the island were life-sized phallic symbols or depicted warriors. It is interesting to note, however, that when the Corsicans sought a leader in their first great liberation struggle against the Genoese, they were unable to find a man worthy of the role.

While history attaches a great deal of glamour to the swashbuckling deeds of male freedom-fighters of the likes of Sampiero Corso, the heroism of Corsican women in the revolts of the past and in the resistance of the last war was every bit as great as that of the men. But legend also ascribes an almost male toughness to Corsican women. After all, was it not the wife of General Gaffori who sacrificed her own child for liberty? Didn't women pour molten pitch over the heads of French soldiers as they stormed the fortress? And wasn't it the woman who would dip a piece of a dead man's clothing into his own blood and pass it on to a younger member of the clan, the signal that it was now his turn to carry out the *vendetta*?

The woman's power no longer manifests itself in such extreme ways. Be that as it may, when it gets to eight o'clock the confident man in the bar will put his empty glass to one side, wipe his *boule* ball clean and put of the

into the seemingly secure realm of men. While it may once have been enough for a Corsican man to rely on a barely justified rank within the clan to assign him work, more and more women, particularly younger women, have acquired real skills. In the world of today, their training and abilities liberate them from the constraints of the man's world and the system of allocation of the political families or the clans, and enable them to stand on their own two feet.

Even in local politics, their matriarchal awareness enables them to have a clear view of proceedings. Sitting on the district council for the first time, a woman is far less vulnerable than a man who has only obtained his

next little conspiracy until tomorrow in order to race back home for dinner. And woe betide him who comes too late! And although she may not sit down to eat with her husband, the *mà* usually directs proceedings from a standing position, apron and all; she listens and absorbs, and when it comes to making a decision she often has the last say.

Break with tradition: Over the past few years, precisely because up to now they have kept to their traditionally accepted roles, Corsican women have brought some uneasiness

Left and above, the cafés and park benches are good venues for discussion.

title primarily as a pawn in the game of parish-pump politics. At the same time, one will rarely meet a Corsican woman who flaunts her emancipated position. She was always conscious of her traditional value and has no need to boast. She is also too clever for that. Now that she brings her metropolitan, almost provocative chic into play, she can treat the old power game between the sexes as a bit of a joke.

"*So Corsu, no se fieru*" – "I'm Corsican and proud of it": this profession is based on the knowledge that despite all the centuries of oppression and annexation, the essential Corsican identity has remained intact.

Girls in jeans sipping Coca-Cola in a disco-theque; dare-devil motorcyclists cutting the corners along the narrow island roads and risking foolhardy overtaking manoeuvres; youthful rally fans trying out their skid tech-niques in the residential districts of towns; skateboard addicts demonstrating their art in an equally breakneck manner on the Place du Diamant in Ajaccio with the aim of impress-ing the cliques sitting in front of the cafés: at first sight the younger generation on Corsica hardly seems different from that in France or anywhere else in Europe.

What is noticeable, however, is the con-trast with the traditional society of the island. The elderly appear to observe the restless activity of their grandchildren with particu-lar suspicion. The men on the park benches discuss the problem, whilst the women at the windows shake their heads, unable to com-prehend the permanent desire for ever-new sensations, the addiction to speed which seems to hold the young in thrall.

Flight from the villages: Corsica's youth is no longer to be found in the countryside; today more than 80 percent of young people live in towns. The exodus of the island's younger generation aged between 15 and 25 from the mountain villages happened re-markably quickly. The hamlets they left be-hind are quiet places today; the inhabitants are mostly pensioners enjoying a contempla-tive retirement. For some time now, young Corsicans have been forced to move to the coast or even to mainland France in order to find a better education, jobs and the means of making a living. The "depopulation of the mountains" is linked to the declining impor-tance of agriculture. In Niolu, for example, wheat and oats are no longer grown as they were during the 19th century; for several decades now, imported cereals have been cheaper than those grown with much effort on the upland terraces.

Some young Corsicans are sad at heart as they follow the migration. Seventeen-year-old Antoine, who lives in Ajaccio, where he attends grammar school, is homesick for his

Left, students are the driving force behind the "Libertie" movement for more freedom.

village: "The mentality there is quite different from that in the towns. Relationships are more personal; everyone speaks Corsican. And you can spend more time outdoors, hunting, fishing or playing football." About a quarter of the island's urban youth spends its holidays in the village from which its family originally came.

Exile is out: Despite the high unemployment rates and shortage of jobs on Corsica, where there is little manufacturing industry and where tourism offers only seasonal work – and although almost half the young people on the island today work in positions for which they are over-qualified – most 15–25-year-olds now refuse to seek their fortunes in

out its limitations, permits the young of today to enjoy a more relaxed attitude to life. The restrictions of island life still annoy some of them, for example 16-year-old Michèle: "Here, everybody knows everybody else, and everyone knows what the others are doing." Dominique, also 16, sees the familiarity in a positive light. "At home, people help each other. Where I live there is an old woman who lives alone, and we all help to look after her."

From 1981, the migration of young people wishing to study was checked by the opening of the university in Corte – a victory for Corsica's newly-regained self-confidence. After the French had purchased Corsica from

"exile". A survey carried out not long ago on behalf of the Corsican weekly magazine *KYRN* and the regional station FR3 revealed a transformation in the attitudes of young Corsicans: they refuse to succumb to the fatalism traditional among islanders.

Most of those interviewed said that, despite the gloomy career prospects and restricted leisure opportunities, they were happy and satisfied with life on the island. One possible explanation is that the penetration of modern urban life has brought a new permissiveness into the hitherto rigid customs and strict rules governing behaviour. The new freedom, admittedly still not with-

the Genoese in 1769 and broken the islanders' resistance by force, they hastened to close down Paoli's university because they saw it as a hothouse for Corsican awareness and as such a potential danger for the central French government. Over 200 years later, patriotic Corsicans were tired of sending their children to the "continent" to study. They organised seminars and courses under the umbrella of a "summer university" in Corte. The pressure on the government in Paris grew until it finally agreed to the founding of a new university in Corte.

Between two stools: Jacques Thiers, the socio-linguist and writer, is a professor at the university, at which the study of the Corsican language plays an important role. He has observed amongst the students an increased interest in the island's culture. Should this be seen as a trend towards a new wave of nostalgia? Is there a move towards conservatism developing amongst students to counterbalance the international youth culture which has engulfed the island?

Of the almost 500 participants in the survey, 45 percent claimed to be able to speak Corsican; by contrast, only 16 percent have a command of the written language. And yet the vast majority (72 percent) agrees with the nationalist movement's demand that Corsican should be afforded equal rights with

over, but they are also increasingly attracted to the music of groups singing in Corsican, such as *I Muvrini* or *I Chjami Ahgjalesi*. This is just one indication of their search for a clear identity. Of the young people interviewed, 40 percent regard themselves as hybrids – either "French-Corsican" or "Corsican-French". A smaller proportion considers itself exclusively Corsican, and only 5 percent would like to be pure French.

The other side of the coin: Apart from the lack of career opportunities, young Corsicans complain of the limited range of leisure activities available on the island. Sport is very important, but in the evening – apart from reading, watching television or playing

French as the island's second official language. For the island's youth, Corsican is an important symbolic element in their resistance to foreign influences.

They are unanimous that "Corsican traditions should be upheld". This includes the rediscovery of the island's traditional occupations: young people can now be found restoring old farmhouses, producing cheese, pressing olive oil, growing kiwis or keeping bees. In the discotheques they dance to the same music as their contemporaries the world

cards – the only pastimes available are meeting friends in bars, visiting the cinema or going to a discotheque. Outside the tourist season, the latter are only open at weekends. You will not see any posters advertising large-scale rock or pop concerts on the island, for there are no suitable concert halls.

Many young people are unable to take advantage of any prestigious leisure activities which are on offer, because they cost money. Those who have the means also have an expensive motorbike, trendy clothes with the right labels, a fancy surfboard. Those who cannot afford such glamourous toys may perhaps feel tempted to acquire them by

Left, the youth of Ajaccio. **Above**, soon they'll be on their mopeds, too.

illegal means. In Ajaccio and Bastia, the capitals of the *départements*, pickpockets and car thieves are rampant; many use motorbikes for a speedy snatch and getaway.

"Everyone wants to be like everyone else, to wear fashionable clothes, zoom around on a motorbike and to let their hair down in the disco at night. Why shouldn't we be able to do all that too?" Twenty-year-old X justifies his lifestyle in these terms; he is one of those who knows how to look after himself. The increase in juvenile crime over the past few years is noticeable. It is not merely a matter of petty offences, but includes breaking into shops and flats, increasingly by organised gangs of thieves. Recently crimes by minors

have ceased to be the preserve of towns and cities, but have spread over into tourist villages during the holiday season.

"It's not just a question of money, or wanting to impress the girls," explains one boy. "There's an element of risk in it, the thrill of winning." He personally does not want to become involved in major felony, because of the shame it would bring his family. "If I didn't have them it would all be much worse. There'd be no limit to what I would do."

Honour thy family: The *KYRN* survey revealed the continued importance of the family to young Corsicans. The family was men-

tioned as "the most important thing in life" even before health, love and friendship. Only 5 percent of those questioned claimed to experience problems with their family or to feel repressed. This is an astonishing result, for in the past a large number of Corsicans left the island because they were no longer prepared to accept the authoritarian regimentation imposed by the head of the family.

Nowadays it is the girls and young women in particular who are rebellious, questioning their traditionally subservient role in the clan-ridden Corsican society. Sixty percent emphasise that they do not share their parents' political views; in the case of the young men, 5 percent fewer take this attitude. Politics is a subject discussed with great passion amongst young people on Corsica. More than half of them wish for a larger degree of autonomy for their island; almost as many are of the opinion that politically motivated acts of violence are sometimes justified. Twenty percent are prepared to concede that such acts are often, or always, correct. Jean-Claude, 17, states: "You can't just condemn the acts of violence without considering what has driven people to resort to this ultimate weapon." Michèle (16) is one of those who condemn political action of this nature: "You can't just blow up everything which gets in your way."

The *KYRN* survey concluded from its comprehensive study and its contradictory results that the youth of Corsica today is undergoing a fundamental transformation. But it adds that "although the island has not remained untouched by the trend towards uniformity which is penetrating to the farthest corner of the planet, it has nonetheless offered more resistance than one could possibly have expected. Today's youth seems even more conscious than the previous generation of the cultural erosion which began some decades ago on Corsica."

More freedom: yes, please. But leave the confines of the island in order to achieve it? Not necessarily. To be like one's contemporaries "on the continent" in Paris, London, Berlin or elsewhere? On one hand yes, but on the other, there are a number of distinctly Corsican characteristics which the young would be sorry to have to abandon.

Above, modern girls in Bastia. **Right**, locals can enjoy the beach as well.

THE "SANTA" FESTIVAL

The broad, picturesque, upland plain of Calacuccia, the largest community in the Niolu, is surrounded by a chain of high mountains soaring up to altitudes of over 2,000 metres (6,500 feet). In former times the peasants and shepherds up here lived from the forests, largely comprised of chestnut trees, from modest cereal and fruit farming and from their large flocks of sheep and goats which grazed on the mountain pastures. In this remote fastness they had no need to fear attack by enemy invaders. And so they built their houses scattered at random across the mountain slopes. Here, in contrast to the coastal areas, you will find no fortified castles perched on the hilltops.

A gathering place for shepherds: "In this region dwell the strongest men on Corsica, patriarchal shepherds who have faithfully maintained the tradition of their forebears," wrote Ferdinand Gregorovius in his history of Corsica in 1852, describing the rugged inhabitants of the Niolu. Every year on 8 September, the Festival of the Nativity of the Virgin Mary, they still celebrate the largest and most important folk festival on the island, at which customs and traditions handed down across the centuries are brought back to life. The people gather together, not only to honour the Madonna, but also to commemorate the old traditions which united Corsicans for many hundreds of years. The festival, which takes place in the tiny hamlet of Casamaccioli to the south of the lake of Calacuccia, occurs during the season when the flocks are being driven back down into the valleys from the mountain pastures.

In former times the sheep and goats spent the entire summer grazing the mountainsides, watched over by the shepherds. In September, when the days become shorter and the arrival of autumn heralds the beginning of the cold season of the year, they would begin the withdrawal to the milder coastal regions. It was an occasion for rejoicing, and also an opportunity for the shepherds and upland peasants to exchange news and views before

the flocks embarked upon the hazardous descent via the Scala di Santa Regina.

There are many places away from the road where even today you can still see the staircase-like footpaths by which the mountain-dwellers and their flocks ascended and descended the slopes. Nowadays the vast herds of animals which once migrated up and down these ancient paths no longer exist. The Festival of *La Santa du Niolu*, however, has remained the meeting point for shepherds and upland peasants, and also for many Cor-

sicans who have left the island in search of better living conditions, and who return specially for the Festival of the Nativity of the Virgin. The modest hamlet of Casamaccioli attracts up to 10,000 visitors for the three-day event.

The traders erect their stalls on the spacious market place. Local handicrafts and Corsican ham and cheese specialities are offered alongside clothes, toys and cheap plastic items. An essential part of the scene are the pious pictures and religious items in sugary hues scaling all the colours of the rainbow, and which at least serve as reminders of the reason for the market. Hidden away

Preceding pages: flowers for the Virgin. Left, the "Santa" is carried through Casamaccioli. Above, a veteran of the times sings his piece.

in the farthest corners of the square, roulette tables are put up, for the Corsicans are passionate gamblers. The more money the relations have brought with them from the mainland, the higher the stakes. There also used to be a big cattle market here, but this has now disappeared.

A festive folk mass: The bustling activity between the stalls and displays does not begin until after the religious service, which is celebrated according to tradition on the spacious square in front of the parish church with its free-standing tower. The brightly painted wooden statue of the Virgin Mary is carried with great ceremony out of the church and placed next to an old crucifix in front of

The voices mostly sound rough and hard, occasionally becoming gentle or strangely nasal. The origins of the music, which follows an octosyllabic verse rhythm, lie buried in obscurity. It may well have developed from the Italian madrigal, or from elements derived from oriental music.

At the end of the mass, a group of men shoulders the pedestal upon which stands the statue of the Virgin Mary. They carry it round the village square to the rhythmic ringing of bells. Between the colourful fairground stalls the procession of white-robed penitents of the Fraternity of St Anthony forms the so-called *granitula*, a spiral procession common to many Corsican religious

the altar. The congregation throngs into the square surrounding the church.

As soon as the mass begins, a group of five men strikes up a traditional chant. On holy days only the upland shepherds sing the folk mass, known as the *paghiella*. It is regarded as the purest example of true Corsican folk music, which despite the lack of written records has been preserved in its simple, archaic form across the centuries. It follows an ancient, polyphonic tonal system. The first voice – *a prima* – sets the rhythm and the pitch. It is underlined by the bass – *u boldu* – whilst the third voice – *a terza* – sings a high-pitched contrapuntal melody.

gatherings. The column coils up in the form of a sea-snail, unrolls and then coils up again in a visual allegory of life from its origins until death and the resurrection.

The story of the *Santa*: The local priest relates to curious listeners the story of the miracle-working statue in whose honour the festival takes place. On a stormy night back in the 15th century a ship had been blown off course near Galéria. Its situation seemed hopeless, but the captain prayed to the Virgin Mary for assistance. In his despair he vowed to donate the most beautiful statue of the Madonna he could find in Genoa. Immediately a strange light appeared above the

Franciscan monastery at the foot of the forest of Tafonatu. The captain kept his promise, and the statue was duly erected in the monastery church.

During the 16th century, when the Turks destroyed the monastery, the statue of the Madonna was saved. It was carried by a mule high up into the mountains of the Niolu, where it remained in safety. When the beast reached the village of Casamaccioli, it suddenly threw its burden to the ground. The statue was placed in the Chapel of St Anthony, near the cemetery. The next day it miraculously reappeared in the middle of the village. After this had happened several times, the shepherds of the Niolu built a church

notonous melody, to which the participants improvise their own lyrics. The *Chiam' e Rispondi* are above all sarcastic musical dialogues, in which they demonstrate their wit and repartee. Comments and responses fly thick and fast. The aim is to demonstrate one's quick wit and to bring in contemporary subjects which will arouse the emotions of the listeners.

The verses invented by the older men are full of poetry and wisdom; however, there are also a few younger bards who have mastered this traditional art of musical dialogue, which only comes to an end when no one can think of an answer. The singer who is best able to express himself in a cutting,

dedicated to the Virgin. Ever since then, they have celebrated the festival of the Nativity of the Virgin.

The singing contest: During the afternoon of the first day, on a square shaded by spreading chestnut trees, the mountain shepherds gather to compete with one another in poetic improvisation and oratory. With microphones belonging to the Corsican radio station in their hands, they stand ready to broadcast their singing talents in the language of the island. Musicians strike up a simple, mo-

Left and above, spectators watch expectantly as the singing contest gets underway.

striking manner will be rewarded by the applause and laughter of the onlookers. This musical form, cultivated above all by the shepherds, is part of the island's folkloric tradition and has been handed down from generation to generation.

Women are excluded from the patriarchal contest (in days gone by their lyrical talents were put to use in the singing of lullabies and lamentations of the dead), and the circle of listeners is also predominantly male. The strange songs of the Corsican mountain-dwellers do not fade away until the sun has finally disappeared behind the ridges of the surrounding peaks.

Three drops of oil fall from the fingertip on to the plate filled with water. According to the laws of physics they ought to flow together on the surface of the water. But on the contrary! They disintegrate into a thousand minute globules which suddenly cannot be seen. As if they had never existed. Is there a rational explanation for such a phenomenon? At such a moment words like "reason" and "rational" cease to have any meaning.

The laws in operation are those of the *Signadora*, who is engaged in the process of

And yet – the tears of the *Signadora*, the relief of the *occhju* victim, the repetition of the theatrical demonstration with the drops of oil, which this time flow instantly together – does this not show that something very mysterious has taken place here? That an unknown force, incomprehensible and yet effective for a few moments, has healed by its exorcism of evil, by its banishment to an indescribable place?

Although any observer can follow the apparent procedures making up the ritual and

freeing someone from the Evil Eye, the *occhju*. The disintegration of the oil on the china plate tells the *Signadora* that the customer sitting opposite her is the victim of malevolent powers. And she sees it as her task to set him free.

This ritual, which cannot be explained by science, has its origins in the deepest depths of the collective island memory. Religious references play a role in the proceedings; signs of the cross are used as part of the ritual, but they do not explain everything. Is there an explanation at all? Who could analyse and confirm procedures before which the human intellect capitulates?

its trappings, it is pointless to try to understand the lip movements of the *Signadora*. When they start to utter what sounds like a prayer, the moment has arrived when the door to a magic universe is opened, only to close again immediately. Evil has admitted defeat, leaving room for a feeling of well-being. The tiredness and exhaustion, the entire malady, all the manifestations of the *occhju* are no more than a bad dream.

But the *Signadora*, who has absorbed these harmful vibrations, must now rest in order to free herself from them once more. For a brief moment it is as if she has fulfilled the role of a sort of lightning conductor for some unseen power. As an initiate who is certain of her abilities she is not only able to drive out evil, but also – when necessary – to heal physical ills, to treat sunstroke or alleviate the pain of a burn.

The *Signadora* is not a witch. She is the guardian of an ancient tradition which can only be learned on Christmas night, when the evil spirits go into hiding. At any other time the handing down of the magic formulas would have no effect. Although it will only seldom be required, one must show the supernatural power that one is worthy.

For those who have never experienced the performance of the *occhju* ritual, a moment in which time stands still, in which centuries converge upon each other, there is one further method of protecting oneself against evil. Most Corsicans, both men and women, wear a carved branch of coral around their necks: a reddish "hand" which will ward off all evil. These talismans are a gift at birth and are preserved throughout one's life as magic symbols.

Magic? Is that not just a term to cover everything which one does not understand? In other words, things which cannot be explained with reason and logic. Should one see the *Signadora* as some sort of magician?

And what is a *Mazzeru*? A man of whom it is said that his baptism took place in sinister circumstances without the blessing of the Church. And who, from a certain night during his life onwards, is able to see into the "Beyond".

He is feared, the *Mazzeru*. The word is probably best translated as "Wizard". His shamanistic powers are demonstrated in dreams, when a mysterious power forces him against his will to go out in the middle of the night and to observe scenes which only he can see: the funeral of a villager who is as yet still unaware that he will die. The *Mazzeru* is a man to be avoided, for no one wants prior warning of such events.

"Villager" is a very important word. Outside the settlements in the interior, the *Mazzeru* no longer exists. And even in the

hamlets strung out along the steep mountain sides he is no longer to be feared, because here, too, he is almost forgotten.

There are still a few of these unusual men – not many, for they are a dying race, following the inevitable fate of so much that has disappeared from the remote villages of the interior through the inexorable exodus of the inhabitants. In the very places where nothing seems to have changed very much, there has been a huge transformation which affects people, their traditions and their beliefs, and

which means that the *Mazzeru* will also one day cease to exist.

Really? Are there not still shadows in the depths of the collective memory, which at night are roused to life once more? They populate the twilight for those who wish to hear and see them. What remains is the mysterious character of the island, its *macchia*, its mountains, its rocks, all of which acquire a soul as night falls. And what can one say about a region which appears alien even in bright sunshine? Where there are no shadows and where man, surrounded by the *macchia*, can forget the world for a moment in order to sink back into the irrational.

Left, the mysterious ritual of the *Signadora*.
Above, defying the laws of physics.

The traveller who wishes to get to know a country really well should be prepared to embark upon a culinary adventure and to try the local food. The experience could well prove instructive. The much-travelled writer Kasimir Edschmid was of the opinion that the imagination demonstrated by a nation's kitchens was closely linked to its deepest emotions. Corsica is a part of France, it is true, but it does not share the sophisticated cuisine of *La Grande Nation*.

Corsican cooking is much simpler. It could be described as unrefined Mediterranean in style: home cooking, in fact. All superfluous trimmings are avoided. The food is mostly prepared and served in a natural way; the composition of the various dishes follows the pattern of the seasons. It is remarkable that, despite Spanish, French and Italian influences, the island has been able to preserve its own culinary individuality – thanks largely to its characteristic spices and seasonings.

Soup, glorious soup: You are most likely to be able to sample traditional Corsican dishes in a small restaurant well away from the holiday centres on the coast. A transparent plastic cover is usually spread over the table-cloth, which is clean and carefully pressed but meticulously darned in several places. The waitress – often the proprietress herself – will bring, along with the menu, a small wicker basket containing slices of *baguette*, placing it beside the *Pinot* ashtray. Sometimes there is no written menu at all; in this case, she will recite a list of all the specialities the chef has to offer. As on the French mainland, there is usually a menu comprising several courses for a set price, with a choice among the individual courses.

A hearty soup can be recommended as a first course. Usually a terrine is placed on the table, and as most Corsican soups are very filling you will hardly need anything else afterwards. One typical example is *aziminu*, a sort of bouillabaisse containing all varieties of local fish. Otherwise, the *suppa corsa* is usually a vegetable soup so thick that you

can stand your spoon in it. The ingredients vary from region to region, from family to family and from season to season: potatoes, cabbage, onions, tomatoes, pasta and broad beans, combined according to the chef's imagination in accordance with what the garden can offer that day.

Supreme example amongst the island's typical cold *hors d'oeuvres* until recently was blackbird pie (*pâté de merle*). Black-birds were considered a great speciality on the island, and were offered as "game" on the

market during the winter months. Traditional recipes (*merle à l'usu corsu*) bear witness to the well-established custom of consuming the little songbird, which now enjoys legal protection and therefore may not be captured. Instead, you may well find, for example, snails with anchovies (*escargots aux anchois*) or snails with mint sauce (*escargots à la menthe*) on the menu. Corsican ham has a unique flavour, for it is marinated in wine with rosemary, garlic and pepper before being smoked over a fire made of wood from the *macchia*.

Gourmet pigs: If your hunger is only moderate, you could decide to try a main course

Preceding pages: grapes have been grown on Corsica since time immemorial. **Left,** smoking ham. **Above,** the bounty of the sea.

of Corsican sausages, the *figatelli*. These are small sausages which are eaten raw, fried or grilled. The main ingredient is finely chopped pig's meat, fat and liver, which is laid in a marinade of wine, fresh garlic and peppercorns. Afterwards the liver is stuffed into sausage skins and smoked over a fire of aromatic wood from the *macchia*.

The traditional black pudding (*sanguin, boudin*) of Corsica also includes its own particular ingredients. Apart from fresh pig's blood and small cubes of bacon, it also includes – according to region – raisins, chopped apple, onions, milk, nuts or brains, packed together into a skin and placed in boiling water.

The pork on Corsica has a highly individual and unusual taste, for the domesticated pigs are allowed to roam free across the island. They feed in the woods on chestnuts, acorns, roots and herbs. Most menus include a pork chop (*côte de porc*). Prepared on the grill, and seasoned with the piquant spices of the *macchia*, the homely-sounding dish becomes a gourmet speciality. Amongst the typical stews is ragoût of pork with haricot beans (*tianu di fave*).

Travellers who have encountered sheep and goats during their journeys through the interior will not be surprised to find that they also feature prominently on the menus of the various restaurants. There is, for example, a ragoût of lamb and peppers, known as *piverunata*, or *riffia*, a skewer upon which lamb's offal is roasted. A particular speciality is the *mesgisca*, or fillet of goat. Certain rules must be observed in grilling the meat; it must be turned on myrtle branches above a fire which is made of juniper and mastic or strawberry tree.

Fisherman's bounty: Fish and seafood (*fruits de mer*), such as mussels (*moules*), sea urchins (*oursins*), crabs (*crabes*), spiny lobsters (*langoustes*) and oysters (*huîtres*) should all be sampled on the coast, where the freshness is more or less guaranteed. A colourfully assorted plate of all the sea creatures with which the waters surrounding Corsica abound is not the cheapest of luxuries, but probably one of the more rewarding ones. In small, relatively simple restaurants you can often make your own selection.

If you are really lucky, the chef will even join you at your table for a few minutes, wiping his hands on his none-too-clean apron

before gesturing expansively as he describes the state of the day's catch. Particularly delicious are sole (*sole*), gilthead (*daurade*), mullet (*rouget*) and sea bass (*loup de mer*). The method of preparation? As you like it. If you choose to have your fish grilled or deep-fried, you will discover that no one is prepared to economise on the garlic and herbs from the *macchia*. To be recommended if you decide on fish whilst far from the coast are the delicious trout (*truite*) from the local rivers and streams.

Many-sided brocciu: By now you are actually more or less satiated, but could no doubt find just a little more room for a small dessert. Cheese is an excellent end to a meal; the sheep and goat cheese of Corsica are as famous as their aroma is notorious. Part of Roquefort, for example, is produced from Corsican ewe's milk. The uncrowned king of the island's cheeses is undoubtedly the *brocciu*, a soft cheese of sheep or occasionally goats' milk, which is seasoned with aromatic *macchia* herbs. Its uses – as you will gather from the study of many a menu – are almost limitless. *Brocciu* is used in the preparation of a number of sweet specialities, including *fritelles au brocciu* – little doughnuts made with chestnut flour and deep-fried in olive oil, or *fiadone*, a delicious cheesecake with rum, gin or brandy and lemon juice.

A quick glimpse at the cheeseboard, containing a wide range of mild and strong varieties, will suffice to disprove any sceptical visitor's assertion that the Corsicans have only a single type of cheese to offer. If you order cheese after a meal in a restaurant, the owner will probably come to your table with a selection on an old wooden board, so that you can make your own choice.

As far as sweet desserts are concerned, you will certainly find plenty of suggestions on the menu. Most typical are the cakes and pastries made of chestnut flour; apart from the *brocciu* doughnuts mentioned above, *canistrelli* are another popular choice. They are prepared from a dough of chestnut flour, yeast, aniseed schnapps, oil, water and a pinch of salt, small spoonfuls of which are placed in boiling water. The cakes are cooked when the dough rises to the top; after being dried in a cloth, they are then deep-fried in hot oil for 10–15 minutes. If you are offered fresh *canistrelli*, your dessert choice has really already been made, although another popular speciality are the local *crêpes* or pancakes, which on Corsica are also often made with chestnut flour and coated with citron liqueur.

Honey is another of the island's specialities. The many aromatic plants growing on Corsica – mint, lavender, orange trees, chestnut, rosemary, etc. – produce a honey with an unforgettably spicy tang. The colours range from white to dark brown; the flavours are just as varied, from mild to very strong.

Vin de Corse: The island can also offer a wide range of local vintages to accompany your meal. Corsica's wines are certainly worth trying, although this was not always

quality are tested annually – in other words, so-called *AOC* wines (*Appellation d'Origine Contrôlée*). They must have a natural alcohol content and a yield of no more than 50 hectolitres (11,000 gallons) per hectare (2.47 acres). Wine of excellent quality is awarded the description *VDQS*.

Among the best grapes used on Corsica is the *Vermentinu*, which produces a dry, fresh wine, particularly on Cap Corse. Then there is the *Sciacarellu*, a grape grown especially in the region surrounding Ajaccio and Sartène. *Nielluciu*, a black grape grown principally in Patrimonio and the Casinca, is often compared with a good Chianti. In the Patrimonio district the muscat grape is used

the case. During the 1960s and 1970s they acquired a bad reputation as the result of a series of adulterated wine scandals. The root of the problem lay in the production of a number of cheap wines, introduced by French Algerians, along the east coast. However, the number of small wine producers on the island who continued to grow traditional types of grapes, has since increased. New standards for judging the wines were laid down and the wines subjected to continuous stringent controls. *Vin de Corse* is a label applicable only to wines whose origin and

Above, tasty morsels from the *charcuterie*.

to produce a delicious dessert wine. Mild red wines with a fine bouquet are produced in Sartène, whilst the white wines from Porto Vecchio are particularly good accompaniments to fish dishes. *Nielluciu* and *Vermentinu* grapes are also found on the east coast.

Other alcoholic specialities of the island include the apéritif *Cap Corse*, as well as citron and myrtle liqueurs. A schnapps is distilled from the fruits of the strawberry tree (*arbouse*). Whichever spirit you choose to match your mood, remember that in Corsica – as elsewhere – a toast to your health is always appropriate. On the island, that means "*A a saluta!*"

The earliest literary account in which Corsica is mentioned is probably Homer's *Odyssey*. The poet tells of the experiences of the Greeks in the land of the Laestrygons, a wild race of man-eating giants who consumed several of Odysseus' companions.

In later descriptions from classical literature the island and its inhabitants are described in slightly more flattering terms, but its sinister, eerie and unruly character are always of prime importance. Seneca, who was exiled on Corsica for eight years in AD 41, describes the island as a "treeless corner of the earth, where virtually nothing grows on which its inhabitants can feed." In his *Epigrams* he curses it as a "terrible place, surrounded by rocks, where you will find nothing but barrenness". His antipathy was, of course, largely due to the fact that he lived here against his will and saw the island as a prison. And yet it seems likely that at least part of the Stoic philosophy which characterises his work can be traced back to the mark left on his mind by the solitude of Corsica.

A study of the history of Corsica and the customs of its inhabitants will explain why for centuries the island was ignored in the development of European literature. The Corsicans' traditional poems and songs – the *voceri, ballate* and *lamenti* – were passed on from generation to generation in an exclusively oral tradition, arising primarily in the mountain villages which were cut off from the outside world. The perpetual struggle against attacks and conquest from across the sea prevented the development of an independent literary tradition on the island.

Exotic travellers' tales: During the 17th century there appeared the first travel journals written by soldiers stationed on the island, or by adventurous individuals who dared to visit the remote interior regions. It was not until 1729–1840, however, during the years between the beginning of the Corsican War of Independence and the year in which Napoleon's ashes were transported back to Paris, that the island appeared as a separate entity

on the European – in this case primarily French – literary scene. Numerous writers visited Corsica. They created a picture of the island as a paradox, both radiant and shadowy, idyllic and demonic. The strange habits and customs, strict moral code, love of freedom, tradition of banditry and above all the *vendetta* combined to produce an exotic portrait in which the boundaries between reality and myth became strangely blurred.

The authors of the 18th century preferred to people their novels with legendary or

historical heroes. The unaccustomed traditions of the Corsicans were depicted in a more or less naturalistic manner: their blood feuds, devotion to honour and close family ties as well as their hospitality and loyalty.

Balzac, Mérimée and Flaubert: The years 1838–39 and 1840 marked the visits of three famous French writers to the island: Honoré de Balzac, Prosper Mérimée and Gustave Flaubert. For Balzac, Corsica was just a stopover on the way to Sardinia. Prevented by untoward conditions from continuing his journey, he spent two weeks in Ajaccio. He describes his impressions in various letters to Madame Hanska, later published in the

Left, for Honoré de Balzac, Corsica was the "back of beyond". **Above**, Prosper Mérimée also wrote about the island.

form of a travel diary. For Balzac, Corsica is above all the birthplace of Napoleon: "Here I am in Napoleon's native town!" In an outburst of lyricism he praises the island as "one of the loveliest countries on earth"; mostly, however, he sees it as the "back of beyond", mysterious and hostile, inhabited by wild, unknown men who suspiciously shut themselves off from foreign influence.

The experience of loneliness and solitude, far from familiar civilisation, impressed him as strongly as the uncompromising sense of fairness and traditional code of honour. Whilst none of Balzac's novels is set on Corsica, traces of the island's landscape and people do occur in the works set in Brittany as well

stranger hiding in the *macchia*. The bandit – alone, persecuted and betrayed, the victim of the child's misdemeanour – becomes a hero. The boy, despite his youth, must die a traitor's death. Mateo Falcone has only one son, whom he loves passionately, and in whom he has placed all his hopes. But the family honour requires that he be put to death. The novella, in which Mérimée develops a dramatic description of the merciless nature of Corsican laws, convinces by its restrained, detached narrative style, which makes the portrayal of the island all the more sinister.

Prosper Mérimée created a lasting monument for the island in his novel *Colomba*, published in 1840. The theme of the story is

as in *La Vendetta*, which is set in Italy.

The writer responsible for creating for the island a permanent place in the annals of literature was Prosper Mérimée. He was the first to succeed in transposing the customs and laws of Corsica from a mist of exoticism by providing an explanation of their origins. In 1829, a decade before Mérimée arrived on the island as the Inspector General for Public Buildings, he was inspired by the novels and travel accounts of his predecessors to write the novel *Mateo Falcone*.

Family honour: In the novel, a father kills his own son because the latter has broken the honourable tradition of hospitality towards a

an authentic family feud in Fozzano, a village in the Sartenais. The main protagonist is Colomba, a young Corsican girl, who tries to incite her brother, returned to the island after a number of years in France, to avenge their father's murder. Orso, conditioned by the laws and customs of France, refuses to comply, but is nonetheless aroused by the passion, mercilessness and cunning of his sister, progressively succumbing to the spell of the traditional values of his Corsican homeland. Columba is obsessed with thoughts of the *vendetta*, and he duly becomes her agent.

Her "serious, sad beauty" symbolises her native island. The central scene in the novel is the lamentation for the dead, led by Colomba at the deathbed of a deceased neighbour. A passionate *voceratrice*, she weaves into the lament her sadness and anger at the unavenged death of her father, awakening in Orso the long-forgotten "wild instincts".

An atmosphere of latent hostility pervades the novel. The author reveals with great precision the deep-seated roots of the hatred which moves Colomba, the "black dove". The prevailing sombre tone is enlivened by the humorous and ironic portrait of the bandits, the *seigneurs de la montagne*. They relate a number of stories elaborating upon the customs of the shepherds and outlaws and revealing the natural character of the

Poetic dreams: Gustave Flaubert's experience of the island was quite different. He visited Corsica in 1840, at the age of 19. Whilst his predecessors attempted to come to terms with Corsican customs, he was overwhelmed by the beauty of the countryside, the sea and the transparent Mediterranean air. His impressions are recorded in his letters to his sister, eventually being published for posterity in his *Mémoires d'un Fou*. Corsica aroused in the young traveller a remarkable talent for describing the natural world, a hallmark of his later work.

Apart from nature, what interested Flaubert most was the lawlessness hidden in the *macchia*. He elevates the bandit to the posi-

island dwellers, whom neither Church nor aristocracy have been able to tame.

Mérimée regards vanity as one of the fundamental characteristics of the Corsicans; it is a trait which also dominated Napoleon's character. The writer sees it as one of the principal explanations for the *vendetta*. He sees revenge as a primitive form of duel and, at the same time, a result of the unjust rule of the Genoese, which made it necessary for so long that it eventually became custom.

Left, the drama of Corsica reflected in this engraving of Sartène by Edward Lear (1868). Above, the island retains its romance today.

tion of an "honourable man", celebrating him as the "hero of the Land of the Sun". Flaubert, a young man seeking adventure and fleeing from the norms of civilisation, turns his attention to the outsider whose lifestyle, far from society, personifies for him the longed-for life of freedom.

Flaubert's description of the island, full of natural scenes and anecdotes, in which women play only a subordinate, sketchily presented role, reflects the romantic dreams of a traveller of the time. He was the first poet to portray the island, its light, its scents and its unique beauty of mountain and sea with such sensitivity and poetic enthusiasm.

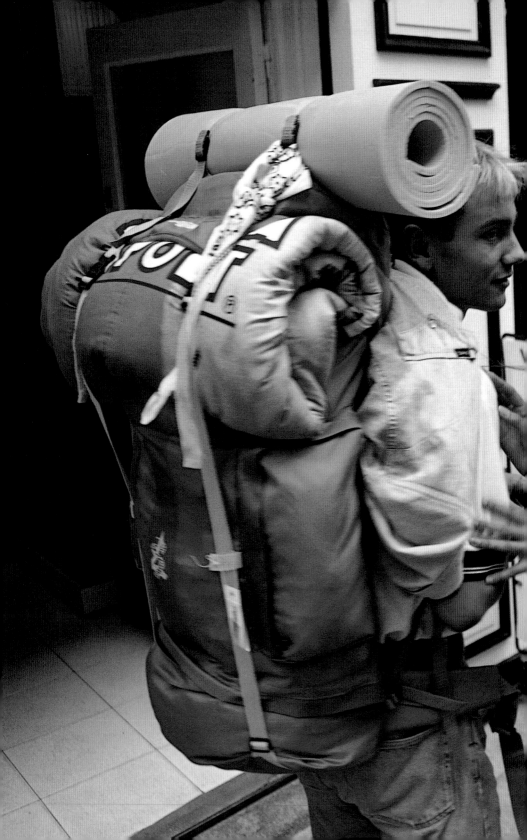

In winter, when the mountain tops are capped with snow, the Corsicans have their island to themselves. Between October and Easter, most windows of hotels and holiday apartments remain shuttered and barred. Mountain villages and coastal resorts go into hibernation. But no sooner does the spring sunshine begin to rouse the sleepy island to new life, than the first visitors from the mainland begin to appear. They are above all sports lovers who are impatient to take on the challenge of Corsica's untamed nature.

The thawing snow, which swells the rivers of Corsica into roaring torrents, first attracts canoeists. Teams from all over Europe, the USA, Canada, New Zealand, Argentina and many other countries come to compete in the *Tour de Corse en Cayak*. The participants in international sporting events of this nature invade the island like a new army of occupation, causing excitement and confusion for a few days before disappearing again just as suddenly.

Sporting visitors: The uninitiated may suddenly find themselves lost for words when, in April, their peaceful enjoyment of the warm sun on a bench by the harbour in Ajaccio is suddenly shattered by the appearance of a hundred frogmen who come trotting towards them. They throw themselves from the mole into the none-too-warm water, swim a wide circuit of the harbour, have their time noted as they emerge and then – still running – throw off their wetsuits before leaping onto bicycles placed at the ready on the Place Foch, which has been specially cordoned off for the occasion. The energetic sportsmen are participants in a triathlon competition, who have come across to Corsica from the mainland on a special ferry.

From the mainland, too, come the sailing yachts of a youth regatta, which put into several harbours on the island, transforming each in turn into a scene of celebration after the daily competition. They are followed by the official *Virée Corse*, a regatta in May whose course is set between a harbour on the

French Riviera and Calvi. For the Corsicans these sporting events are a colourful diversion after the silence of winter. Not all islanders are delighted, however, when the touring vehicles of the *Rallye Corse* career over the island's roads in May; the latter are closed in stages to normal traffic, including herds of goats. You will seldom see or hear criticism in the local media, however, and no mention is made of the ecological after-effects or the potential dangers the racing drivers present their voluntary or captive

audience. This seems less surprising when you take into account that almost half of the total of over 100 teams which tackle the 1,300-km (813-mile), extremely challenging world-championship circuit of the island, comprise Corsican drivers. Furthermore, the daily newspaper *La Corse* acts as patron of the event.

The hazardous slalom on wheels "brings a good deal of money to the island, and ensures plenty of international press coverage", explains a local journalist. The organisers are relieved if the headlines are not filled with reports of injuries or even deaths (as has already happened). "Heaven and the gods

Preceding pages: Corsica is a backpacker's paradise. **Left,** the ardours of climbing. **Right,** the delights of yachting.

have been watching over us." That is the thankful comment of Jean-Marie Balestre, President of the French and International Rally Drivers' Association following the 35th *Tour de Corse Automobile* in May 1991.

After this invasion, which guarantees a turbulent interlude in spring, peace returns to the island for a while. Early-season holidaymakers are notorious individualists, most of them also keen sportsmen. The car number plates and official statistics reveal that apart from mainland French, most visitors at this time are Germans, Swiss or British.

If you ask any tourist who is visiting Corsica for the first time why he chose the island for his holiday, he is likely to name the

Corsica, you can sometimes ski in the mountains and surf on the beach on the very same day until well into May. During these weeks, paragliding and parasailing enthusiasts can set off amidst a winter landscape and land on a sunny beach. Less energetic types may have their fishing rods or walking boots with them. A factory owner from the Odenwald and his wife, who discovered their love for Corsica for the first time 18 years ago, indulge in every kind of water sport and fit in a round on the golf course at Bonifacio by way of a change.

Of the large number of German visitors to Corsica, 21 percent claims to be keen to "experience something new". They explore

"natural beauty and wild scenery" as the main reason. The same applies to long-standing Corsica fans. A high percentage of visitors to the island are regular guests. A dentist and his family from the Rhine-Main area in Germany have been spending their holidays on Corsica for 15 years now, because "here there are no smoking factory chimneys, no atomic power stations and – except in the towns – the air is clean. For us, that means that the holiday is doubly valuable."

A glimpse at holidaymakers' luggage provides a clue as to their plans for their stay. In spring you will sometimes see surfboards and skis side by side on the roof rack: on

the island by car, motorbike, bicycle or mountain bike, on horseback or on foot. Even those who have been coming for years do not have the feeling that they have already discovered all there is to see. They fix an engine to a rubber dinghy and set off in search of lonely bays which can only be reached from the water.

The summer crush: Particularly along the coast, there is little chance of solitude when holidaymakers from mainland France and Italy descend on the island like a swarm of locusts in July/August. Between 1977 and 1990 the number of summer tourists (from June until September) doubled, from 623,000 to 1,285,000. Traditionally, the largest contingent has consisted of mainland French; they currently comprise 58 percent of all holidaymakers, whereby a considerable number are expatriate Corsicans visiting their native land.

A recent phenomenon is the invasion of Italians (getting on for 300,000 a year), which nowadays exceeds all other foreign tourist contingents. From a geographical point of view this may not seem surprising, for Corsica lies only a stone's throw from the Italian mainland. The shortest crossing is that between Livorno and Bastia, which only takes three hours. What is it, however, that drives these hordes of Italians to the beaches of

lessly overcrowded. Since the accommodation available for tents and caravans is almost as great as in hotels, many of the visitors are self-caterers. Shoppers' cars litter the roadside on the outskirts of the villages, and there are long queues in the supermarkets. Whereas in other places residents buy in large supplies in order to survive the winter, Corsicans stock up before the summer holidays begin, filling their deep freezes in July in order to avoid the crush in the shops. The locals feel themselves trampled on, and the visitors complain about the poor service. The dirty beaches often lead the islanders to complain loudly about Italian bathers who seem to have no conscience

Corsica? The massive price increases in Italy are doubtless one factor. The fact that the summer holidays of schoolchildren in both France and Italy are uniform rather than staggered according to region has led to an unfortunate concentration of the peak season within a period of only 45 days in summer.

At this time, although the beaches – particularly those along the east coast – never become as crowded as those in Spain, for example, nonetheless hotels, campsites, holiday villages and naturist enclaves are hope-

**Left, surfing without the crowds near Ajaccio.
Above, peace and quiet in the mountains, too.**

about the environment. The vast rubbish tips in the interior, however, are not produced by holidaymakers.

Those who wish to make a profit from the tourist industry, it can be argued, should ensure better facilities for guests as well as better disposal facilities for the refuse they leave behind. The average Corsican can hardly be regarded as possessing the ideal character for a service industry, but tourism is the island's most important industry and source of revenue; during an average year, the resulting income is about 5 billion francs. By extending the hotel capacity it would be possible to induce this source of income to flow even more generously. Before this can happen, however, improvements to the infrastructure are essential to avoid overloading and bottlenecks during the peak season.

Those who think in purely economic terms, however, have failed to take the landlord into account. In past years, tourist facilities have often been blown sky-high. It is exceedingly difficult for an outsider to understand the reasons behind these "plasticages" (bomb attacks using plastic explosives). What is clear is that they are not planned with the aim of harming the tenants: attacks on holiday villages mostly occur whilst the island is hibernating during the winter months. Should guests or staff happen to be in the building,

islanders this radical attitude to the tourism "blight" finds widespread support, or at least understanding.

Tourism under strict control: Everyone is only too pleased that Corsica's coastlines have been spared the reinforced concrete, bunker-like hotels and other concomitants of mass tourism. One result of the desperate resistance to the continued extension of the "white industry" was that, during the 1980s, the capacity of the hotels decreased by 10 percent, but this figure is now back at its former level. A further effect was the withdrawal from the island of a number of travel companies, but now they have returned and at the end of the 1990s new records were

they are given plenty of advance warning, or even temporarily "kidnapped" for their own safety.

Without doubt, these acts of violence are directed at the owners of property which in the opinion of nationalists and environmental protectors has been constructed following incorrect procedures. They generally object to the erection of a concrete jungle strip along their coasts, and in particular to illegal practices on the part of speculators who fail to observe the local building or environmental regulations. They justify their violent methods by pointing to the lack of activity by legal and administrative authorities. Amongst

being broken in tourism with about 2 million visitors and 27 million overnight bookings. There are still changes to be made. In addition to the rather expensive peak season fares on flights and ferries, there is a transport tax. Introduced in 1992, it has had a detrimental effect on tourism and may yet be abolished. More and more visitors are using camp sites, which have increased their capacities to cope with extra demand; the practice of camping wild has been curtailed by strict controls designed to reduce environmental damage and especially to prevent bush fires.

The landlords of holiday flats are also enjoying a boom: in the last quarter of the

20th century occupancy trebled to around a quarter of a million holidaymakers choosing this type of accommodation, accounting for a total of 4 million overnight stays.

The other side of the coin is that back-packing and camping holidaymakers, not to mention visitors staying in holiday flats or on sailing or motor yachts who are also in a position to cater for themselves, spend far less money; surveys have shown that a hotel guest is likely to spend nearly three times as much each day as a camper. Many campers and motorists bring food from home, since the items on sale in the shops on the island must all be transported from the mainland, which makes them more expensive. It is not

difficult to guess which category of tourists is regarded by Corsican businessmen as desirable, and which less so.

Many islanders strongly opposed the "all-tourism" projects of the late 1960s, which proposed the construction of extensive holiday resorts along the beaches of the Agriates. The land was bought back from investors and is now protected.

The newspaper *La Corse* summarises current opinions when it says, "A tourist boom and protective measures for the island

Left, the rivers are a tough test for canoeists.
Above, for skiers, Asco provides the pistes.

must be brought into harmony with each other, and the season must be extended over a longer period." Among initiatives planned to lure more visitors to the island during the early and late season are – apart from international sports competitions – sports programmes for amateurs, attractive special offers from hotels, music festivals and other cultural events, and the attempt to attract congresses and conferences.

Staying for ever: Long-term Corsica lovers invariably attempt to avoid the peak season. A considerable number of them have transformed their relationship with the island into a permanent affair. They may be the permanent tenants of a campsite on which a caravan is pitched throughout the year, or they may be the proud owners of a holiday home which makes them independent of the seasonal offers made by hotels. But anyone who has hopes of purchasing a plot of land or even a house will need tremendous reserves of patience and considerable staying power. Corsican families are seldom prepared to sell to a stranger even a property which has been standing empty for many months and which is on a neglected site. The old ties are just far too strong.

The outsider who proves himself worthy of such an acquisition will still have to leap a number of bureaucratic hurdles, whilst downing vast numbers of glasses of *pastis* with the neighbours or workmen before he can settle back in a deckchair on his terrace to enjoy a carefree holiday. His affection for Corsica may well develop into a passion which does not even exclude the island's winters. Some of them may even tell you "We could still swim in the sea at the beginning of November". Others may well enthuse over "ski mountaineering" with furs, crampons and ice axes.

The next stage is the "staying for ever". Who can afford to do that? Only pensioners? Well, among the foreigners who have taken up residence on the island are freelance journalists, hardworking craftsmen, bakers and butchers. They have been bold enough to abandon their previous way of life and have made new friends in the process. Nonetheless, they will continue to be excluded from Corsican society. The islanders' reserve towards all foreigners guarantees that this immigration is unlikely to turn into another invasion.

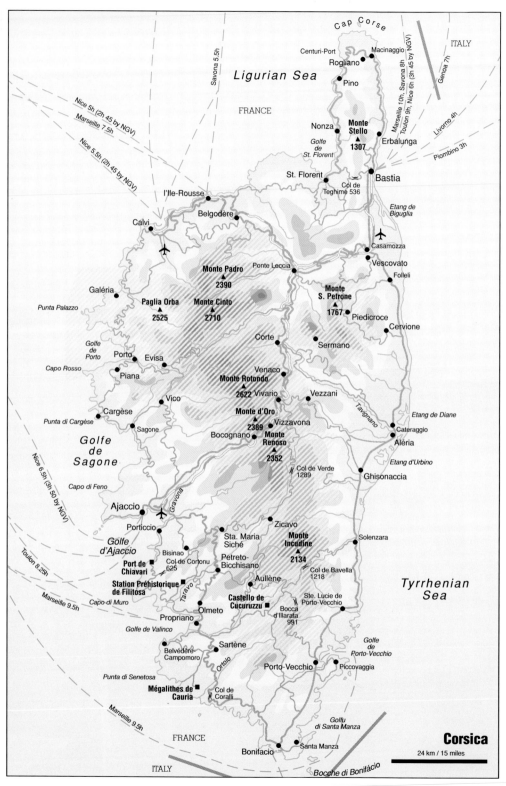

Cap Corse

ITALY

Ligurian Sea

Centuri-Port
Macinaggio
Rogliano
Pino

FRANCE

Savona 5.5h

Nice 5h (2h 45 by NGV)
Marseille 7.5h

Nice 5.5h (2h 45 by NGV)

Marseille 10h, Savona 8h
Toulon 9h, Nice 6h (3h 45 by NGV)

Genoa 7h

Livorno 4h

Piombino 3h

Nonza
Monte Stello
1307
Erbalunga

Golfe de St. Florent

St. Florent
Bastia
Col de Teghime 536

l'Île-Rousse

Etang de Biguglia

Belgodère

Calvi
Casamozza

Monte Padro
2390
Ponte Leccia
Vescovato
Folleli

Galéria
Paglia Orba
2525
Monte Cinto
2710
Monte S. Petrone
1767
Piedicroce
Cervione

Punta Palazzo

Golfe de Porto
Porto
Evisa
Corte
Sermano

Capo Rosso
Piana

Venaco
Monte Rotondo
2622
Vivario
Vezzani

Etang de Diane

Vico

Cargèse
Punta di Cargèse
Sagone

Monte d'Oro
2389
Vizzavona
Bocognano
Monte Renoso
2352
Cateraggio
Aléria

Golfe de Sagone

Tavignano

Capo di Feno

Col de Verde
1289
Etang d'Urbino

Ghisonaccia

Nice 6.5h (3h 50 by NGV)

Ajaccio
Porticcio

Gravona

Zicavo

Golfe d'Ajaccio
Bisinao
Sta. Maria Siché
Monte Incudine
2134
Solenzara

Toulon 8.25h
Port de Chiavari
Col de Cortonu 625
Petreto-Bicchisano

Col de Bavella 1218

Tyrrhenian Sea

Marseille 9.5h
Station Préhistorique de Filitosa
Aullène
Ste. Lucie de Porto-Vecchio

Capo di Muro
Castello de Cucuruzzu
Tavaro
Olmeto
Bocca d'Illarata 991

Propriano
Golfe de Valinco
Sartène

Golfe de Porto-Vecchio

Belvédère-Campomoro
Ortolo
Porto-Vecchio
Piccovaggia

Punta di Senetosa
Mégalithes de Cauria
Col de Coralli

FRANCE

Golfu di Santa Manza

Marseille 9.5h

Bonifacio
Santa Manza

Corsica

24 km / 15 miles

ITALY
Bocche di Bonifacio

WELCOME TO CORSICA

Even the Ancient Greeks, who arrived here in the 6th century BC, called Corsica *Kalliste*, "the beautiful". The chances are that they were inspired to this epithet even before they landed on the shore. Certainly, the visitor approaching the island by sea today, particularly from the north or west, can feel nothing but a sense of awe at the sheer magnificence of the landscape as it rises steeply from the coast and only stops at the gleaming mountain summits as high as 2,500 metres (8,000 ft) above. Viewed from the railings of a ship, such grandeur is bound to entice all but the most fanatical of beach-goers to set out and explore.

While much of the coast is indeed very beautiful, it is in the interior that the true drama of Corsica unfolds: in the towering peaks, in the unfathomable gorges, the weird rock formations, green valleys, blue glacial lakes, dark forests and lonely mountain villages. It is also in the interior that many of the historic treasures of the island – the menhir statues with their mysterious expressions, the old Genonese bridges, the Romanesque chapels and Pisan churches – are to be found. They are monuments in stone to a long and eventful past, which has not only witnessed the grief and suffering caused by centuries of foreign occupation, but has also seen the development of a strong sense of identity amongst the islanders. Despite the vicissitudes of history and the problems of the modern world, this identity has endured, as have many of the customs and traditions that surround it.

Despite the fact that some Corsicans have resorted to violence as a means of expressing their disenchantment with certain modern developments, the vast majority of the islanders accept and welcome the fact that tourism now plays such an important role in the local economy. The Corsicans are a warm and friendly people and receive their guests with courteous dignity. Even back in the 18th century, when the War of Independence against the Genoese was raging, the Scottish man of letters James Boswell could only find positive things to say about the island and its inhabitants. "I had got upon a rock in Corsica and jumped into the middle of life," he wrote. Visitors who wish to discover the island and all its wonders for themselves, rather than simply lying on the beach, can be sure to experience a similar sensation.

Preceding pages: the mountain village of Sainte Lucie de Tallano; an impressive mountain backdrop to the Gulf of Calvi; high-season down on the beach; fishing boats in Ajaccio.

PLACES

Because of its extremely diverse land-scapes, Corsica might easily give the impression of being much larger than it actually is. But wherever you happen to land on the island, nothing is very far away. Having scarcely even arrived at a place like Ajaccio and done the tour of the museums and monuments to Napo-leon, you can be off, doing whatever your heart so desires; seeking out some lonely beach on the west coast, negoti-ating the hairpin bends of some moun-tain road, or even beating your way through the *macchia* in search of the remnants of past civilisations.

The following pages allow you to take your pick from the island's wealth of sights and sites. Leaving Ajaccio, the tour starts by heading south, via the monuments to the island's megalithic past in the Ornano, through the rugged Sartenais and on to Bonifacio, precari-ously perched on its clifftop above the waves. Then it's up the rugged west coast, past such wonders of nature as the Calanche cliffs of Piana, and on to Calvi, dominated not only by its Genoese cita-del, but also by the impressive hills of the Balagne rising in the backgound and studded with picturesque villages and their bold, Pisan churches.

Before the tour of lonely Cap Corse, the next port of call is the pretty port of Saint-Florent and its equally enchant-ing hinterland, the Nebbio, where the very best of Corsica's wines can be savoured. Bastia is a convenient launch-ing pad for a drive down the east coast with many an opportunity for a fascinat-ing detour into the interior, including the Castagniccia, the land of chestnuts. Then it's up to Corte, Corsica's "secret capital", once the stronghold of Pasquale Paoli, and today the centre for explora-tions of the island's high mountains and valleys. Impressive country this, as any-one with stamina enough to tackle some of the hiking trails is bound to testify.

Preceding pages: Catering for all tastes at a news stand in Ajaccio.

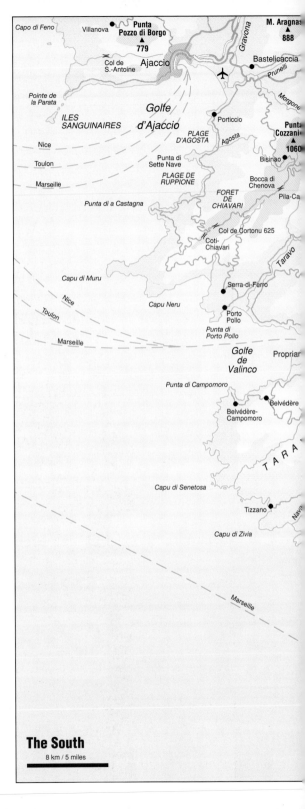

The South

8 km / 5 miles

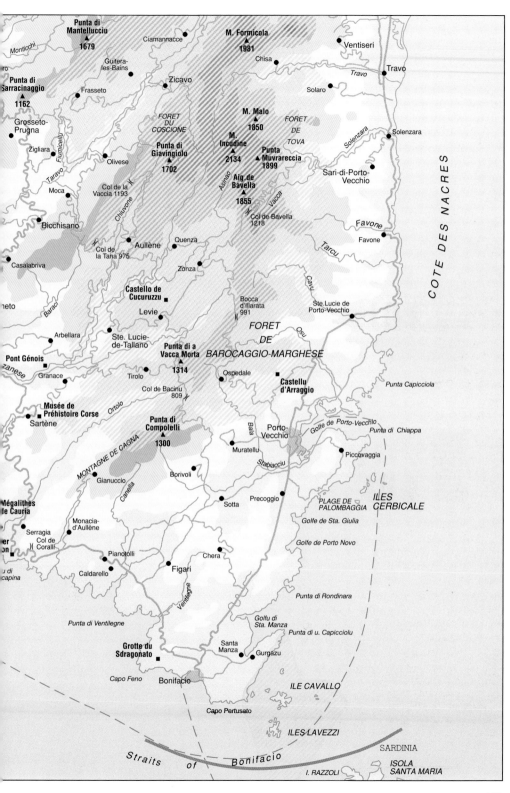

Punta di
Mantellucciu
▲
1679

Ciamannacce

M. Formicola
▲
1981

Ventiseri

Chisa

Monticchi

Guitera-
les-Bains

Zicavo

Travo

Travo

Punta di
Sarracinaggio
▲
1162

Frasseto

Solaro

Grosseto-
Prugna

Zigliara

M. Malo
▲
1850

FORET
DE
TOVA

Solenzara

FORET
DU
COSCIONE

Punta di
Giavingiolu
▲
1702

M.
Incudine
▲
2134

Punta
Muvrareccia
▲
1899

Olivese

Sari-di-Porto-
Vecchio

Moca

Col de la
Vaccia 1193

Aig.de
Bavella
▲
1855

Bicchisano

Aullène

Quenza

Col de Bavella
1218

Favone

Col de
la Tana 975

Favone

Casalabriva

Zonza

Castello de
Cucuruzzu

Bocca
d'Illarata
991

Ste.Lucie de
Porto-Vecchio

Levie

FORET
DE
BAROCAGGIO-MARGHESE

Arbellara

Ste. Lucie-
de-Tallano

Punta di a
Vacca Morta
▲
1314

Pont Génois

Granace

Tirolo

Ospedale

Castellu
d'Arraggio

Punta Capicciola

Col de Bacinu
809

Musée de
Préhistoire Corse

Punta di
Compolelli
▲
1300

Bala

Porto-
Vecchio

Golfe de Porto-Vecchio

Punta di Chiappa

Sartène

Muratellu

Piccovaggia

Gianuccio

Borivoli

Stabiacciu

Mégalithes
de Cauria

Sotta

Precoggio

PLAGE DE
PALOMBAGGIA

ILES
CERBICALE

Serragia

Monacia-
d'Aullène

Golfe de Sta. Giulia

Col de
Coralli

Pianotolli

Chera

Golfe de Porto Novo

u di
capina

Caldarello

Figari

Punta di Rondinara

Punta di Ventilegne

Golfu di
Sta. Manza

Punta di u. Capicciolu

Grotte du
Sdragonato

Santa
Manza

Gurgazu

Capo Feno

Bonifacio

ILE CAVALLO

Capo Pertusato

ILES LAVEZZI

SARDINIA

Straits   of   Bonifacio

I. RAZZOLI

ISOLA
SANTA MARIA

COTE DES NACRES

129

AJACCIO

The best way to appreciate Ajaccio's setting in its broad, magnificent gulf is to view it as one arrives by ferry. The ship enters the semicircle of the harbour, which is protected by the citadel and the harbour mole; behind it the houses extend up the slopes, and the town towers above the yachts and fishing-boats below. Palm trees along the quayside, street cafés, fishermen mending their nets: a first walk along the mole (**Jetée de la Citadelle**) is an intensely Mediterranean experience. From here one can get the very best impression of the town as a whole, and of its "two-storey" appearance: the colourful facades of the Old Town below, and the rather less picturesque modern, concrete housing blocks further up.

"Resting place" to harbour town: The town's name could have come from a Roman camp that was once situated here, if one takes the word *adjacium* (resting-place) as its root. But the Corsican word for sheep-herding, *agghjacciu*, also comes very close. Whatever the derivation, the town as we know it today was founded as late as 1492 by the Genoese, who ceded administration of the island to the private Bank of Saint George. Many members of the Genoese nobility and around 100 families from Liguria settled here.

Corsicans were not allowed to live here at first, and stayed outside the town for security reasons. But in 1553 Sampiero Corso captured the town, marking France's first ever intervention in Corsica, and the French started building the citadel. In 1559 Ajaccio was once again in the hands of the Genoese, who extended the fortress still further. Today, the citadel is still being used for military purposes by the French army, and is closed to visitors.

In 1769, just a few months after France had annexed the island, Napoleon Bonaparte was born in Ajaccio. Even though the town's most famous son did very little that was beneficial either to Ajaccio or Corsica in general, his birth-place still revels in his fame to this day, proudly styling itself *Cité Impériale*, a title more than emphasised by all the monuments and museums here. However, the crown in the city's coat-of-arms (above a pillar supported by two lions) dates back to Genoese times. In 1811, Napoleon honoured Ajaccio by making it capital of the whole island – or rather of the French Département Corse. The harbour thus gained rapidly in importance. Since 1975, however, the island has been made up of two *départements* once again, and Ajaccio is now the capital of Corse du Sud.

Seen in terms of its population figure of 58, 300 inhabitants, Ajaccio is really little more than a provincial town. But one very soon notices just how lively this former resting place can get when one drives off the ferry and plunges headlong into the tumult of the town's traffic, which only slackens off briefly at lunchtime. There's a colourful market every morning in the **Square César Campinchi** – directly opposite the harbour ferry building. The stalls here offer

Left, a calm Ajaccio morning. **Right**, Napoleon is the town's most famous son.

not only delicious fruit and vegetables but also such Corsican specialities as *macchia* honey, chestnut cake and Corsican wine. The sausages and the fresh, white *brocciu* cheese are garnished appetisingly with green ferns or leafy twigs, possibly a reminder of the fact that pigs, goats and sheep enjoy a great deal of freedom in the woods and meadows of the island's interior – something that lends their meat and their milk a particularly fine flavour.

There's a fine selection of seafood in the fish market hall: Ajaccio is the only town on the island that can afford these hygienic, tiled displays. Fish of every size and colour lie on ice here waiting to be sold, along with oysters, mussels, crabs and lobsters. At weekends, the "non-food section" of the market becomes the focus of attention. Textiles, belts and all sorts of appliances are laid out on the ground for sale, mostly by North African traders.

Napoleon souvenirs: The rear side of the same building is a lot grander, housing as it does the **Hôtel de Ville**, or Town Hall. It lies on the **Place du Maréchal Foch**. This long square, sloping upwards slightly, is the finest way to enter the town from the direction of the sea. Its centre, full of palm trees and plane trees, is perfect for strolling or relaxing.

The Town Hall is a good place to start our "Tour de Napoléon", with its inevitable town stroll. The white marble statue of Napoleon's brother Jérôme Bonaparte, King of Westphalia, greets the visitor here with outstretched arm. Then on the first floor there is the **Musée Napoléonien**, containing several momentos of the town's most famous son, including a copy of his baptism certificate and the death mask taken at Saint Helena. On the red velvet walls of the Great Hall (*Grand Salon*) there are portraits of various members of the family, and hanging from the ceiling is a highly ornate chandelier made of Bohemian crystal – presented by Czechoslovakia on the 200th anniversary of Napoleon's birth. Other highlights of this museum include a collection of medals and coins,

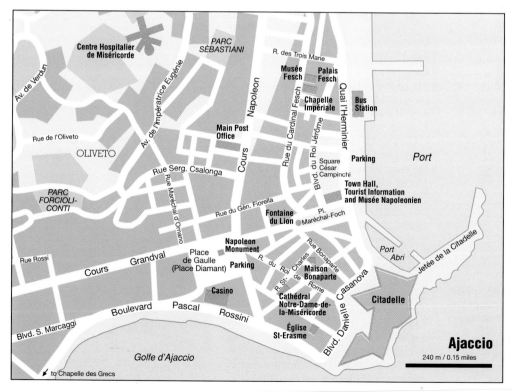

the latter commemorating outstanding events from 1797–1876.

We bump into Napoleon yet again at the other end of the Place Maréchal Foch: a statue of him in marble, dressed as the First Consul and wearing a Roman toga, towers above a fountain with four lions spouting water. It's at this point that the visitor must decide whether he wants to start off by visiting Corsica's only really good art museum, or by following the Napoleon trail back to the house where he was born.

Those in favour of the museum should turn right into the Rue du Cardinal Fesch, which leads to the old harbour quarter *(borgu)*. The tall houses here, with their partly crumbling, partly restored facades, contain tiny handicraft shops, boutiques and cafés. Narrow, dark alleys and stone staircases branch off this street until – somewhat surprisingly – a broad square opens out on to the generously-proportioned **Palais Fesch**. The black bronze statue of Cardinal Fesch, Napoleon's uncle, stands out in stark contrast against the yellow facade of

Place Foch.

this edifice, which was built by Napoleon III. It has been undergoing extensive renovation work since 1980.

Joseph Fesch was a half-brother of Letizia Bonaparte, the *Madame Mère*. His nephew Napoleon I, who was only six years younger, not only helped him reach his high rank in the Church but also lent his support to Fesch's extremely secular passion for collecting Italian paintings from the 15th to the 18th centuries, many of which were spoils of war. The **Musée Fesch** contains an extensive selection from this collection, including works by Botticelli and Titian. Ajaccio itself is only represented in one rather modestly-proportioned painting by Peraldi, hanging next to a corridor window facing the sea: it shows a view of the town around 1882.

In the north wing of the Palais Fesch is the **library**, founded by Lucien Bonaparte in 1801, which numbers several valuable antique books among its treasures. The south wing of the building is taken up by the **Chapelle Impériale**, the Bonapartes' funeral chapel, where

Fesch lies buried in the crypt alongside Napoleon's parents and various other members of the family.

Much less tranquil than the Rue Fesch is the Cours Napoléon, the town's main traffic artery, which runs above it. Even here, though, cafés have placed their wicker chairs out on the pavement, forming little oases amid the turbulence of the busy street.

The Maison Bonaparte: To reach Napoleon's parents' house from the lion fountain one simply has to set off in the opposite direction – into the Rue Bonaparte, where a little niche set into the wall of the house on the corner contains a small statue, the **Madonuccia** or "little Madonna", as the town's patron saint is fondly named. The **Maison Bonaparte** is not situated in the Rue Bonaparte, however, but on the small Place de Letizia in a side-street, the Rue St-Charles. Opposite is a small, tree-shaded square containing a bust of Napoleon's son, the *Roi de Rome*. The facade of the house is decorated with the family's coat-of-arms, and a memorial plaque situated above the entrance announces that Napoleon was born here on 15 August 1769.

The vestibule contains the sedan-chair in which his mother, Letizia, feeling the pains of oncoming childbirth, was swiftly carried home from a service in the Cathedral. The furnishings are, however, no longer the same as they were during Napoleon's childhood. The Casa Buonaparte was destroyed in 1793 when the family were forced to flee from the Paolists and leave Ajaccio because of their French sympathies.

The family country house was their first point of refuge. This estate, known as **Les Milelli**, in an olive grove only 10 km (6 miles) from Ajaccio, on the D61 in the direction of Alata, may also be visited today. It was only five years later that the Bonapartes were able to return to their house in Ajaccio, and Letizia had it renovated and extended with the aid of reparation money from the Paris Directorate.

Go up the stairs now and enter the first hall on the first floor, and you will find

Café in the harbour district.

a highly elaborate family tree of the Bonaparte family, with entries made as recently as 1959. These upstairs rooms, with their memorabilia in glass cases and family portraits on the walls, are furnished more as museums than living quarters. Then we see the rooms designed by Letizia when she returned from her years in the countryside: her living-room furnished in the Paris *chic* of the time, her sleeping-chamber and also the room in which she is said to have given birth to Napoleon – assuming, of course, that it hadn't already happened in the sedan chair on the way back from church.

We now enter the 12-metre (40-ft) long salon, in which Napoleon is said to have eaten a meal with friends on his last ever visit to the house in which he was born, and then "taken French leave". He left his hat on the table as a decoy manoeuvre and disappeared down to the floor below through a trapdoor, in order to reach his ship unobserved and travel off to further adventures on the mainland. This secret escape route ends up in a vaulted cellar, where a Corsican oil-mill can still be admired today.

The Cathedral: If you follow the Rue St-Charles you will reach the **Cathédrale Notre-Dame de la Miséricorde**, an unpretentious-looking Renaissance edifice consecrated to the town's patron saint. *La Madonuccia* is meant to have protected Ajaccio from a plague epidemic in 1656. Above the altar of the first chapel to the left is a valuable *Vierge du Sacré Coeur* by Delacroix. The chapel is decorated with stuccos thought to be the work of Tintoretto. In the second chapel we see a marble statue of the *Madonuccia*. Her feast, 18 March, is celebrated each year by the citizens of Ajaccio.

Napoleon was baptised in this cathedral on 21 July 1771, in the marble font to the right of the main entrance. He also wanted to be buried here if Paris were to "exile his corpse" – this request can clearly be read on a plaque to the left of the entrance to the cathedral; this never did become Napoleon's final resting place since Paris, as is well-known, did

An ideal coast for anglers.

not wish to do without its dead emperor.

Napoleon has returned to Ajaccio in another sense, though: a huge variety of statues of him can be found in all the squares of the city. In the **Place du Général de Gaulle** (known locally as the Place du Diamant) he's been on horseback since 1865, dressed as the Emperor of Rome, wearing golden laurels, and surrounded by his four brothers dressed in togas. This generously-proportioned square – a skateboarders' paradise – affords a fine view of the sea. It also doubles as the roof of a car park.

The most imposing Napoleon memorial was erected as recently as 1938, however, on the Casone, officially the **Place d'Austerlitz**. The broad Cours Grandval leads from the Place du Diamant straight to this square, at the end of which we see Napoleon – high on a white pyramid – in a familiar pose: wearing his frock coat and bicorne hat, the fingers of his left hand thrust inside his jacket. Between the steps on the way up, his famous deeds are engraved in stone. He used to enjoy playing hide-and-seek here as a child – in a **grotto** at the base of the monument.

Anyone interested in learning more about the history of the town and the island should certainly visit the **A Bandera Museum** in the Rue Général Levie (near the Place Général de Gaulle), which documents a great deal of military history. A private collection belonging to an old established Ajaccien family (furniture, paintings, sculptures, tableware) can be seen at the **Musée du Capitellu** near the Citadel. There are also some remarkable watercolours and portraits by Aglaé Meuron, a woman artist born in Ajaccio in 1836.

Blood-red islands: The town doesn't just revel in its past glory, though – and certainly not in the summertime, when life here primarily revolves around the sea and the beaches. Anyone who is not just passing through should at least take an excursion out to the **Iles Sanguinaires**, either by boat or on the *Petit Train des Iles*, a small open-top train with a warning bell. Both begin at the harbour ferry.

The **Route des Sanguinaires** runs along the north coast of the Gulf of Ajaccio, and passes the **Chapelle des Grecs**, where the Greek Orthodox community used to pray. The Greeks first settled in Ajaccio after their expulsion by the Turks in 1731, before finding a permanent home in Cargèse. Founded in 1632, some lines from Joseph Bonaparte's memoirs are engraved above the entrance. Just beyond the chapel is the impressive **cemetery**, with its many family vaults and tombstones spread over the steep hillside facing the sea.

The route then passes several more beaches, and ends at the **Punta de la Parata**, crowned by a Genoese watchtower built as a defence against the Moorish raiders, with the Iles Sanguinaires in the middle distance. *Sanguinaire* means bloodstone, and the name turns out to be very apt at sunset, when the rocks turn a reddish-ochre colour – an experience that really should not be missed. It can be enjoyed from the restaurant and bar by the car park, or from any of the many paths that lead through the *macchia* here.

Left, Napoleon as an artificial *taffoni*.

THE NAPOLEON CULT

There is hardly a street or square in Ajaccio which does not recall Napoleon and his clan. At the foot of the monuments, the eternal gratitude of his native island is proclaimed – but what reason does the Corsican people have to be grateful to the Emperor of France? Because he "carried out our vendetta on all those who caused our downfall", as Paoli asserted? Or because today he can be marketed so successfully – as a sight, a motif on T-shirts, postcards and mugs, as the inspiration for the names of cafés and bars? Napoleon himself is hardly likely to turn in his grave, for as he once remarked, "Providence created in me a Corsican rock, from which all strokes of Fate simply run off like water."

But what was Napoleon's relationship to Corsica really like? "I was born as my fatherland lay dying." The words of the young man express an ambivalent attitude to his native island which was mirrored in the career of his real father. Carlo Buonaparte was a descendant of a Tuscan family who became involved in the Corsican struggle for independence. He became the confidant of Paoli; whilst pregnant with Napoleon, his wife Letizia Ramolino accompanied him to the Wars of Independence. On the day of the defeat at Ponte Nuovo she felt the child struggling "as if it wanted to fight before it was even born".

Napoleon was born in 1769 on the Day of the Assumption; he was the second son in the family. The fight for Corsica was over for the moment; his father, Carlo Buonaparte, did not follow Paoli into exile, but chose to stay in Ajaccio and to adapt to French rule. Napoleon's childhood on the island was a happy one. Of all Letizia's children – she bore thirteen – "Nabulione" was the most boisterous. A ruffian and a precociously cheeky child, he soon acquired the nickname "Rabullione". When he was nine, he went to the military academy at Brienne. He always remained somewhat aloof from his fellow-pupils, wrapped up in his dreams of Corsican independence and imagining himself as the saviour of the island. He adapted his name to the French much later, when he was a general in the French army.

He took advantage of the revolutionary turmoil in France to enjoy an extended period of home leave in Corsica, meeting up with Paoli, who had been his idol during his youth, and who had returned from exile. The bubble burst when Napoleon's brother Lucien spread the rumour in the Jacobin Club in Toulon that Paoli wanted to hand Corsica over to the English. The warrant for Paoli's arrest gave rise to a *vendetta* on behalf of the Paoli clan against the Bonapartes, who were forced to flee from Ajaccio.

Napoleon's comet-like career began in Paris; as commander-in-chief and later as emperor he finally forged the links between Corsica and France. His compatriots were forced to adapt to his plans to make France a major power. But Napoleon remained a Corsican in his concern for his clan: irrespective of their abilities, he elevated his relatives to the thrones of Europe. At the end of his life, during his exile on the island of St Helena, he often felt homesick for his homeland: on Corsica, the earth smelt different. He was certain that even with his eyes closed, just by the smell alone, he would recognise his native island. ∎

137

ORNANO

Apart from having the odd busy beach during the summer-time, the **Ornano** – the area between the Gulf of Ajaccio and the Gulf of Valinco – is a lonely part of the island. But although sparsely populated, the area has a long history. Hunters, shepherds and farmers lived here more than 7,000 years ago. They left some mysterious menhir statues in Filitosa. The quickest route from Ajaccio to the most important prehistoric site in Corsica is the rather sinuous but still relatively wide N193 *route nationale*, that runs via Cauro and Petreto-Bicchisano.

On the trail of Sampiero: This busy island road passes through the homeland of the island's hero, Sampiero Corso. **Bastelica**, his birthplace, can be reached via a detour into the mountains from **Cauro** (35 km/20 miles on the D27). Sampiero is immortalised in bronze in the square below the church, in a warlike pose, his sword held high. The house in which he was born used to stand in the hamlet known as **Dominicacci**. A plaque on the wall of the house, which was later rebuilt, reminds visitors of "the most Corsican of Corsicans", though it doesn't say why he was nicknamed Corso (The Corsican).

We find the explanation in Ferdinand Gregorovius' historical sketches: all the typical Corsican attributes were apparently combined in "this man of primeval granite: a wild daring, an unshakeable tenacity, a glowing love of freedom and of his native land, penetrating insight, indigence and modesty, ruggedness, a hot temper, and truly volcanic passion", as well as a strong vengeful streak which eventually led him to strangle his young wife, Vannina, whom he suspected of having been in league with his hated enemies the Genoese.

Anyone coming from Ajaccio who is only planning to do this excursion can combine it with a drive back along narrow roads through the gorge of the **Prunelli River** (D3) which has been dammed up to form a reservoir near

Tolla, thus providing a round trip through superb landscape. **Eccica** lies on the D103, a small connecting road leading to the N196. It was in this small hamlet that the heroic life of Sampiero Corso came to its end: in 1567 he was ambushed here and fell victim to a family *vendetta* in which his enemies, the Genoese, played a large part (*see page 45*). A memorial tablet in the middle of the *macchia* marks the spot where he was murdered by his wife's avengers.

Vannina came from **Santa-Maria-Siché**. The road leading to this village branches off the N196, 12 km (7 miles) after Cauro, in the direction of Propriano. The hamlet of **Vico** contains the ruins of the fortified house that Sampiero built for himself and his family.

The N196 to Propriano passes through only very few villages, and provides hardly any opportunities to stop and eat. A modest-looking Hôtel de Tourisme awaits guests seeking salvation in the sulphur springs of **Bains de Taccana**. Beyond **Casalabriva**, on the **Col de Celaccia**, the D302 branches off to the

Preceding pages: Sunset at the Iles Sangninaires. Left, a calm anchorage at Porto Pollo. **Right**, a quick glance in the mirror.

right, leading to the Taravo Valley and Filitosa. Nearby **Sollacaro** is a fine old Corsican village steeped in history. It used to be a seat of the d'Istria family; its most famous member was Vincentello d'Istria, a 15th-century viceroy of the King of Aragon. It was in Sollacaro that the first meeting took place between the Scottish biographer James Boswell and the hero of Corsica, Pasquale Paoli. They had been introduced to each other by Rousseau, and Boswell's subsequent *Account of Corsica* (1768) had immediate success and was translated into several languages.

Sollacaro was also the scene of a nasty drama of revenge, if a medieval legend is to be believed. It is the tale of the beautiful Savilia. She apparently enticed a count of the d'Istria family to her castle by promising to marry him. On visiting her, however, he did not end up in the marital bed as expected but in the castle dungeon instead. And every morning the beautiful mistress of the castle would parade naked in front of his prison in order to mock him for his ugliness: how could he even have dared hope to possess such a wonderful body as hers? The humiliated Count managed to escape at some point, though, thus clearing the way for his revenge. He returned with his men, destroyed his tormentress's castle and put Savilia in a hut at a crossroads on a pass – so that all the men who passed by could have their way with her. Word of this must have spread very quickly among the local male population: the unfortunate Savilia is said to have survived the onslaught for just three days.

Armed stone figures: Many old shepherd legends also revolve around the menhirs on Corsica, which date from the megalithic period. In 1946 Charles-Antoine Cesari discovered several of them on his land in the hamlet of Filitosa. The **Station Préhistorique de Filitosa**, the Cesari family's well-preserved prehistoric site, which has been the subject of archaeological research by Roger Grosjean since 1954, is the best place to study the development of the island's megalithic culture and its replacement

Among the menhirs of Filitosa.

by the "Torréen" civilisation – so named by Grosjean because of the tower-like fortresses they built (*see page 34*). You can buy Grosjean's excellent book *Filitosa, haut lieu de la Corse préhistorique* in the Cesari family's bar and restaurant. More up-to-date and richly illustrated is *Lumières de Granite* by the archeologist Lucien Aquaviva and Filitosa owner Jean Dominique Cesari. Stone-Age monolith carving reached its high point around 1400 BC, when statues began to take on increasingly human form. Between 1300 BC and 800 BC, however, the megalithic culture gradually declined.

The small museum at the entrance is best visited after a stroll around the whole area. To make it easier to distinguish between them, the menhirs, all of which represent men, have been quite simply numbered, and an avenue of pine trees leads us first to Filitosa V: a massive, 3-metre (10-ft) high rock statue with a head divided into two halves, upon which the chiselled outlines of a long sword and a dagger in its sheath are clearly recognisable. On the back of the statue there are faint indications of a shoulder blade and also of the spinal column.

The "Torréens", Grosjean believed, streamed into southern Corsica between 1600 and 1400 BC, and were far superior to the megalithic population. If the armed granite statues were supposed to represent the invaders and help defeat them via some kind of magic spell, then this turned out to be a rather futile defensive strategy. The "Torréens", according to this theory, invaded Filitosa, once populated by shepherds, and smashed their menhirs or used them in the construction of their own places of worship.

The East Monument resembles a walled-in burial mound. The ramp leading up to this tumulus is remarkable, as is the 15-ton block of stone forming part of the wall. No one is really certain what took place here. Taffoni rocks were used as hiding places by the megalithic people, while the Torréens later built dwellings from them. Foundations can be seen to the left.

The beach at Propriano.

Under the shade of olive trees we now reach the Central Monument, a round "Torréen" building used for religious purposes. Fragments of simple menhirs and menhir statues – face down – were incorporated into the walls, but have since been retrieved, and are now either upright once more or leaning against the monument. The statues are unarmed and may have represented the megalithic dead, or served as tomb guardians. The midday sun is weathering them more and more, and those with oval faces are the easiest to define. The grim but clearly defined features of Filitosa IX (to the right of the entrance) are very arresting. On the other side of the "Torréen" building are the three fragments of the menhir-statue Filitosa VI, a sword-bearer with a very realistic, almost clown-like expression.

The most important "Torréen" complex is the West Monument, a labyrinthine structure composed of three chambers, two rock caves and a spring. The main chamber, the Cella, is divided into two sections. Connecting passages lead to underground cavities, which may have been used for storing food, weapons or cult objects. The remains of a fireplace may point to it having been used as a temple of fire.

Below, in the valley of the Barcalojo stream, the five menhir statues first discovered here stand in a semicircle in front of an olive tree. Their facial features are scarcely recognisable, but daggers and swords can be clearly seen. The statue Tappa I (named after the place it was found, roughly 400 metres away), with its strange head, is particularly striking. A faceless "mummy" or a phallic symbol erected by farmers for fertility purposes?

The museum (**Centre de documentation archéologique**) contains more menhir-statues that have been restored: Scalsa-Murta holds a sword, his back is protected by armour and a helmet containing two holes can be made out; they may once have contained Viking-style horns. Filitosa XII was discovered – split into two lengthwise – in a shepherd's hut, where it was being used as a door lintel. Particularly distinctive here

are the positions of the arms and hands. Finally, Tappa II is impressive for the manner in which its facial features are only hinted at, in a similar way to some modern sculpture. Alongside the mysterious statues there are glass showcases displaying pottery fragments, millstones and other finds documenting daily life in Filitosa from the Early Neolithic period to medieval times.

Coast roads: Anyone keen on a swim in the sea after this visit to the Corsican megalithic period won't have far to go to get to the next beach: try the **Plage du Taravo** at the mouth of the river, or the small semicircular bay at the delightful seaside village of **Porto Pollo**, situated just before the promontory at the northern end of the Gulf of Valinco. There are a few hotels, and a restaurant.

To get back to Ajaccio, there are some narrow and very romantic back roads. One possibility is to follow the course of the Taravo River along the D757 until the left turn via **Pila-Canale**. The D302 winds its way up to quite a height at several points, the highest being the **Col d'Aja Bastiana** (640 metres/2,100 ft), after which there is a fine view across the Gulf of Ajaccio.

A route closer to the coast runs via **Serra-di-Ferro** (D155) and **Coti-Chiavari** (D55), a terraced village 500 metres (1,640 ft) up on a steep slope. The aptly-named Belvedere hotel overlooks the sea here. The route then continues via the Chiavari Forest and down an avenue of eucalyptus trees to the village's old fishing harbour. A road to the left leads to the picturesque bay at **Portigliolo** and to the **Punta di a Castagne** with its Genoese tower.

The coast road to Ajaccio now runs parallel to the beaches of **Ruppione** and **Agosta**, which are separated by the **Isolella** peninsula. Finally one reaches **Porticcio**, the popular resort opposite Ajaccio. The internationally famed **Institute of Thalassotherapy** on the tiny promontory **Punta di Porticcio** does seawater cures. Anyone driving through the resort must take care not to lose their way in the veritable maze of billboards, all of them advertising campsites, hotels, supermarkets and discos.

THE SARTENAIS

After being spoiled by the dramatic landscapes of the mountains and the west coast, many visitors to the Sartenais tend to be somewhat disappointed. The landscape south of Ajaccio has only a few scenic highlights. Among them are the Gulf of Valinco and, down in the very south, the white cliffs along the coast near Bonifacio. Between these two there are still some fine beaches to be found where the various rivers and streams join the sea, but Corsica's reputation as "the isle of beauty" really needs to be appreciated on a miniature scale in this region, where some of the meadows contain so many flowers in springtime that the grass hardly has room to grow.

The highlights of this relatively large area, alongside its old "capital" of Sartène – or Sartè as the Corsicans call it – are the structures left behind by the megalithic peoples, early settlers who were defeated and subjugated by the warlike Torréens. There is extensive evidence of both cultures in the area around Sartène, and the fact that it lies so far away from urban centres and tourist routes makes visiting it somewhat difficult, but all the more rewarding too, since it is so impressive.

The Gulf of Valinco: Propriano is a tourist town first and foremost, but an attractive one all the same. The town centre with its church up on the hill gives every sign of having developed quite naturally, and many people from the surrounding countryside come here to do their shopping. The bars often contain genuine sailors, because the harbour – which was developed as a centre of the export trade for the south of the island – is now busy once more, ever since French Algerians began cultivating cereal, fruit and wine in the vicinity.

Olmeto is situated high on a slope above the Gulf of Valinco. One of the castles belonging to the powerful della Rocca family stood here in former times; today only ruins remain. Much olive cultivation goes on in the area surrounding the town. An inscription on a simple house on the right-hand side of the road announces the fact that Colomba Carabelli used to live there: she was a heroine of the *vendetta*, and Prosper Mérimée met her in 1840. The events upon which his tale *Colomba* were based took place in a small village north of Sartène called Fozzano. One can also drive up there from the valley of the small Baracchi river and see the fortified houses that belonged to the rival families. The detour leads via Arbellara across into the valley of the Rizzanèse.

The river flows along peacefully through forests and meadows; cows stand in the water; a family uses buckets and wicker-clad bottles for scooping up water to irrigate a small garden nearby. High above, spanning this tranquil scene, is the stone arch of the **Spin' a Cavallu** bridge. The name means "horse's back", but the nag that gave it its name must have been pretty gaunt-looking. The road leading to this 13th-century Genoese bridge goes up steeply, makes a bend at the top and then dips straight down again just as steeply to the other

bank. The road is very narrow and really only suitable for carts, horse-riders and mule trains. Many such bridges were built on Corsica during Genoese rule, and this one, the best-preserved of all, still serves its original function.

Grey town with a heart: The hilly landscape here is so cheerful and inviting that the first sight of **Sartène** up on its mountain can often come as quite a shock. Could this really be Mérimée's *"la plus corse des villes corses"*? It not only looks grim and forbidding, it's actually quite ugly, too, at first glance. The high blocks of houses seem to be clustered together very haphazardly. First impressions are deceptive, though: as one rounds the final few bends before entering the town it already looks very different, with its parks and gardens full of palm trees, orange trees and bright flowers, and by the time you reach the square it becomes clear that the town is far more in harmony with the landscape than initially seemed to be the case. It may turn its back to it in one sense, but in another it shows it its heart. For this

central square, the focal point of town life with its plane trees and palm trees, is only built up on three sides. The fourth, open, side faces the valley, affording a magnificent view far across the hills and the plain. This open centre is typical of mountain towns in Corsica, and it can sometimes even be found in small villages as well.

The finest house in the square, apart from the town hall, is the palace that once belonged to the Genoese governor, and today the building houses the headquarters of Sartenais wine. The dark, cool vaults here are a good place for some *dégustation*, wine purchasing and information-gathering before one travels off to the vineyard of one's choice out in the countryside.

Also in the square is the town's main church, the **Eglise Sainte-Marie**, an austere structure built of grey granite. The wooden cross and iron chain in the doorway, often the subject of curiosity among tourists, are used for a very serious procession: the *Catenacciu*, or Grand Penitent, dressed in a red robe and hood

Sartène can look grim and forbidding.

through which only his eyes can be seen, drags the cross and the chain through the town barefoot on the evening of Good Friday each year.

Upper versus lower town: A gateway below the town hall leads through to the lower town, the medieval Old Town – or rather, one of the two Old Towns, for the upper town is equally old. Power and wealth, influence and political importance were distributed between the two parts of the town at different times, and the question of whether living down in Sainte-Anne is nobler than living up in Borgo is probably still a bone of contention even today – though no longer the excuse for wholesale slaughter it was in former days. Sartène's notoriety as capital of the *vendetta* stems from its divided Old Town.

Feudalism was still rife here as late as the 19th century. The town was run by just a few families, some of them genuinely noble, others self-styled nobles because of the sheer amount of land they owned. Each family had its own supporters and dependants among the

simple townsfolk, and so the various rivalries, combined with the *vendetta* tradition, cut through every social rank, and for tactical and practical reasons, straight through the entire town as well. The two quarters became fortresses, and people were still barricading themselves into the houses here as late as the 19th century. It was only in 1834 that the French finally succeeded in getting the two rival sections of the town to sign a peace treaty. A solemn announcement to this effect was made in the church, and an oath was sworn.

The lower part of the Old Town gives every indication of having had a shady past, too: any sunlight that does manage to penetrate the high walls of grey granite very soon vanishes in the narrow streets and winding passageways. The Old Town is very much alive, however. Children play on stairways, and women carrying shopping bags go in and out of the houses.

The old people are the only real locals left, however. Many of the young families come from the Maghreb states, and

All-terrain vehicles are useful in the Sartenais.

THE CATENACCIU

The *Catenacciu* procession in Sartène isn't the only Easter-week custom the visitor can experience on Corsica, but it is certainly the most spectacular. *Catenacciu* means "The Chained One". The event takes its name from the 14 kg (30 lb) iron chains which for the rest of the year can be viewed in the church. Even the weight of the cross is common knowledge: 32 kg (70 lbs). It requires little fantasy to imagine what it must be like to drag such a burden through the Old Town of Sartène.

Only one man enjoys the honour and the torture of completing this penitential circuit on Good Friday each year. It is an anonymous honour, for he is enveloped in a red hooded robe from his head to his naked feet. He drags the chain attached to his ankle. Nobody knows who he is apart from the parish priest and the monks in the monastery perched up above the town. The priest selects the man in question – supposedly from a long waiting list which stretches out well beyond the year 2000. Having been chosen,

the winner spends a day and a night in prayer in St Damian's monastery preparing himself for the procession.

From the late afternoon the town centre is closed to traffic and crowds of spectators begin to assemble at the best vantage points. At nine o'clock the lights are all extinguished. Everyone falls silent. There is a sudden flickering as candles are lit. Twinkling lights can be seen at windows and in doorways.

Then comes a surge of movement, whisperings. And finally he appears, the *Catenacciu*, the Grand Penitent in the red robe. Bent double under the weight of the cross, he sways, stumbles and finally falls to the ground. That is part of the ritual – and may even be genuine. As he collapses, only one man comes forward to help him: the Little Penitent. Dressed in a white, hooded robe, he represents Simon of Cyrene. The red- and white-robed figures are followed by eight men in black, the *Penitents Noirs*, bearing a wooden effigy of the dead Christ wrapped in a shroud. Behind follows the procession of those whose participation is based on piety rather than curiosity: men, women and children, bearing candles and quietly chanting the invocation *Perdono mio Dio, perdono mio...*

The priest, by contrast, is far from quiet as he takes up the microphone as the procession approaches the half-way point, the square in front of the church. Question, answer, incantations – the strange ritual of the Stations of the Cross. Then they move off into the darkness once more, their voices echoing in the narrow alleyways, the candles flickering under archways. The two historic town centres, the lower and the upper, are linked by the route of the *Catenacciu* – no wonder, after the feuds between the different districts during the past. The journey of the *Penitent Rouge* ends where it began, beside the parish church of St Mary. The entire procession lasts three hours. In the meantime, the onlookers have dispersed: the pious have taken their places in the church, whilst the less pious have gone for dinner.

The next day, the photo of the *Catenacciu* in his red robe will adorn the front page of the local newspaper. Not even the reporter knows his identity, so there will be no startling revelations. Respectfully – and wisely – he too will stick to the rules. ■

The Grand Penitent bears the cross.

work on farms owned by *Pieds Noirs*. As is the case in many small towns in Western Europe, the immigrant workers have been left with the shoddier housing. The odd craftsman here and there attempts to make some money from tourism, and cheese and honey are also on sale.

In the Borgo quarter it is not so much the old streets but the newer *palazzi* that strike one at first. When the barred windows are flung open here to let fresh air into the salons, and the family arrives in a state carriage drawn by majestic horses to play its role in the town for several days, one can sense that the power structures haven't really altered very much.

Above the Borgo quarter is a building surrounded by trees, so attractive that one would scarcely believe it was used as the town prison until only recently. Today it is the **Musée de Préhistoire Corse** – a remarkable museum, well laid-out and definitely worth a visit.

Menhirs and dolmens: The journey continues south-westwards away from Sartène, along the valley of a small river, bordered by scrubland, meadows and macchia, interspersed with new stretches of vineyard. The fishing village of **Tizzano** is gradually developing into a holiday resort, one especially popular with divers. A series of small sandy beaches can be reached from here along attractive clifftop paths.

The monuments are further inland – a signpost on the road points down a smaller road in the direction of the **Alignements de Palaggiu**. It leads through a vineyard, where a sign asks visitors to close the lattice-gate behind them. Leave your car where the signs tell you to do so. It was Roger Grosjean, the first archaeologist to undertake a serious study of Corsica's megalithic culture, who unearthed many of the menhirs here and had them placed upright once more.

And there they are: an army of 258 stone men, standing firm in a lonely stretch of landscape. Some of them are wearing daggers and swords. Their weapons are only vaguely hinted at with scratch marks, possibly to enhance their

Discussing events on Sartène's main square.

effectiveness, at least if we are to believe Roger Grosjean's theory that they may have been some kind of magic deterrent. The stone men are arranged in groups and face in various directions, some towards the rising sun, and others towards the Uomo di Cagna, the most striking peak in the chain of mountains to the south.

A little further to the north, the road branches off towards **Cauria**. Here, you should leave the car at the end of the road and continue on along one of the scenic footpaths signposted to various prehistoric sites. They include dolmens, *alignements*, groups of menhirs, all of them possibly forming part of a central place of worship and once again pointing towards certain salient features of the landscape: the Uomo di Cagna, the Lion of Roccapina. The summer solstice, of course, also plays an important role in many prehistoric sites (more information on the significance of this from an anthroposophical point of view can be found in the work of Adalbert Graf von Keyserlingk).

One dolmen is placed in such a way that it catches the first rays of the sun after the winter solstice. This **Dolmen de Fontanaccia** is the largest on the whole island. Granite blocks as high as a man support a crossways slab 3.4 metres (11 ft) long and 2.6 metres (8.5 ft) wide. Cauria is the name of this mountain area across which these monuments are distributed. A path leads through a grove of chestnut oak, along the edge of which 36 smaller standing stones can be seen, the **Menhirs of Rinaggiu**.

Stone warriors: On the way back to the parking place – or starting from there to Rinaggiu – you will meet impressive rows of unarmed Stantari ("petrified ones") and Paladini, menhir-statues with swords and daggers. At the foot of one of the menhir statues a vessel was found which had apparently served as a painting bowl more than 3,500 years ago. Two statues still bore traces of red paint. The stone warriors were not only painted, however, they also had horns, judging by the impressions in their helmets.

Alignements de Palaggiu.

Indeed, some of the stones are so well carved that it is even possible to tell what kind of weapon the megalithic masons wanted to depict.

Grosjean came up with the theory that the megalithic people wanted to represent their enemies with these statues – the "Torréens" who had invaded their island. And it was also the stone statues of Cauria that suddenly reminded him of similarities in an Egyptian temple relief of Medinet-Habu, leading him to suppose that the Torréens may have been identical with the Shardana.

The **Uomo di Cagna**, a mountain peak in the Cagna range which seems to have played an important role geometrically in the layout of these extensive megalithic cult sites, is remarkable in its own right: it is a huge spherical rock that has been eroded so much by wind and weather that it now balances on top of a very slender base. Apparently it used to serve as a landmark for ships arriving from the south; it is certainly the most noticeable feature of the landscape for miles around.

The Lion of Roccapina: The Cagna range is no place for mountain hikers. It is far too hot, and far too thinly populated. Here people tend to stick to the river valleys. The final foothill of the range ends up near the coast in the form of a rocky spur known as the **Lion of Roccapina**. It really does look like a huge, petrified lion, and unsurprisingly it, too, played a major part in the megalithic people's extensive geometrical calculations. Today it guards the large beach at the mouth of the Otolo River.

One worthwhile detour here leads along the coast south of Propriano to **Belvedere** and **Campomoro**. Belvedere, with its superb view across the Gulf of Valinco, more than lives up to its name. Campomoro lies in a broad sandy bay, sheltered by a high hill with a Genoese tower at the top. Tourism here is still contained within reasonable limits.

The wilderness proper begins just beyond the village. This whole stretch of coast is grazing land, all the way down to Tizzano: *macchia*, heather,

The beach at Campomoro.

herbs, flowers, thorny thickets and green valleys. The only village in the area is **Grossa**, a grey-looking little place with touristic ambitions. Much of the grazing land here is still used by shepherds, and most of the routes are unsurfaced roads and rough tracks. Nevertheless, anyone travelling through Corsica in the early part of the year (up until the beginning of June) really should hazard a trip across this part of the island. Near Grossa is one of the old churches built at the time of the Pisan occupation and then neglected.

If you follow the road to Sartène you will pass a sheep-herding area; a Torréen building was unearthed here during the 1960s. Not one of the larger structures, true, but it still exhibits all the typical features, especially the combination of roughly-assembled sections of rock and carefully-built wall. Four passageways with bends in them fan out, swastika-like, from an unwalled, almost circular central area.

A gigantic fortress: Far more impressive are the Castelli of the Corsi that can be visited from Sartène as part of an excursion into the upper part of the Rizzanèse Valley. Between Sainte Lucie de Tallano and Levie, a side-road branches off to **Castellu de Cucurruzzu**. From the car park, the route to the site leads through shady pine and then oak forest, past blossoming briers and tall rockroses, for about half a mile.

Like other, similar fortified settlements, Cucurruzzu, which dates from the 14th century BC, utilises a rocky hilltop to incorporate the natural rock into the structure of the town. The walls are made of huge granite blocks, some of which weigh several tons. Entrance is via a roughly-formed stairway between a huge split rock. It leads past subterranean chambers, casemates, billets, and niches for storing provisions.

A walkway leads round to the east side of the fortress to a terrace, which is bounded on one side by the Cyclopean walls of the central monument, surrounded by the cult area. The chamber is entered through two successive openings framed by huge lintels set on massive vertical rocks that serve as pillars. The interior vaulting is quite ingenious, particularly when one considers that the stones are held in place without any kind of mortar.

Outside, the summit of the monument can be reached by a kind of staircase. From up here the visitor can really appreciate the strategic location of the site. On the eastern extremity of the rocky spur it is possible to make out the basic foundations of the houses of the former village, and also the remains of the fortifications that once surrounded it. In every direction the view stretches far across the *macchia* and forests, valleys and mountains.

A further Cyclopean structure, the **Castellu de Capula**, can be reached either directly from Cucurruzzu (20 minutes) or from the car park. Unlike Cucurruzzu, the site was continuously occupied from the Bronze Age right up to medieval times, when the castle was finally destroyed after a long period of clan warfare in 1259. Archaeological finds from this area can be viewed at the museum in **Levie**.

Left, Fozzano is the setting for Prosper Mérimée's *Columba*.

VENDETTA

Not so long ago, firearms could be seen hanging not only above bar counters and bistro fireplaces, but also behind bank counters and church pulpits. They may have been old, decorative carbines, but they were unmistakable symbols of a traditional readiness to take the law into one's own hands if need be, as cowboys did in the Wild West of yore. Here, too, the principle of self-administered justice grew up in an atmosphere of uncertainty. On Corsica, however, it was not the powerlessness or cowardice of a sheriff which induced the citizens to take up arms, but rather the partiality and venality of a well-established judiciary.

The courts of justice established by the occupying forces which ruled the island for over six hundred years, the maritime republic of Genoa and the Bank of Saint George, showed a marked tendency to favour those from their own ranks who were on the winning side. Injustice on the part of these gentlemen was of as little concern to the courts as affairs of honour amongst the Corsicans themselves. They were only prepared to take on such matters upon payment of hefty fees, but how many Corsicans were in a position to find the necessary cash? And so the native islanders, accustomed to self-defence since time immemorial, resorted to settling matters of personal vengeance by means of the bullet or stiletto.

Vendetta corsa is still written on the penknives in the island's souvenir shops. If the murder of a Genoese enemy led to military retaliation, the killing of a fellow-Corsican would lead just as inevitably to a counter-assassination. Constant retaliation meant entire clans were extinguished. Between 1683 and 1715 there were almost 30,000 victims of arbitrary law. Pasquale Paoli was the first to end this self-destructive butchery by establishing a legal system which was beyond bribery and which guaranteed justice for everyone.

But when France annexed the island and tyranny reared its head once more, so too did the principle of "an eye for an eye". This time it was a true *vendetta* in highly personal affairs of vengeance where the local inhabitants were reluctant to allow a foreigner to pass judgment. Furthermore, the penal code introduced by the new rulers seemed too weak to the passionate Corsicans. The blood of the perpetrator was the only way of cleansing a besmirched family honour.

A man marked by the curse of the vendetta took refuge in the *macchia* – but he knew that his death was only a matter of time. Into the undergrowth fled, too, the *bandits d'honneur* who had killed a gendarme, a customs officer or some rich oppressor. The silence of the populace was as impenetrable as the thorny vegetation.

Prosper Mérimée, the poet who created *Carmen*, based his novella *Colomba* on a tribal drama of this kind. Balzac, Dumas and Maupassant also carved for the Corsican vendetta a place in literature. But there is no concrete evidence that the *vendetta* continues to exist in its original form today. Nowadays, it manifests itself not so much in killing but in the destruction of things like property; the supermarket that gets burnt down the day before it's due to open because it provides unwanted competition in a seaside resort, for example. But the perpetrators of such deeds can still be fairly sure of the silence of their fellow-citizens. ∎

Right, Jeanne Fioravanti as Columba in Ange Casta's film.

BONIFACIO AND PORTO VECCHIO

The only people to start their tour of Corsica at its southernmost tip will be those who arrive by boat, from Sardinia. On the journey over, their eyes will have already grown accustomed to the stunning view of Bonifacio, and they may therefore not be quite so overwhelmed on arrival as visitors who approach by land. But however you get here, you'll feel bound to concur with the sentiments of the French poet Paul Valéry: "as far as sheer beauty is concerned, Bonifacio is the unrivalled capital of Corsica".

The builders of Bonifacio converted this wonderful natural setting into a magnificent theatre stage. The Old Town consists of a small cluster of houses, built on the topmost overhanging ledge of white chalk cliffs, a dizzying 65 metres (200 ft) above the sea. Whether viewed from offshore or from the clifftop promenade, their location on this perch looks decidedly precarious; it seems that almost at any minute they might just drop off the edge. The sea pounds against the cliffs from two sides. In the course of millions of years the waves have eroded the soft chalk. But the town has endured; like a crown, man has triumphantly set it here upon the cliffs as if his sole aim were to stubbornly defy the forces of nature.

Tales from *The Odyssey*. But nature didn't only produce the cliff face; behind, it moulded a protected harbour in the form of a 1,600-metre (1-mile) long inlet, where the water remains calm even if there is a storm raging out on the open sea. It is thought that this is the harbour referred to in *The Odyssey* when Odysseus tells of arriving at the fortress called Lamos, which was held by the Laestrygons, and entering a good harbour protected by an unbroken wall of rock with two headlands guarding the narrow entrance. The Greeks were actually forced to beat a hasty retreat by the Laestrygons; their king was a cannibal and he wanted to have them for his supper.

The Old Town: The **Old Town** can be reached by car by following the winding Avenue Charles de Gaulle. But a more impressive, though less relaxing way, is on foot, via the steps of the **Montée Rastello** that lead up from the harbour. The mighty ramparts above were built by the Genoese in 1195 to thwart any attempts at resistance by the "uncolonisable" locals whom they had banished from the town and replaced with Ligurian families (the little church on the right of the steps is that of the fishermen barred from the town).

Having passed under the Avenue Charles de Gaulle, a further flight of steps, the Montée Saint Roch, leads up to the **Col Saint Roch** and the natural belvedere which looks over the harbour on one side and out to sea on the other. Towards the south, the green coast of Sardinia can be made out across the narrow Straits of Bonifacio. Italy is only 12 km (7 miles) away. The colour of the sea changes from turquoise blue to emerald green, from cobalt blue to pale aquamarine, then loses itself somewhere in the sandy coloured current.

The view from up here can leave nobody in any doubt about the fact that this channel was created by the sea itself; it simply washed over, broke over and finally tore away the narrow isthmus that once connected Corsica with Sardinia. Islands and islets were created, but they too eventually succumbed to the power of the sea. One of the tiny islands remaining is aptly called "Perduto", the lost one. From the Col Saint Roch, the visitor can continue to savour the view of the sea by following the cliff path towards the **Pertusato Lighthouse**, a 45-minute walk.

The Old Town itself is entered through the **Porte de Genes**, which until the 19th century was the only gate; the 16th-century drawbridge and gates can still be seen. The Ligurian settlers constructed their tall, narrow houses packed next to each other to create a defensive shield. On the **Place d'Armes** to the right of the gate are the plinths of the four grain silos that provisioned the inhabitants during times of siege. The town's most testing time came in 1553

Preceding pages: The Porto Vecchio marina. Left, the chalk cliffs near Bonifacio.

when it was besieged from the sea by the French and Turks under the command of the notorious corsair Dragut, with the Corsican freedom fighter Sampiero Corso mounting a rearguard action from the landward side. But the siege was a waste of time because the whole island was handed back to the Genoese in 1559. This all occurred at the time when Henri II of France was waging war with Charles V of the Holy Roman Empire.

The emperor himself had actually once stayed in Bonifacio: on returning from his campaign in Algeria in 1541, he was driven to these shores by a storm. Count Filippo of Bonifacio, who was known locally as *Il Alto Bello*, offered the emperor his house as lodgings, and presented him with his favourite horse to ride on. The story goes that when the emperor departed, the count had the unfortunate animal killed because nobody else should mount his steed once the emperor had sat on it.

Napoleon's sojourn in Bonifacio is recalled by a plaque on the house in which he stayed. At that time he was the commander of the second batallion of Corsican Volunteers, and laid siege to the tiny Italian islands off Sardinia, which he intended to capture for the French crown. It was here that Napoleon sampled his first bitter taste of defeat.

Successive generations of builders added their own touches to the town. Beautiful patrician houses with balustrades and arcades with splendid portals and loggias testify to the wealth of their former owners. The magic of the old streets is compounded by the arches which span the alleys from one house to another. Many of the houses in the Old Town bear the patina of age; some have fallen into complete decay.

However, since central government in Paris declared Bonifacio a "national monument" and offered cheap grants to the house owners, a great deal of restoration has taken place; some of the old palazzi have been returned to their former splendour. The attraction of the town as an international tourist destination has also encouraged the locals to do

Left, close neighbours. **Right**, a precarious location.

the place up. But Bonifacio's essential character is still there; a certain amount of dull-pink, morbid decadence remains to remind one of the fact that we are still in Corsica, in Europe's beautiful, if somewhat sleepy south.

Sights in the Old Town include the **Church of Sainte Marie** in the Rue du Corps de Garde which was begun by the Pisans in the 12th century and subsequently refashioned in Gothic style by the Genoese. Meetings of local notables used to be held in the large loggia in front, which was also where proclamations were made and justice dispensed. The palace of the ruling magistrate was situated directly opposite. The church contains a Roman sarcophagus from the 3rd century and, above it, a beautifully sculpted Genoese tabernacle representing the torso of Christ.

An ivory and ebony casket said to have contained the relics of Saint Boniface is kept in the sacristy together with the relic of the True Cross which used to be carried up to the **Belvedere de la Manichella**, 65 metres (213 ft)

above the waves. Here the waves were blessed in the hope of bringing calm. And here on this very same terrace once stood a certain first-lieutenant Bonaparte; he had just been defeated by his enemies, but was madly in love.

Until 1963, the **citadel** at the western end of the promontory was the main garrison of the Foreign Legion, and so could not be visited. Although there is still a military presence, it is now possible to walk right to the end and to visit the two old windmills as well as the ruins of the **Franciscan Monastery** and the Church of St Francis. The **Church of Saint Dominique** on the south side of the citadel was begun in 1270 by the Knights Templar and completed by the Dominicans in 1343. The pillars of the nave are decorated with delicate paintings of the Fifteen Mysteries of the Rosary and there is also a particularly fine Resurrection and a wonderful Descent from the Cross. The 800-kg (1,763-lb) wooden sculpture Martyre de St Barthélémy is carried in the Good Friday procession. Tradition has it that St

Rock with a view.

NECROPOLISES

The cemetery at Bonifacio lies next to the Church of St Francis, perched high above the sea at the far end of the limestone plateau. As they enter, visitors will feel themselves transported to a miniature city outside the main town. The tombs stand cheek by jowl, their roofs surmounted by gables topped by a cross. A place of rest, deaf to the roaring of the surf at the foot of the cliffs – and also a mirror-image of life on this side of the grave. The tombstones tell of how the deceased must once have lived. If they were rich, stone edifices of hewn granite or white stuccoed walls soar heavenwards.

Sometimes such a mausoleum has been built in the shape of an elegant villa – maybe even with shutters or curtains at the windows – or perhaps resembling a sacred monument, almost a cathedral in miniature. If it is open you can peer in at free-standing sarcophagi adorned with wreaths of pearls. On the graves of the less well-to-do, a massive stone slab, sometimes carved, declares who has been laid to rest below. If the

dead man was poor, his burial place will be marked by a simple wooden cross, sometimes decorated and simply pushed into the ground, or one of iron, its arms rusted by the salty sea breeze which wafts across the memories, along the frequently abandoned footpaths, caressing the pine trees, its wailings echoing like an eternal prayer.

For the Corsicans, as for other Romance peoples, death was never a tragic moment in which a loved one passed over into what they hoped would be a better life beyond. No! Death was a constant companion on this island where tragedies were a daily occurrence. Death is a familiar figure. He is feared because the ancient spell of Corsica has always waged war against the *imbuscata*, the evil with which the dead can curse the living.

And yet, death is also honoured. Death is never far away, recalled in monuments both simple and grand. Apart from the many isolated tombs on the island, standing in solitude by the wayside or even in the middle of the *macchia*, each community has its own *campu santu*, its *cimteriu*: a place of respect, a place where the living recall the dead. It is a meeting place where the Corsican is carried away by his memories. But the dead are not only present here. The islander believes they exert an invisible influence on the living. Until recently, death was to be heard in the *lamenti*, the moving dirges; it also formed the main theme of traditional folk poetry, and it gave rise to superstitions.

The cemeteries along the Mediterranean, formerly avoided because of its perils and the infertile soils of the coastal margin, are more recent than those in the interior. The Corsicans seldom turned towards the sea. Apart from the residents of Cap Corse, the islanders preferred the mountain valleys, where they found protection and safety. Only in the vicinity of the towns built by the Genoese or near the settlements built during the 19th century will you find necropolises beside the sea, facing out across the water.

In the past, towns like Bastia, Ajaccio, Calvi and Bonifacio, whose Genoese pedigree explains their fortifications, buried their dead in such a way that there was no contact between the two worlds on either side of the grave. But by ensuring that the cemetery lay not too far from the town they still gave their heirs the chance of honouring the dead with their presence. ■

You can tell how they lived by their tombs.

Bartholomew was flayed alive while working as a missionary in Armenia, and the sculpture depicts the infidels fulfilling their gruesome task.

The harbour: The centre of the action in Bonifacio is undoubtedly the **harbour**. There are bistros and restaurants, souvenir shops and smart boutiques, a number of bars and the odd hotel. Boats to neighbouring Sardinia leave the harbour just about every hour, and there are services offering other trips as well; the islands of Lavezzi, Bainzo and Cavallo are interesting for their flora and birdlife and the **sea caves** beyond the inlet are also fascinating for their mysterious play of light.

Providing many of the inhabitants a secure income, tourism has become the mainstay of the local economy. In recent years, fisheries, wine cultivation and the cork industry have suffered a noticeable decline. Many of the fishermen now work on pleasure launches during the summer season and the local fishing boats have now become crowded out by luxury yachts. The nicest time of

day to stroll along the quay is the evening, just before dusk, when the last of the boats have berthed and the area is a hive of activity.

A couple of decades ago, things were much quieter here, although the place was always popular. One sat on hard benches at wooden tables and enjoyed crayfish, bouillabaisse and all kinds of seafood, the specialities of the few bistros down on the waterfront. Much has now changed; for want of space, restaurants have leeched into the old town. But crayfish remains the very special delicacy of Bonifacio. They live – as long as they are allowed to live – in the underwater caves beneath the cliffs and are served freshly caught. But as demand now outstrips supply, extra live crayfish also have to be flown in from further afield.

In the Gulf of Porto Vecchio: But with its rugged chalk coast, Bonifacio has very little to offer in terms of "paradise beaches". For visitors wishing to swim or sunbathe, the best bet lies 10 km (7 miles) to the north, along Corsica's flat

The fishing boats have given way to luxury yachts.

east coast. The Gulf of Porto Vecchio possesses some of the best beaches on the island and for this reason the area has been a prime holiday destination for decades. There is something for everybody here: campsites and nude bathing, marinas, club villages, holiday villages, hotels, small pensions, as well as private accommodation; and all looking out over a deep blue sea that is seldom too rough.

It's hard to believe that once upon a time this stretch of coast was swampland. When Genoa developed the natural harbour and built its first fortress on top of a mighty cliff of porphyritic rock, the entire garrison was wiped out by disease within 10 years. That was in the year 1539. Before the Genoese, Greek seafarers had settled here, and even earlier the Torréens. But they all succumbed to the anopheles mosquito, whose breeding grounds were also the breeding grounds of malaria. The only people who knew how to survive in these parts were the Corsicans themselves, accustomed as they were to the prevailing conditions. In summer they left the coast and lived in the hills above the gulf, not returning until the autumn. It was only during World War II that malaria was finally irradicated. After that the door was open to all.

In the summer the narrow streets of **Porto Vecchio** (population 8,000) are teeming with visitors. Shopping has priority here. The only historical attraction worth seeing is the well-preserved **fortress** ranging above the town. Apart from that, the town is dominated by the creations of the booming tourist industry: supermarkets, filling stations, holiday apartments.

What counts here are the beaches. From the swamps of old has emerged a seaside paradise, so synonymous with holiday enjoyment on Corsica. Shallow sandy beaches, perfect for the family holiday. One doesn't have to pay much attention here: not much can happen to the little ones. Aromatic Laricio pines provide shelter when the sun gets too hot, and the crystal-clear water offers welcome refreshment. The beach at **Palombaggia** and those further south

in the **Gulf of Santa Guilia** are considered to be the best. The latter also caters for nude bathers.

Castelli sites: For those who prefer not to spend their time in the water or on the beach, a journey into the past presents itself only a few miles from Porto Vecchio. Located in the hills behind the coast, there are a number of archaelogical sites which are easy to reach. Start at the place from which the "Toréen" civilisation was actually given its name; the little hamlet of **Torre**. To reach it take the N198 from Porto Vecchio towards Bastia and fork right after about 8 km (5 miles). The road stops, and after the car park there is a short climb up to the site. Situated against a granite mass, this is the best-preserved and most complete tower-like structure in Corsica. Amazingly, some of the original stone roofing slabs are still in place.

A further fascinating fortress is **Castellu d'Arraggiu**, a fortified living settlement. At 245 metres (803 ft) above sea level, it lies well above any dangers presented by the erstwhile marshy ground. In places the walls are 5 metres (17 ft) high and have a circumference of 120 metres (394 ft). They were created out of the existing crags and large boulders. Once again take the N198 towards Bastia; 1.5 km beyond La Trinité take the D759 to the hamlet of Arraggiu and from here it is a half-hour uphill walk to the site.

Three further "Torréen" sites can be found in the valley of the Stabbiacco stream that flows into the Gulf of Porto Vecchio. These are **Tappa**, **Ceccia** and **Bruschiccia**. This area was where the invaders were supposed to have settled when they arrived on Corsica in the middle of the second millennium BC.

So for those who wish to escape the noise of the holiday villages, the bars and the discos, there is plenty to do on the southern tip of the island. And one isn't just limited to the creations that the Torréens left behind or the charms of Bonifacio; just a trip up into the forests is like visiting another world, a world enveloped in the sweet fragrance of the *macchia* and the Laricio pine.

Right, mending the nets.

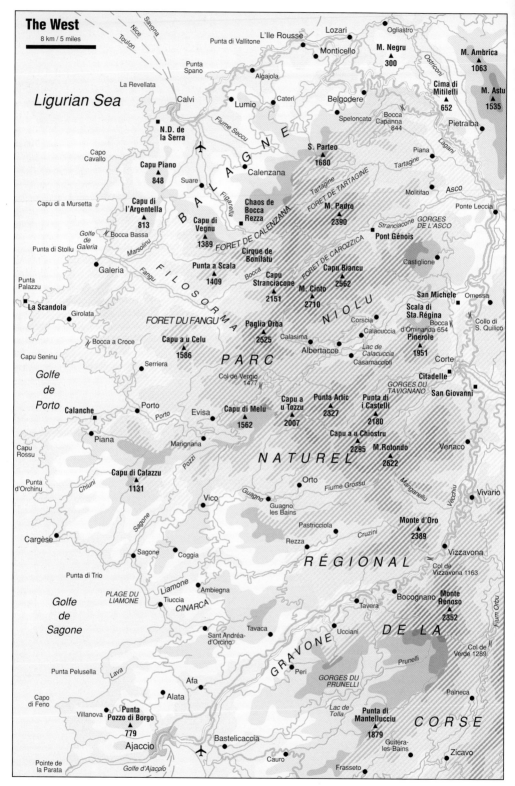

THE WEST COAST: AJACCIO TO CALVI

Corsica's west coast is one of the finest pieces of natural landscape in the entire Mediterranean. Popular subjects for photographers along the coast road from Ajaccio to Calvi include: the strange-looking red rocks known as Les Calanques (the Calanche), at Piana; the deep rocky bay at Porto, with its old watchtower; the fishing village of Girolata, which can still only be reached either by water or by mule even today; and last but not least, the view of the town of Calvi from the heights above.

The coastline is markedly jagged, with rocky outcrops enclosing broad bays where good swimming beaches can almost always be found. Best equipped with holiday amenities is the huge Gulf of Sagone, while the narrow Gulf of Porto is also a popular destination for excursions. The high mountains nearby are always part of the dramatic landscape; their white peaks stand out against the sky until well into May each year, and their vast tracts of forest are easily and quickly accessible from the coast.

Gulf of Sagone and surroundings: The road from **Ajaccio** starts off by going inland, and it isn't until the top of the **Col de San Bastiano** that there is the first really good view of the sea. The road then leads down from the pass into the broad **Gulf of Sagone**, where three small rivers meet the coast. Between them, the ranges of hills extend down towards the coast, finishing as promontories surmounted by watch-towers, and dividing the Gulf into several small bays.

The landscape here consists of macchia up on the hills, farmland in the fertile river-valley plains, vineyards and olive plantations here and there on the valley slopes. The villages, though, can only be seen in the distance, situated high up, away from the coast. The coastal strip is an area that was freed from the danger of malaria only relatively recently, and its fine sandy beaches, rather than its fertile flood plains, are the real reason for any housing development taking place here now. Hotels, shops,

bars and apartments are a distinctive feature of **Sagone**, and the smaller town of **Tiuccia** nearby seems to have similar aspirations.

From the southernmost of the bays, with its beach, a detour leads upwards along the River Liscia into the **Cinarca**, once ruled by the mighty counts of the same name, whose castle overlooked their domain from a hilltop. The farmers also settled high up in the valley here, and laid out terraced fields below their villages. If winding roads don't bother you, try doing a round trip inside the Liscia basin along the smaller back roads, from **Sari d'Orcino** to **Ambiegna**, then on to **Casaglione**, past the ruins of the Castello Capraia – seat of the counts of Cinarca – and then back down to the coast again.

Another worthwhile detour leads to **Vico**, historically the most important town in the area. The road curves out of the Sagone Valley and up through macchia-covered hills and forests to the **Col de Saint-Antoine**, a former junction of traffic routes. Behind it lies the

Preceding pages: king crabs are a common catch. **Right**, a dramatic place for windsurfing.

old town of Vico, overlooking the valley and surrounded by forest. The bishopric was moved here from Sagone for a while, when the coast fell victim first to the Saracens and then to malaria. The town still looks serious and dignified today, with its high, grey houses. A short distance from here is the former Franciscan monastery, now inhabited once again by monks, who will gladly show you round the church. Today, on the site of historic Sagone, the former bishopric, only the ruins of its cathedral remain. A menhir statue was used in the foundation wall.

The Greeks of Cargèse: The most interesting place along the Gulf of Sagone is where a tiny, narrow valley faces out towards the sea, with two churches up on the ridges on each side of it, facing each other. Together they form the centre of the small town of **Cargèse**, which stretches away behind them on a small plateau above the steep cliffs. The "gulf" separating the two churches is symbolic, too: one of them is Roman Catholic and the other Greek Orthodox.

Cargèse was founded in the 18th century by Greek refugees from Turkish rule. These days, its protective power is no longer Genoa but France, and the oath of loyalty it once swore to Genoa is now merely symbolic, in the shape of the flag kept in the church and used during processions. An arrangement was swiftly made between the Greeks and the Catholics in Cargèse, and anyone who visits Corsica in springtime can witness a very colourful combined Easter Monday celebration, in which both confessions take part.

The Greek church is definitely worth a visit. The interior is incredibly impressive, and some of the icons are masterpieces – the refugees brought them with them from their homeland. Cargèse, by the way, with its hotels, restaurants and shops is also a very pleasant place to stay. Delicious seafood is served at the restaurants down in the small harbour. Swimming and beach life takes place in the bays some distance away from the town; those who prefer seclusion can find it out along the rocky headlands.

View from the coast road to Porto.

The red cliffs of Porto: For many people, the **Gulf of Porto** is the main reason for Corsica's reputation as the "isle of beauty". It's true that some of the views here sometimes make people forget that they are driving – which is particularly dangerous considering the number of bends along this stretch of road. The reddish colour of the rocks here is at its most vivid and striking, standing out starkly against the deep blue of the sea, and there are many fascinating variants of it, ranging from the bizarre formations of the **Calanche** to the red houses here, built from the local rock.

The coast road goes past the outskirts of **Piana**, and most tourists, with only the Calanche and Porto on their minds, tend to drive straight past – much to the advantage of this village, which has thus succeeded in remaining unspoiled. Men wearing peaked caps sit outside here in front of the cafés in the little village square. Piana is built on a rocky spur 400 metres (1,300 ft) up, overlooking the sea. A small road winds down to a small beach, but it's actually a better idea to enjoy the view of the sea and the rocky coastline from above – while enjoying a hotel breakfast, for instance. Some of the houses here could have come straight from a picture postcard – and they don't cost all that much to buy either.

A narrow valley, almost a ravine, in the red rock; the mouth of a small river; a pebble beach; and a natural harbour. They all contribute to the picturesque beauty of **Porto**. Before the tourists arrived this is all Porto was: a small harbour, where the village of **Ota**, situated further upstream, kept its boats. The people of Ota, prosperous and keen on tradition, have not simply left tourism to its own devices here, but have successfully kept one eye on the architectural planning. Even if the odd modern hotel here may look just a little too box-like, at least its colour suits the general appearance of the place. Even the supermarket is red.

A rocky promontory with a Genoese tower on top divides the bay into two sections. To the south there is the pebble

Beauty on the beach.

THE CALANCHE

Recent research suggests that the islands of Corsica and Sardinia are not, as was once supposed, the remains of a separate Tyrrhenian block, but a part of the granite massive of Southern France that drifted away from the main mass and came to rest in its present position during the Tertiary period. And indeed, the type of red granite which so impressively dominates the landscape of the Estérel hills to the west of Cannes on the Côte d'Azur can also be seen along some stretches of the Corsican coast.

In other areas, however, it appears that the granite block of Corsica has undergone its own special geomorphological development. The most spectacular and best known example is the Calanche of Piana. Here the forces of nature have moulded the granite and porphyry just like a sculptor. Smooth columns and pillars alternate with hideously gnarled forms, grotesque faces, animal-like features and sharp profiles. The kind of erosion that has taken place here can hardly be found anywhere else the world, and can

be explained by the special crystal structure of the rock created by particularly rapid cooling. As far as the variety of forms are concerned, these are further highlighted by the light that penetrates the cliffs. What might resemble a face in the morning can easily have turned into an animal form by the time evening comes around. The colours also change with the time of day. The morning sun produces yellowy-orange tones, which turn to red by the time the sun begins to set, and then fade to violet and as it sinks beneath the horizon.

Maps to trails can be obtained in Piana, although the routes are so clearly marked that there is little danger of ever slipping or falling. The approaches to the cliffs are marked by the Tête du Chien (Dog's Head) in the north and the bridge Pont de Mezanu in the south. Both are served by a car park. The third starting point is the Roches Bleues in between, which, although poor for parking, does offer a magnificent view from the bar. The most popular trail leads from the Tête du Chien to the Chateau Fort, a cliff formation above the coast. While it offers good views of the cliffs and the sea, it doesn't really penetrate the chaotic labyrinth of the Calanche itself. But it is still a walk worth taking, particularly in the springtime when all the fresh vegetation compounds the colour spectacle. Indeed, on all routes it would be a shame to allow the splendour of the rock scenery to totally detract from the flora: in addition to the variety of orchids, there is the rare alpine violet, a kind of clove; the heaths of fragrant rosemary will also delight the senses.

The second of the short routes leads along the top between the Tête du Chien and the Roches Bleues, although you'll actually get better views if you start at the Roches Bleues. Opposite the bar begins a route with a number of possible variants: the northern one is the easiest while the southern one provides the most dramatic scenery. Here it is also possible to join the long tour which runs all the way to the east as far as the summit of the Capo D'Orto. The final ascent itself should only be attempted by experienced climbers, but even if you turn back, it still makes for a memorable walk; here the cliffs become part of the landscape, the scene magnificently framed by the mountains in the background.

Moulded like the work of a ■ sculptor.

beach, the mouth of the river and a eucalyptus grove which until recently was a 3-star camping area. Nowadays it tends to be filled with hikers. On the other side of the outcrop is the business centre of this tourist resort. The connecting road between the coastal route and the town centre is lined with even more shops and hotels: a good place for a stroll and also a permanent headache for the traffic planners, since Porto is not only a very popular holiday town but also a "must" on nearly every Corsican excursion or round trip.

A resting place for hikers: Ota, 6 km (3½ miles) further inland, is a world away from the busy holiday atmosphere on the coast. The people who come here tend to arrive with rucksacks and walking boots, and find their kindred spirits either at the hiking hostel *(Gîte d'Etappe)* or in the pubs.

Ota marks the end of one of the most popular hiking routes on the island. It begins in the mountain village of **Evisa** and leads through **Les Gorges de la Spelunca**, in which several mountain

streams join together to form the Porto River. The walk isn't difficult at all as long as you wear sturdy shoes. Bring a pair of swimming trunks, too, because there are some very inviting places to bathe en route. The path, which leads down through the *macchia* for nearly 700 metres (2,300 ft), should be taken in fine weather: in the rain it quickly becomes slippery. Evisa is situated exactly between the sea and the mountains, and is no more than a stone's throw from either, making it a popular base for tourists keen on combining a swimming with a hiking holiday. The road, lined with hotels and unpretentious restaurants, carries on up through the **Forêt d'Aïtone** to the **Col de Vergio** (1,477 metres/4,800 ft).

There are several fine views to be had from Evisa out across the valley containing the Gorges de la Spelunca, with Ota, huddled on its steep slope, and the sea in the far distance.

The way down into the Spelunca Gorges begins at the cemetery in Evisa and ends at an old Genoese stone bridge.

There is no road to Girolata.

There are some fine places to swim here; indeed, why not make a day of it here, in this marvellous landscape?

No through road to Girolata: There are more fine opportunities to photograph Porto and its bay as the drive continues along the coast road. The next feature of interest is the **Bocca a Croce**, a rocky spur overgrown with macchia dropping steeply down to the sea. From here one can also catch a glimpse of part of the magnificently isolated coastal village of **Girolata**.

It really is: no roads lead to it at all, apart from a hot and dusty mule track. But in the mornings, one excursion boat after the other moors there, and its two fishermen's bars have now become elegant restaurants with terraces. Situated on a promontory and dominated by the coastal hills and its very own Genoese watchtower, this small coastal village still retains its own special charm. The boat trips along this stretch of coast – particularly those from Calvi – provide glimpses of several other completely inaccessible bays, all of them forming part of the enormous **Parc Naturel Régional de la Corse**.

The coast road also leads through this protected area. It is a lonely stretch, punctuated by numerous bends. The next place on the coast is **Galeria**, a village that has opened up to tourism only recently. The centre of the village is still very much intact, and the street leading up to the church, lined with shops and houses several storeys high, projects an astonishingly prosperous image for such a remote place. The village is also famed among connoisseurs for its cheese.

Galeria is traditionally connected with the pastures high up in the Niolu. The sheep used to graze throughout the winter in the green countryside inland from the Gulf; in summer they would then move up to the high mountains *en transhumance*.

Long journeys like these belong to the past now, however, for far fewer sheep are now reared on Corsica, and transferring animals to new pastures in trucks is safer and simpler. Demand for Corsican ewe's cheese has risen a lot over the past few years because of tourism, and since the selection is limited the prices tend to be pretty high. It's still well worth taking some home, though.

The fishing village down by the beach is also part of Galeria, and the seafood restaurant right next to the beach is popular among those in the know.

Bathing-pools in the rocks: The old sheep track used to lead up into the valley of the Fango. Today, a reasonably good road can be found here, as can a section of the hiking route known as **Tra Mare e Monti**. The little river is framed by low-lying red cliffs, and here and there they form attractive bathing pools; the evergreen shrubs here are not the thorny variety, either. A good, old-fashioned *Gîte d'Etappe* lies right on the route, and the two small hamlets situated higher up the valley also provide good, simple food.

From Galeria the route now leads northwards again right above the coast before entering human habitation again at **Argentella**. This is a very odd place: half beach resort, half ghost town. It was named after a silver mine that closed years ago, and this adds a touch of adventure as far as campers are concerned: they can go off silver prospecting on the campsite.

The last section of the coastal route leads through the "Balagne Déserte", so named to distinguish it from its more fertile counterpart further to the east, the "Balagne" proper. It is indeed a desolate landscape, devoid of all human habitation, part *macchia*, part bare rock. Driving conditions are easier on the newly-surfaced road inland, which is joined by turning right just after the bridge over the Fango River.

Doing this, though, does involve missing a highlight which the coast road has been keeping as a kind of farewell present: a small road leads off in the direction of **Notre Dame de la Serra**. This tiny chapel is situated on top of a rocky knoll, and affords a very impressive panoramic view for miles around, with the citadel in Calvi right in the middle.

Right, the cliffs of the Calanche sometimes resemble strange creatures.

CALVI AND THE BALAGNE

On Corsica's north-western coastline, nature has created several areas resembling huge natural theatres, with broad dress circles, narrow stalls, bold balconies and a stage opening out onto the broad expanse of the Mediterranean and mainland Europe beyond. And to cap all these geographical set pieces, whenever there is a change in the weather the snowy peaks of the Alps come into view at the very rear of the picture.

The white and yellow ferry boats only have 180 km (112 miles) of water to cross between Nice and the protected harbours of the Balagne's two main towns, Calvi and L'Ile Rousse – a far shorter distance than the one that brought Columbus immortality. However, local legend has it that the Genoese explorer was born in the citadel in Calvi.

The heart of the Balagne: Calvi, which was already promoting itself as a cosmopolitan beach resort when Saint-Tropez, on the opposite shore, was still a sleepy little fishing village, is the heart of the Balagne. During wintertime, which actually resembles nothing more than one long, drawn-out March, the pace of life here is leisurely.

The many sunny moments of these quiet months combine just about everything that is attractive about the island and its rather old-fashioned charm: the glittering sea, the curving beach, devoid of people once more, the pine-groves behind it and then the foothills gradually sloping upwards, with their oaks and olives, their barren-looking, aromatic *macchia*, their distant villages halfway up the mountainside and above them a chain of 2,000-metre (6,500-ft) mountain peaks, whose snowy summits change colour as the day goes by, progressing from freezing blue to pristine white, then yellow, and then finally a red shimmer in the setting sun.

A sense of cosy tranquillity then descends over the imposing **fortress**, a **contrefort** further inland and the

Preceding pages and left: harbour views.

Chapelle de la Madona di a Serra, situated just on the bend of the town's main street, which stays busy late into the evening.

Garish collage: Calvi's nearby airport brings a lot more visitors to the town than its rather impractical harbour ferry. Even when tourists are already occupying every other chair outside the cafés along the quays during the off-peak season, and a jazz festival at the beginning of June is already providing a foretaste of the crush to come, there are still a huge number of spare seats outside the cafés of L'Ile Rousse, Algajola and Galeria. The terraces outside the bars and bistros, situated next to a narrow one-way street and extending as far as the fishermen's nets right by the water's edge, are set up on a recently re-made traditional pavement and sheltered by colourful sunshades.

During the peak summer months, this tiny coastal resort is filled with the kind of frantic activity favoured by the hordes of tourists that descend on it from France and Italy. Nowhere is free of it, not even the bungalows and campsites right out on the edge of the town. Calvi actually feels rather pleased at its little dose of flair from "over the water", at the suntanned skin being sported everywhere, the smell of suntan oil and expensive perfumes, at the macho motorcyclists from Rome, the blonde, Nordic beach goddesses, and the chic Parisian-style atmosphere.

Fit for a prince: The **Balagne Déserte**, situated only a few minutes' drive to the south of Calvi, could not be more of a contrast. It begins just beyond the promontory called the Punta di a Revellata, which extends far into the gulf; a colony of seals lived in the caves there until not long ago.

Prince Pierre Bonaparte, a nephew of Napoleon, sought isolation here once, a little further inland. After his cousin Charles Louis had become Prince-Président and then the Emperor Napoleon III, thus destroying any political ambition he may once have possessed, Prince Pierre had the castle of **La Torre Mozza** built in the middle of the *macchia*

Left, in Calvi's Old Town. **Right**, from the air force, with love.

for himself and his mistress. Women carried the building materials on their heads – including, for the record, a bathtub from Marseilles – from a jetty up into the hills. Today, even the ruins of this erstwhile dream of a life lived close to nature still have a rather royal atmosphere about them.

In the rear stalls of the huge natural theatre in which Calvi itself occupies the royal box, and the landing strip of Santa Catalina airport forms the centre aisle, the dress circle area rises steeply. Behind it is another, smaller but still dramatic arena: the **Cirque de Bonifato**, providing access to Monte Cinto and, beyond the crest, to the winter sports resort of **Asco-la-Neige**.

On the road leading to the Forêt de Bonifato is the very inconspicuous-looking restaurant "U Spuntinu", on the site of a former sheep farm. In the direction of Calvi the luxurious manor house hotel of "La Signoria" is hidden inside a pine grove. **Calenzana**, stretched out at the foot of Monte Grosso, is the largest village in the Balagne with its small

A ferry docks at L'Ile Rousse.

hotels and hostels, and is also the starting point for the **GR20** and **Tra Mare e Monti** hiking trails. On the clock tower of the the impressive **Church of St Blaise** is an inscription relating to the famous battle fought here in 1732 when German mercenaries, hired by the Genoese to help put down the Corsican revolt, were slaughtered by the locals. Some say that they did it with pitchforks and spades alone; others that they opened their beehives and stung the enemy before finishing them off with knives.

Monte Grosso, which can be seen in the distance all the way from the harbour in Calvi, has also lent its name to a group of three small villages: **Cassanu, Lunghignanu** and **Montemaggiore**. Like the village of **Zilia**, which is even closer to the mountain, they are all around 300 metres (1,000 ft) above sealevel, a popular altitude in former times. This area is connected with the real-life Don Juan, Miguel de Leca y Colonna y Manara y Vincentello: his father came from Calvi and his mother from Montemaggiore before they both moved

THE WIND ROSE

As on the Greek islands, windmills were once an essential part of the landscape of Corsica. The fact that they are now ruins is not because the wind has ceased to blow. It is due to the decline of trade with Genoa during the 19th century, which led to a decrease in the quantities of wheat and olives grown until ultimately there was no more work for the mills.

The winds are as strong as ever. The massive erosion of the rocks, creating grotesque formations which evoke in the mind's eye an Indian's head or a dinosaur, is due in no small part to the "tossing breezes". They blow and roar from all points of the compass – although not at the same time, of course. On Corsica, each of these winds has a name. The *Scirocco*, which blows from the southeast, from the Sahara, brings with it desert sands – an unpopular souvenir amongst Corsicans. In Bonifacio the *Scirocco* only blows an average of four days a year, because Sardinia acts like a protective shield. Along the east coast, however, it is much more

common: in Bastia it occurs, albeit in a mild form, on over one hundred days each year.

The opposite of the *Scirocco* is the wind which blows from the northwest, the *Maestrale* (French: "*Mistral*"), which blows southwards from the Massif Central and the Rhône Valley. It is a rough companion, whose gusts whip up the waves and create a hazard for winter sportsmen. The storm warnings in the weather forecast: "Beware of the *Mistral*!" should not be ignored. By the time it reaches Corsica the *Maestrale* has usually lost some of its strength, but it can still be unpleasant. It is experienced most frequently in Ajaccio – on 36 days a year. The *Mistral*'s easterly neighbour is called the *Tramontana*. It blows from the North, from the cold, wintry plains of the Po. As its name indicates, it comes from "across the mountains" and makes the islanders shiver, particularly the inhabitants of Bastia, who have to face it for two whole months each year.

Continuing round the wind rose in clockwise direction, the next wind is the *Grecale*, which during the winter brings rain from the Apennines across on the mainland. If the wind blows directly from the east it is named *Levante*, after the sunrise. The opposite, the west wind, is known as the *Ponente*. Having set off from Gibraltar, the southwesterly *Libeccio* has crossed the entire western Mediterranean by the time it reaches Corsica. It brings rainfall in winter, which mostly falls on the west coast.

Although that completes the list of the seven winds, there are still two missing. On Corsica, the *Mezzogiorno* is not a southerly, for the wind virtually never blows from that direction. Instead, following the original meaning of the word, it is applied to a wind which blows at noon. The breeze gets up at about nine o'clock, after the land mass has heated up faster than the sea, causing the air to rise and creating a current of air to fill the resulting vacuum. So the *Mezzogiorno* blows from the sea onto the land, reaching its greatest intensity at about midday. In the olden days, sailing ships returned to port at this time. During the afternoon, when the temperatures have equalised, the *Mezzogiorno* dies down again. After sunset the drama is played in reverse, and the land breeze *Terrana* starts to blow, reaching its climax at midnight. And that was once the signal for sailing ships to put out to sea. ■

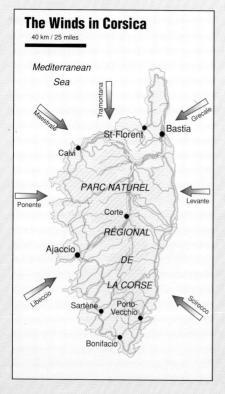

The Winds in Corsica

40 km / 25 miles

Mediterranean Sea

Tramontana

Maestrale

Grecale

St-Florent

Bastia

Calvi

PARC NATUREL

Ponente

Levante

Corte

RÉGIONAL

Ajaccio

DE

LA CORSE

Libeccio

Sartène

Porto-Vecchio

Scirocco

Bonifacio

The winds blow from all points of the compass.

to Spain. There is a very fine view of Calvi and its bay from the church square in Montemaggiore.

A similar sort of place, though closer to the sea, is **Lumio**; in the evening, the light from its windows and street-lamps shimmers across to the battlements and quays of Calvi. The two lions' heads on the Romanesque church of San Pietro e San Paolo also gaze across the bay.

Along the coast: The road forks at Lumio, with one direction leading eastwards into the Balagne and back to the beach at Lozari, and the other sticking close to the coast as far as the Désert des Agriates. Along the coast there are around half a dozen beach resorts, the first of which, called the **Marine de Sant'Ambrogio**, surrounding a fishermen's chapel, was conceived on a drawing board. There is a Club Méditerranée here. Passing through this area, the road then leads through *macchia* and several weird rock formations as far as **Punta die Spanu**, which has a small golf course set into a unique landscape. Along the coast, below the broad and gently curv-

ing road, the *Trinighellu*, the island's little railway – in its summer guise as *Tramway de la Balagne* – can be seen rattling and whistling its way at regular intervals between one holiday village bay and the next.

Algajola is a typical stop: a tiny resort on a long, yellow, sandy beach which actually belongs to the mountain village of **Aregno**. Algajola's small citadel, now privately-owned, was once an outwork of the Genoese fortress at Calvi. It also kept Pasquale Paoli at bay; the latter eventually thought he had found a chink in the armour of the hated oppressors when he founded a Corsican port to rival the Genoese Calvi at the red cliffs of the *Isola Rossa*, today's **L'Ile Rousse**. His plans failed to materialise, however, but the tower that once protected his harbour is now right at the centre of the second most popular tourist destination in the Balagne.

Guarded by a column of tall palm-trees, a white marble statue of Paoli dominates L'Ile Rousse's plane-tree-lined square, situated right next to a fine

High season on the beach at L'Ile Rousse.

promenade and also a sandy beach, divided up by beach cafés and rocky outcrops. From the new harbour, which is now used by enormous ferries, the view across the town encompasses a large area of hillside with two basin-like depressions – one of them beyond Algajola and extending up to Aregno and Cateri, the other concealed behind the Regino Valley, and both of them natural catchment areas for the town, which has now spread far beyond its original borders.

Just as in the Calvi basin, all the people from further inland stream into the shops and supermarkets of this resort, and many for whom the sea is only a distant shimmer from their villages can usually earn a modest income here, though only during the peak season. L'Ile Rousse, which the Romans called *Rubica Rocega*, is hopelessly overcrowded in July and August, its beaches completely covered with sun-hungry bodies. A sewage treatment plant originally built to cater for the local population sometimes cannot cope with up to ten times its working capacity. So it is best to come here out of season for a holiday, even though some of the establishments are closed then. Try swimming off **Lozari** or **Ostriconi**, two magnificent, almost unspoiled stretches of beach further out towards the Cape, where even in June it is sometimes possible to see the snowy peak of Monte Padro to the south.

Like a string of pearls: The meandering road leading inland from Lumio – or conversely from Lozari – is so full of bends that it is more than double the distance as the crow flies (15 km/9 miles), and the villages are strung out along its length like pearls: **Lavatoggio** and **Croce, Cateri, Avapessa, Muro** and **Muratu, Felicetu, Nessa, Ville-di-Paraso** and **Quarcio, Costa, Occhiatana** and **Belgodere**. A *corniche* road hugs the mountainside at the 300-metre (1,000-ft) mark, and the only destination even higher up is **Speloncato**.

This necklace contains the following gems: **Aregno** with its simple but stunning Pisan Romanesque church of La Trinità; **Pigna**, famous as a haunt of **Palasca**.

artists and also for the edible as well as audible joys to be had at its *Casa Musicale*; the monastery village of **Corbara**; and then, up on a 500-metre (1,600-ft) high ridge, the ultimate jewel: **Sant'Antonino**, a village that seems almost to grow out of the rock, with its sloping walls, vaulted passageways and the remarkable views it provides, across the Balagne to the sea and inland to the mountains.

In **Belgodère**, where Maurice Utrillo and his painter-mother Suzanne Valadon eked out a meagre existence shortly before World War I selling paintings of the surrounding villages and churches, the *corniche* begins to descend towards the beach at Lozari. But the Balagne has three more attractive, though less well-known valleys to offer. The road to the **Ghjunssani** begins in the village square of **Speloncato**, right next to the veranda of a restaurant, and is only just wide enough for a car.

But before taking this trip, why not take a break and sit down, either on one of the bar-stools or next to the fountain?

Belgoderè.

This whole square, lined by several picturesque houses, one of the village's two churches and also the private palace of a Corsican cardinal that has now been turned into a hotel, is a sight in itself, and is the focus of village life here.

It's also an ideal place to observe typical Corsican daily life: here you can see women, dressed in practical housecoats which they don't change until lunchtime, shaking out bed-sheets and sweeping up in front of their doorways, chattering uninterruptedly with their lady neighbours. Then the men, who have come back from work in a village further down the mountain, enjoy their first *Pastis* of the day.

Fresh water gets brought along in pails at mealtimes, and children race around. Right up until sunset the square is one big meeting-place filled with noisy, gesticulating people going about their business or sitting in the shade.

Flying above the hustle and bustle from dawn till dusk are the swallows and swifts, which feel very much at ease here and often even nest on hotel win-

dow-sills. The rocks on either side of the village are riddled with numerous grottos (*spelunca*). Twice a year, on 8 April and 8 September, assuming there are no clouds, the locals and their guests wait for the setting sun to reappear through the famous Pietra Tafonata (pierced stone), bathing the village in its light for several extra minutes.

Bird's-eye view from the pass: The road then curves around in several ever-widening loops up the side of the mountain as far as the 1,099-metre (3,600-ft) high **Col de a Battaglia**. If you get out of your car at this point and take a few steps back towards the valley you will suddenly feel you are flying above the Balagne. The bird's-eye view from up here takes in the whole stretch of coast between the **Balagne Déserte** and the **Désert des Agriates** to the north-east. And if you turn round you will find yourself standing opposite the 2,393-metre (7,800-ft) high **Monte Padro**. The valley basin in front of it contains the villages of Piaggiola, Olmi Capella, Forcili and Mausoleo, all surrounded by intense green foliage. Laricio pine covers the slopes of Monte Padro above, and the mountain torrents of Melaja and Tartagine are cool and refreshing even on the hottest days of the year.

Back to the sea now, perhaps via **Palasca**, situated in its own valley among several hilly crests often ravaged by fire, in whose *macchia*-covered folds the sunlight is particularly dramatic. The valley of **Ostriconi**, whose beach is only attractive from a distance these days, has now been turned into a conservation area and is worth exploring.

A new road from Bastia via Ponte Leccia is supposed to cut travel time drastically from one coast to the other. It leads through this formerly remote basin, and has now brought tourism and traffic a step closer to four more Balagne villages. Until early 1999 this highway, known familiarly as the "Balanina", was still incomplete. The road through the Désert des Agriates was a real adventure until 1997 when it was widened and covered with asphalt.

<u>Left</u>, Speloncato.

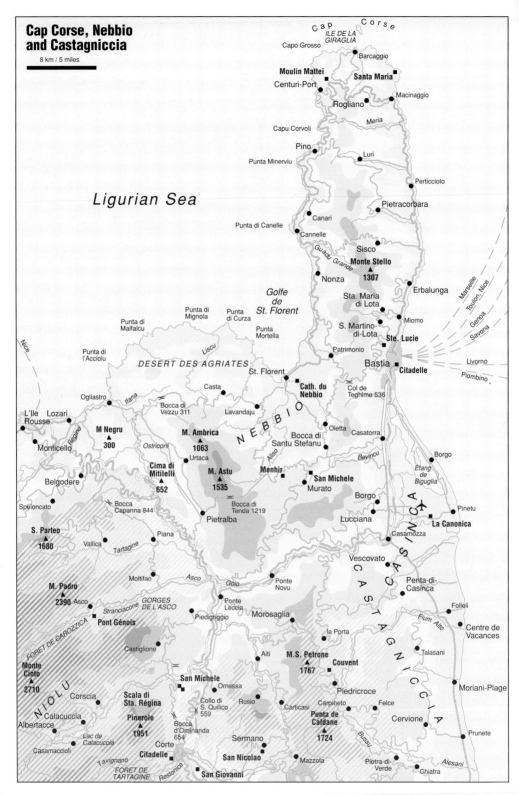

Cap Corse, Nebbio and Castagniccia

8 km / 5 miles

Cap Corse

ILE DE LA GIRAGLIA

Capo Grosso

Barcaggio

Moulin Mattei
Centuri-Port

Santa Maria

Macinaggio

Rogliano

Meria

Capu Corvoli

Pino

Luri

Punta Minerviu

Perticciolo

Ligurian Sea

Punta di Canelle

Canari

Pietracorbara

Cannelle

Guadu Grande

Sisco

Monte Stello
▲
1307

Nonza

Erbalunga

Sta. Maria di Lota

Miomo

Golfe de St. Florent

Punta di Mignola

Punta di Curza

S. Martino-di-Lota

Punta di Malfalcu

Punta Mortella

Ste. Lucie

Patrimonio

Bastia
Citadelle

Punta di l'Acciolu

Liscu

DESERT DES AGRIATES

Casta

St. Florent

Cath. du Nebbio

Col de Teghime 536

Ogliastro

Itana

Bocca di Vezzu 311

Lavandaju

Lozari
L'Ile Rousse

Regino

M Negru
▲
300

Ostriconi

M. Ambrica
▲
1063

Urtaca

N E B B I O

Bocca di Santu Stefanu

Oletta

Casatorra

Bevincu

Borgo

Etang de Biguglia

Monticello

Cima di Mitilelli
652

M. Astu
▲
1535

Menhir

San Michele
Murato

Borgo

Lucciana

Pinetu

Belgodere

Bocca di Tenda 1219

Pietralba

Casamozza

La Canonica

Speloncato

Bocca Capanna 844

Piana

Vescovato

Penta-di-Casinca

S. Parteo
▲
1680

Vallica

Tartagine

Moltifao

Asco

Golo

Ponte Novu

Folleli

M. Padro
▲
2390

Asco

GORGES DE L'ASCO

Strancicone

Pont Génois

Ponte Leccia

Piedigriggio

Morosaglia

la Porta

Fium Alto

Centre de Vacances

Talasani

Castiglione

Monte Cinto
▲
2710

San Michele

Omessa

Aiti

M.S. Petrone
▲
1767

Couvent

Piedicroce

Moriani-Plage

N I O L U

Corscia

Scala di Sta. Régina

Collo di S. Quilico 559

Rusio

Carticasi

Carpineto

Felce

Cervione

Calacuccia

Pinerole
1951

Bocca d'Ominanda 654

Sermano

Punta de Caldane
▲
1724

Prunete

Albertacce

Lac de Calacuccia

Corte

Citadelle

San Nicolao

Bussu

Casamaccioli

Tavignano

Restonica

San Giovanni

Mazzola

Pietra-di-Verde

Alesani

Chiatra

FORET DE CAROZZICA

FORET DE TARTAGINE

C A S I N C A

C A S T A G N I C C I A

Nice

Marseille

Toulon, Nice

Genoa

Savona

Livorno

Piombino

192

SAINT-FLORENT AND THE NEBBIO

Pasquale Paoli was reputedly the first person to refer to the Nebbio as a "golden shell". And the region does indeed resemble a sea-shell as it rises up from the Gulf of Saint-Florent. The hills pile up, higher and higher, into the schist mountains whose peaks form the crest along the top. During Paoli's lifetime, the Nebbio was the bread-basket of Corsica. The Genoese, who pursued a strict agrarian policy on the island, ordered cereal to be grown here, and today golden corn is a typical feature of the island, alongside its fruit and vegetables.

Olives grow further up. The high hills are a mixture of woodland and meadow, especially in the island's centre, where a narrow range of mountains halts the build-up of clouds to the west. To the north is the Patrimonio wine country, and to the west the vast, lonely expanse known as the Désert des Agriates.

Mediterranean harbour: Saint-Florent lies on the gulf of the same name. The town dates back to Roman times, when it was situated higher up, and further inland. It was here that the Pisan bishopric also grew up, thus providing continuity from antiquity via the Early Christian Period right through to the High Middle Ages, which was when Genoa placed its citadel on a rocky projection right next to the coast, and the town, forced to stay close to it, had to extend its housing to the surrounding marshland. Saint-Florent then became a strategically important harbour, and during the various wars that followed it was owned by Genoa, Corsica and France alternately, though its real conqueror was malaria. It was only when the nearby swamps were drained that its harbour was able to function properly once more.

Today's Saint-Florent is very French, very Mediterranean, and one gets the feeling that it is not "pestered" by Corsican problems. Its boutiques have a touch of elegance, and its cafés (bastions of the male population) still have a fishing-village atmosphere about them.

Here one can live in style, the food is good, the holiday crowds never become a crush, and the central square is still predominantly a meeting-place for the locals, for *pétanque*, *Pastis* and *politique*.

The key to the **Cathedral of the Nebbio** can be obtained from the Tourist Office. Although it is a Pisan cathedral, anyone with visions of the cathedral in Pisa will be disappointed. It stands on farmland outside today's town, and is a simple building of pale limestone. Blind arcades adorn the facade and the tops of the graceful pilasters are decorated with a frieze. The Cathedral is actually by no means as plain as it appears at first glance. More and more details catch the eye: the fabulous animals on the capitals, and the symbols, geometrical patterns and marks on the frieze. Inside the building, in a glass case, the mummified remains of Saint Flor can be seen. The patron saint of the town, he was a Roman soldier who was martyred here in the 3rd century.

A tour of the Nebbio: It is possible to take a circular tour of the hills of the Nebbio from Saint-Florent. Take the D81 towards Ile Rousse for about 4 km, along the southern edge of the Désert des Agriates, before turning off to the left along the narrow and winding D62. To the west, the route is dominated by a 1,500-metre (5,000-ft) high mountain range, the highest peak of which is the impressive Monte Astu.

There are a number of tiny villages along the way. After 10 km (6 miles) is **Santo Pietro di Tenda**, whose houses are ranged along the Tenda ridge above the Aliso valley. In the centre of the village, which is surrounded by olive and chestnut trees, are two separate baroque churches joined in a single facade by a square campanile. The route gets more rugged and mountainous as it continues to **Pieve**, 7 km (4 miles) further on. Next to the church are the very weathered remains of two menhirs. Unlike their granite cousins in the south of the island, these ones are made of slate. Now and then one comes across very strangely-constructed shepherds' huts: the ground plan is square, but the roof is round. The walls and roof, made up of layers of flat stones, blend into each other.

The biggest attraction of the journey is without doubt the famous **Church of San Michele de Murato**, situated at a T-junction about 1 km from the village of **Murato**. Considered to be one of Corsica's finest churches, it stands on a grassy spur, elevated in splendid isolation above the surrounding countryside.

The 12th-century church is built of two kinds of stone: pinkish-yellow limestone and dark-green serpentine marble, running in relatively uniform "black-and-white" stripes around the top of the building before becoming more and more untidy and irregular at the base. The whole structure looks weird and highly exotic. Even more remarkable are the numerous motifs chosen by the stonemasons. According to local legend a mosque once stood on this site, and several people have interpreted the reliefs as representing the victory of Christianity over Islam. Severed hands are depicted, for instance, possibly signifying that the church once housed a

court of law. Men, animals and fabulous creatures are all gathered here. Another relief depicts the wine harvest: two men with an enormous grape that they have just hacked down with warlike curved knives. A further scene depicts Eve being tempted by the serpent and covering her nakedness with an oversized hand – naive Romanesque "expressionism".

The cemetery next to the road opposite is also worth a visit. Like so many others on Corsica it is like a small town, where each family has its own special resting place beneath cool avenues of trees. Cemeteries are usually a good way of assessing the prosperity of a village, and Murato is no exception: it is a wealthy farming village. It has profited from the new road to Bastia, and its street-lights are especially modern – each one is equipped with solar cells.

To the east of Murato, the D62 connecting Saint-Florent with Bastia plunges into a deep ravine, the Défilé de Lancôme, and then descends to the eastern coastal plain. Recently a broader, less winding road (D82) on the south

The parish church of Patrimonio.

bank has been constructed to lead down to the plain as well. The traveller can return to Saint-Florent by taking the D82 to the north, past the village of Oletta and the fertile Guadello valley, which is famous for its cheese.

Barren wilderness: Les Agriates – also referred to as the **Désert des Agriates** – is the name given to the strip of land to the west of the Gulf of Saint-Florent. This area, which measures roughly 10 by 20 km (6 by 12 miles), was once fertile land but is now a barren wilderness – for several reasons. The farmers who grew their wheat here used to live beyond the gulf, on the steep slopes of the Cap Corse, where the sunny slopes were more suited to wine and figs than corn. For sowing and harvesting purposes they thus travelled across to the coast. The farmers shared the Agriates region with shepherds, who brought their flocks here to winter pasture.

The fact that the shepherds began to burn tracts of forest to give their flocks more room to graze probably did not **San Michele.** concern the farmers unduly at first –

until the resulting erosion starting affecting the water balance. Increased karstification also limited grazing possibilities. The farmers abandoned the region, and the valleys degenerated into steppe. Recently, however, the Agriates region has become more interesting again – thanks to tourism.

Excursions by boat from Saint-Florent mean that the area does some business in the summer. And in the winter-time, a few herds of sheep do still graze in this wilderness. On the road leading from Saint-Florent to L'Ile Rousse, which passes along the edge of this region, there are only very few houses. They include several establishments selling Corsican cheese, honey and wine. In **Casta** there are restaurants, and you can join a horseback ride or an excursion in four-wheel-drive vehicles; the tracks that lead from this road through the Agriates and over to the sea are unsuitable for normal cars. Hikers should take sufficient drinking water with them. There are a few observation points along the road, though, affording fine views across

the gulf, and over mountains and valleys, all the way to the mountain range on Cap Corse.

The vineyards of Patrimonio: The wine country of Patrimonio, in the north of the Nebbio, is a complete contrast to the barren wilderness of the Désert des Agriates. Wine has been produced in Corsica since antiquity; it played a role while the island was under Pisan domination, and Genoa turned the Cap Corse peninsula and its surrounding area, as far as the corn land in the Nebbio, into a wine-producing region. In 19th-century French Corsica, more Corsicans were employed in wine production than in any other trade. But then, in 1874, the *phylloxera* (vine louse) arrived and destroyed as much as 85 percent of the crop. Most of the island's vintners gave up. Many emigrated. The few who stayed were faced with unexpectedly tough competition after World War II.

But it wasn't long before people who knew how to apply modern cultivation methods arrived: the *Pieds noirs*, French emigrants returning from newly-independent Algeria. They also introduced new grape varieties, and gave winemaking on Corsica a huge boost – but in many cases the island's wine was now being mass-produced. Several local vintners called in the bulldozers, cut away large areas of macchia and planted the cheap varieties. It took the shock of a bomb attack to get people to begin considering a change of policy.

Now even France has remembered that Corsica used to have a tradition of quality wine-growing, and honour has finally been restored to the island once more: Corsican wine now has a legal claim to the AOC *(Appelation d'Origine Contrôlée)* title. Patrimonio received its AOC in 1968. Most of Corsica's AOC wines are made from the island's original grape varieties, and several of them can only be obtained on the island itself.

The wine region of Patrimonio today comprises not only the central area around the village with its church but also the surrounding slopes. Some vines here grow on shale, but limestone tends to predominate. The soil is a favourite **Rockery by the wayside.**

with *Nielluccio*, a variety that probably came here from Tuscany centuries ago, and which today gives Patrimonio red wine its distinctive character.

Wine from this region is definitely worth buying – especially red wine. The Muscat is also popular. But the real classic alongside the Nielluccio is the *Vermentinu*, also known as *Malvasiu*, which may even have been brought to the island by the Greeks. Here in Northern Corsica it produces a white wine of distinction that is also strongly acidic. As far as taking wine home is concerned, it is best to stick with those vineyards that have experience in the wine export business, and to ask which wines are susceptible to long-distance travel and which are not.

The menhir in the vineyard: Patrimonio is probably the only village on the island to have maintained and retained its prosperity for any length of time. Lots of small, dignified-looking vintners' houses, separated by ancient trees and encircled by vineyards, dot the slopes surrounding the village and its elegant parish church. There are a few craft shops, and also several restaurants providing Corsican cuisine. And it's also a good place for those interested in Corsican prehistory: a few years ago, a menhir statue was found in one of the vineyards here. It has now been erected just below the church.

A human head with shoulders can be made out on the top of a column – one of the "stone warriors" that are so numerous in the southern part of the island. This one, hewn out of pale-coloured limestone, is "only" 3,000 years old, and is now protected by a roof. When it was created the island's sculptors had already been producing menhirs for 2,000 years. Possibly forced to leave their settlements in the south of the island, the megalithic peoples brought this expression of their culture along with them and guarded it closely, while all around them a new epoch – the Bronze Age – had already been ushered in. The menhir of Patrimonio is thus the last reminder we have of a very advanced Stone-Age civilisation.

The church of San Michelle de Murato.

THE CAP CORSE

The Cap Corse, the northernmost tip of Corsica, is not a cape but a peninsula, pointing at the Italian mainland like an index finger. A range of schist mountains runs along this 40-km (25-mile) long and 15-km (9-mile) wide tongue of land from north to south, dropping steeply down to the sea in the west, and more gently so in the east. The villages here, their houses built from the local grey or green stone, are either hidden along the slopes of the lateral valleys, or situated majestically out in the open with a commanding view.

The sea is always close at hand on this slender promontory, and each municipality here has its own small harbour, with fishing boats, where the Cap Corse's products (wine, oil, wood, fruit and fish) get exported. Magnificent mansions, castle-like villas and elegant-looking mausoleums remind the visitor of the region's former prosperity.

From the end of the 19th century onwards, however, the Cap Corse suffered a steady economic decline: trade with Genoa was *passé*, and the vine louse put an end to almost all wine exporting. Some of the local inhabitants emigrated overseas. These days, however, tourism has offered a new source of income, and the Cap Corse's grapes are producing good wines once more, as well as the island's favourite aperitif, "Cap Corse".

Watchtowers and pebble beaches: A day-long excursion around this peninsula, with superb landscape viewing, can be undertaken from either Saint-Florent or Bastia. The whole trip, along the D80, is only 128 km (80 miles) long, but the road is just as sinuous as most others on Corsica, so if you are planning to make detours into the villages, take a few leisurely photographs and possibly do some hiking too, the best thing is to plan on at least one overnight stay. The harbour at Centuri is an idyllic stopping-off point in this respect, and there are several pleasant, small hotels to choose from.

Photographers should proceed anti-clockwise around the Cap Corse, because the sun shines on the east coast in the morning and the west coast in the afternoon. The first beach after leaving Bastia is at the little fishing port of **Miomo**: it is strewn with pebbles, and dominated by a well-preserved Genoese watchtower. Right next to it is a small chapel, built in 1780, with touchingly naive stucco work in its interior. The church of Notre Dame des Grâces in the neighbouring hamlet of **Lavasina** is more than a century older, but has unfortunately been provided with an ugly modern concrete *campanile*, surmounted by a white statue of the Virgin that can be seen for miles around. On 8 September, Corsicans make the pilgrimage here to the "Madonna of Lavasina", an altar painting darkened with age. The picture is credited with miraculous powers and is thought to be a product of the school of Perugino (16th century).

A favourite subject for landscape painters is **Erbalunga**, situated on a schist promontory jutting out into the

Preceding pages: the lonely west coast of Cap Corse. **Left,** one way of touring the peninsula. **Right,** the excellently preserved tower at Losse.

sea. A Genoese tower, now in ruins, once used to protect access to the tiny fishing harbour. Many of the buildings seem to rise directly out of the water because of the limited space available. The small marina here can be observed from a square filled with snack bars, cafés and pizzerias. The balcony of the restaurant called "Le Pirate" affords a particularly fine view.

Anyone interested in observing the whole of the Cap Corse from its highest peak, the **Monte Stello** (1,307 metres/ 4,300 ft), can travel along the D54 from Erbalunga as far as the hamlet of **Silgaggia**, from where the ascent takes around three hours to complete. Since the climb is in full sunshine, the earlier one starts the better.

The next small harbour on the route is the **Marine de Sisco** with its short, greyish-coloured pebble beach. The village itself actually lies several kilometres further inland. It was a metal-forging centre in medieval times, producing weapons, armour and jewellery. Right into the 18th century, Sisco's flourish-ing crafts and far-reaching trade connections made it one of the richest villages on the Cap Corse. Just behind the marina, a statue of Saint Catherine of Sisco, wearing a sword, can be seen standing on a rock above the promenade. The relics brought to her by sailors returning from Palestine in the 13th century are no longer housed in the Romanesque church of St Catherine, a former monastery, but are now locked away in the parish church of Saint-Martin, up in the village.

Cap Corse's colourful history: The route now continues past various other small harbours, with sandy beaches this time, ideal for swimming: the **Marine de Pietracorbara** and the **Marine de Porticciolo**. Five kilometres further inland lies the village of **Cagnano**. According to a recent theory, it was here – and not in Genoa or Calvi – that Christopher Columbus was born.

This new angle in the dispute as to his origins has been introduced by Corsican historian Lucien Saladini, and there is a reasonable amount of evidence to sub- **The pebble beach at Miomo.**

stantiate the claim: during his youth, Columbus was apparently called Colombo de Terra Rossa, and he once mentioned that he was not the only admiral in the family. The former manor known as Terre Rosse is situated in Cagnano, and was built by an admiral in the Genoese fleet roughly 200 years before Columbus was born. So was Columbus really a Corsican from Cap Corse? Wherever he hailed from, he made such a mystery of his origins that the speculation is guaranteed to go on for years.

After passing the well-preserved **Losse Tower**, the traveller will arrive at **Santa Severa** with its small port at the estuary of the river Luri. The D180 leads west from here across to **Luri** and **Pino**. Anyone keen on seeing the northernmost point of the Cap Corse should stay on the D80. The **Marine de Meria** lies in a small, sheltered bay. **Macinaggio** possesses a relatively large marina, several small hotels, restaurants and souvenir shops, a disco, and also one of the Cap Corse's rare petrol sta-

tions. The harbour here has certainly had its share of VIP visitors: it was at Macinaggio in 1790 that Paoli set foot on Corsican soil once again on his return from England; Napoleon visited the harbour only three years later, breaking his trip back from Egypt for a short visit to his homeland; and the Empress Eugénie also arrived here in 1869 from Egypt, where she had attended the opening of the Suez Canal, because a storm forced her ship to seek refuge in the harbour. The Empress and her retinue walked up to **Rogliano**; the way was steep and arduous, and Eugénie later had a road built. The latter has since been known as the *Chemin de L'Impératrice* ("Empress Way").

It's definitely worth making a detour off the D80, which runs inland near Macinaggio, to see the hamlets of Rogliano, with their towers, churches and slate roofs. The ruins of the castle of **San Colombano** can be seen high on a rocky crag; it was once the seat of the da Mare family, who used to own a large section of the Cap Corse.

Nonza clings to the hillside.

The landscape up at the northernmost point of the Cap Corse is barren and bleak. If you turn off in **Ersa** you can go on a short, 16-km (10-mile) tour of the area. The D153 leads through the *macchia* to the small fishing harbour of **Barcaggio**, and then on to **Tollare.** Both these hamlets, with their grey slate houses, are situated on the estuaries of small rivers. Greenish, shimmering serpentine rocks stand at Corsica's windy "Land's End" and can also be seen on the **Ile de la Giraglia** further out, with its mighty lighthouse.

Back on the D80 one then arrives at the **Col de la Serra** (365 metres/1,200 ft), from which a footpath leads to an old ruined windmill, the **Moulin Mattei**. From here the view extends across the west coast of the Cap Corse. The picturesque and colourful **Port Centuri** lies directly below – the perfect backdrop for a meal of delicious seafood, or even just a short coffee break.

Stories about Seneca: Beyond **Morsiglia**, which extends up from the sea on a series of terraces, the road rises to quite a height, curving its way along the jagged, steep rocky coastline. Just before **Pino** the D180 branches off towards Santa Severa. Only a few kilometres further along this road is the **Col de Sainte Lucie**, and not far away, on the peak of the Ventiggiole, the ruins of the famous **Seneca Tower** (Tour de Sénèque), can be seen. To reach it you need to drive to the *Maison d'Enfants* at Luri, from where the entire steep climb takes a good hour there and back. The famous Stoic is said to have lived here during his exile from Rome between AD 41 and 49. The tower itself could hardly have provided Seneca with shelter considering that it was only built in the 15th century, but it does stand on the site of an earlier structure.

"Inhospitable" and even "horrible" were just two of the words Seneca used to describe the island on which he involuntarily spent eight years of his life, far from the *dolce vita* in Rome. "Where else is there anything as bare, as overwhelmingly grim as this rocky land?", he wondered. The Corsicans avenged **A loner on the cape.**

themselves for this unfriendly description of their homeland with an uncomplimentary little tale about Seneca: apparently the philosopher had his evil way with the daughter of a Corsican shepherd. When her brothers discovered the hanky-panky they massaged Seneca's bare buttocks with a particular variety of stinging-nettle that still grows in the vicinity of the tower. The Corsican name for this species of nettle is a reminder of the whole scandalous affair: *Ortica di Seneca*.

Pretty **Pino** is surrounded by altogether more pleasant vegetation: planetrees provide refreshing shade, and olives, figs and oranges grow on the terraced slopes. The baroque facade of the church of Sainte-Marie is painted a welcoming white. Down at the harbour, the village's old Genoese tower and its former Franciscan monastery stand opposite one another.

Beyond Pino, there is another Genoese tower at the **Marine de Giottani**, with its grey pebble beach. Then a little further along the road is **Canari** with its two churches, which are definitely worth visiting. Santa Maria Assunta is a fine example of 12th-century Pisan Romanesque: its cornices have curious human and animal faces. The baroque church of Saint-François, formerly part of a Franciscan monastery, contains 15th-century altar paintings depicting St Michael subduing the dragon and weighing human souls, and also Christ dressed as a penitent. A Cap Corse noblewoman, Vittoria di Gentile, holding her child, is depicted on a 16th-century tombstone in front of the choir.

A tower and its hero: A grey wasteland and old, dilapidated buildings and machinery are all that remain of an asbestos mine on the coast road which was abandoned in 1965. The overburden has created a beach of black sand that extends as far as **Nonza**. It forms an ideal surface on which to draw and write using white pebbles. Now the cliffs of Nonza come into view. The imposing square tower perched on top was defended single-handedly against the French in 1768 by the resourceful Corsican lieutenant Casella. Using just one

cannon, and several flintlocks, Casella delivered such an incredible show of strength that the besiegers did not dare storm the tower. They eventually offered everyone inside it safe passage, and were amazed and very embarrassed when, instead of the whole team they had expected, the cunning old trooper limped out alone.

The church in Nonza is consecrated to St Julie. She was actually martyred in Carthage around AD 300, but legend has shifted her death to Nonza. A double fountain (Fontaine Sainte-Julie) is supposed to have sprung up at the place where the stubborn young Christian apparently had both her breasts severed from her body.

Shortly after Nonza, the Bay of Saint-Florent comes into view, and the vineyards of the Patrimonio region begin. To get back to Bastia, the D81, which borders the Cap Corse to the south, first has to climb over the **Col de Teghime** (536 metres/1,750 ft). There is a fine view to be had of both coasts from up on this pass.

A discovery on the beach.

BASTIA

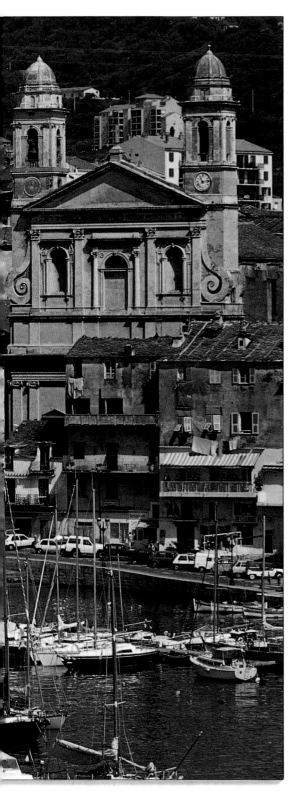

Bastia is an honest town, not a spruced-up, shiny tourist haven. There are fewer luxury yachts in the harbour here, and there's not a sandy beach for miles around. It is a busy port with real Neapolitan flair, economically the most important town in Corsica, although with a population of only 38,000, it can hardly be called a major metropolis. On weekdays the town is one massive traffic jam – although since the construction of the road tunnel, this problem is nowhere near as bad as it used to be.

A town to arrive in: Bastia is the first contact many visitors will have with the island. This is where most of the ferries from the mainland arrive, and the holidaymakers headed for the beaches on the east coast all land at Bastia-Poretta airport. Anyone arriving in Bastia by car who gets sucked down into the **Voie Rapide** (expressway) will have missed the best view of the town, which is the old, semicircular harbour with the church of Saint-Jean Baptiste. This church, visible from miles away across the water, has greeted homecoming seafarers for centuries. The streets of the Old Town with their tall, narrow houses rise up behind it like a huge amphitheatre, and high above them, in stark contrast, are the modern, white apartment buildings. But it is the old, dilapidated buildings that make Bastia so picturesque.

Bastia was founded by the Genoese. Their governor, Leonello Lomellini, occupied what was then a rocky crag above the fishing village of Cardo, and had a bastion erected at this strategic location. The Italian word for "bastion", *bastiglia*, gave the town its name. The watchtower soon developed into a mighty fortress with high walls and battlements. In the 17th century the Genoese moved the seat of their Corsican governors from Biguglia to Bastia, and Pope

Preceding pages: the people of Cap Corse were always involved with the sea. **Left,** it's the dilapidated buildings that make Bastia so picturesque.

Clement VII then awarded the settlement civic rights.

Even after Corsica had fallen to the French in 1769, Bastia still remained chief town of the island. Following the division of Corsica into two *départements* in 1797, Bastia remained capital of the northern one. Then, much to its displeasure, the town had to content itself with being a *sous-préfecture* when Napoleon I selected his native town of Ajaccio as Corsica's new capital.

It was only in 1974, when Corsica was divided anew into two separate regions, that Bastia once again became the administrative centre of the northern part of the island, or Département Haute Corse. There is considerably less jealousy and resentment between Ajaccio and Bastia now that each administers one of the two *départements* on the island, but the two towns are very different: Ajaccio in architecture and atmosphere is very French while Bastia is far more Italian.

Trade and industry: The town's new port (Nouveau Port), was constructed between 1850 and 1870, and it very soon became the most important marine traffic and trading centre in Corsica. Over half of all the goods exported or imported by Corsica pass through Bastia. The economic boom, and Bastia's reputation for being Corsica's leading trading port, have both left their mark on the town's demographic structure. In contrast to other towns and even regions on the island, Bastia still provides enough jobs, and is thus succeeding in staunching the flow of young emigrants to the French mainland.

Bastia could be termed a workers' city, for working people do make up the largest section of the population here, at 39 percent (roughly 30 percent in Ajaccio). A cliché attitude on the island considers Ajaccio to be the cultural centre of Corsica and Bastia the industrial capital where "feet are on the ground and hands at work". Two-thirds of Bastia's working population are employed in companies within the region, most of them small craft businesses and industrial firms. However, the town also offers its visitors a whole host of sights,

and its colourful markets, quays and squares are full of bustling life. A day in Bastia (the average amount of time most tourists spend here) is certainly not a day wasted.

In 1983, the new road tunnel was built in order to cope with the town's appalling traffic, which used to be quite unbearable whenever the big ferries docked, or during rush hour. It runs directly from the docks under the old harbour and the citadel. Not everyone in Bastia was happy about this development, since it meant that many tourists by-passed the town centre entirely. Restaurant, café and boutique owners manned the barricades, but in the end the arguments in favour of the tunnel outweighed the complaints.

A favourite rendezvous point: To get to know Bastia the best place to begin is the **Place Saint-Nicolas**, right in the centre of town. The 300-metre-long square, built on a terrace overlooking the port, is shaded by palm and plane trees. Together with its cafés and shops on the landward side, it is strongly remi-

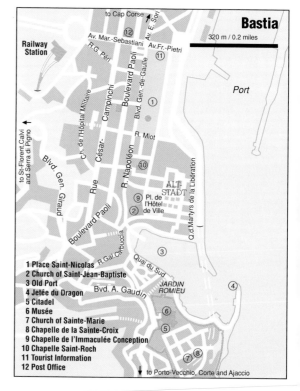

Bastia

320 m / 0.2 miles

to Cap Corse

Railway Station

Av. Mar.-Sebastiani Av.Fr.-Pietri
R.G. Péri
Campinchi
Boulevard Paoli
Blvd. Gen.-de-Gaulle
Ch. de l'Hôpital Militaire
César-
Rue
R. Miot
R. Napoléon
Blvd. Gen. Giraud
Boulevard Paoli
R. Gal. Carbuccia
Quai du Sud
Bvd. A. Gaudin
Q.d Martyrs de la Libération

Port

ALT-STADT
Pl. de l'Hôtel de Ville

JARDIN ROMIEU

to St-Florent, Calvi and Serra di Pigno

1 Place Saint-Nicolas
2 Church of Saint-Jean-Baptiste
3 Old Port
4 Jetée du Dragon
5 Citadel
6 Musée
7 Church of Sainte-Marie
8 Chapelle de la Sainte-Croix
9 Chapelle de l'Immaculée Conception
10 Chapelle Saint-Roch
11 Tourist Information
12 Post Office

to Porto-Vecchio, Corte and Ajaccio

niscent of squares on the Italian mainland. And there's a lot going on here, particularly in the evenings: young people, fashionably dressed, go strolling up and down, past the bandstand and the marble statue of Napoleon, indulging in the age-old ritual of flirtation. The older and wiser ones take up their observation positions on the benches around the square where they have a good view of the Corso while discussing everything under the sun. One subject of lively debate is the game of *boules*, usually played by the older men in various parts of the square.

In the afternoons, the Place Saint-Nicolas is bathed in a warm, soft light that is typically Mediterranean. The statue of Napoleon, by the way, is not the work of a Corsican, but of the Florentine sculptor Lorenzo Bartolini. It is the only reminder the inhabitants here have of the erstwhile Emperor of France. At the bottom of their hearts they've never really forgiven him for choosing Ajaccio as the island's capital instead of Bastia.

It's certainly worth making a short detour at this point to the shop on the western side of the square called **Louis-Napoleon Mattei**, where Corsican products of all kinds can be purchased. There is the spicy wine known as *Cap Corse Mattei*, for example, and also candied citrus fruits, myrtle or cedrat liqueur, olive-wood sculptures, ceramics and several different types of honey. The particular attraction of this shop, apart from its excellent assortment of genuinely Corsican products, lies in its interior, which has not been altered since the business first started around the turn of the century. There is also a **Tourist Information Office** on the north side of the square, opposite the Centre Administratif; the main Syndicat d'Initiative is on the Boulevard Paoli, between the Rue Abatucci and the Rue Miot.

Busy markets: Anyone keen on rummaging through old junk and knick-knacks should definitely take a stroll across the Place Saint-Nicolas on a Sunday, when the flea market takes place. It's at this time that the numerous bars

Boat at Bastia.

and street cafés along the **Boulevard de Gaulle** do particularly good business. Sitting down here for an aperitif or a coffee is not only an excellent way to wind down, it also provides a very good opportunity to come into contact with the locals.

Parallel to the Boulevard de Gaulle is the **Boulevard Paoli**, a shopping street that is usually one enormous traffic jam, with all the accompanying exhaust fumes.

The **Old Town** is a lot more romantic: this complex labyrinth of narrow streets and passageways, with its tall 16th- to 18th-century buildings showing every sign of their age, tends to confuse most visitors. Right at the centre of it is the **Place de l'Hôtel de Ville** (Town Hall Square). A food market is held here every morning except for Sundays and public holidays. Farmers from the surrounding countryside sell fresh fruit, vegetables, meat, cheese, honey and *macchia* herbs. Since Bastia has no market hall, the seafood here is sold in the open air. In the afternoon the whole commotion suddenly stops as if by magic, and the square is eerily deserted once more.

Now it's time to take a look at the largest church in Bastia: the church of **Saint Jean-Baptiste**, down by the **Old Harbour** (Vieux Port). Its ornate 17th-century baroque facade, with its two striking towers, has become a symbol of the town. The interior – gilded stucco, Corsican polychromatic marble – is 18th-century.

St Roch, protector of plague victims, gazes down at passers-by from several houses down at the harbour. The tradition whereby each captain greeted the saint and prayed for a safe return before setting sail has, however, long since been forgotten. If you take a seat in one of the numerous restaurants here, which serve all kinds of different seafood dishes, you'll find it a good place from which to observe the colourful fishing boats and the busy harbour.

Up in the fortress: Photographers should really walk across the Quai du Sud as far as the harbour mole (Jetée du Dragon)

Left, the Old Town bears the patina of age. Right, the upper levels of Bastia's amphitheatre.

in order to take in the whole of the *Vieux Port*. The best place to take a comprehensive photograph of the entire Old Harbour is from the top of the flight of steps known as **L'Escalier Romieu**, which leads from the **Quai du Sud** up to the citadel. The view from up here extends across the broad expanse of the New Harbour, where the large ferries dock, all the way to the mountains on the Cap Corse.

Today the **citadel**, surrounded by a defensive wall, and referred to by the Genoese as the **Terra Nuova** to distinguish it from the older harbour settlement, is another "Old Town" all on its own. It covers a relatively small area and is strikingly different from the rest of Bastia: the streets are narrow, short and easy to walk along. At the top of the steps on the right the first building one sees is the 14th-century **Palais des Gouverneurs**. The round tower at the right-hand corner is the oldest surviving part of the original Genoese fortifications. It is in a remarkably good state of repair.

Today the palais houses a museum, the **Musée d'Ethnographie Corse**. The geological, historical and folkloristic collections are not all that well laid out, but one can still find informative details illustrating Corsican history. A valuable exhibit here is the tattered flag once carried by Paoli and his troops in their final battle against the French, a symbol of Corsica's struggle for independence. At the other end of the inner courtyard, the conning tower of the submarine "Casabianca" can be seen – a reminder of the fight to liberate the island from foreign occupation during World War II. On the night of 13–14 December 1942, the French submarine had anchored off Cargèse in order to supply the Corsican resistance with arms.

Solemn processions: The Rue Notre-Dame leads to the 15th-century **Church of Sainte-Marie**. It served as an episcopal cathedral until 1801, when the status of bishopric was conferred upon Ajaccio instead. The church underwent extension work in the 17th century, when it received its tall *campanile*. A great deal

A local fisherman.

of marble (from Corsica and from Carrera) was used for its magnificent interior. An 18th-century Assumption of the Virgin in silver can be seen behind protective glass; it is carried through the town in a solemn procession on 15 August every year. Some of the paintings, taken from Cardinal Fesch's collection, date from the 17th century; the ceiling decoration is 18th-century.

The **Chapelle Sainte-Croix** is situated directly behind this church, and its unimpressive exterior belies the magnificence within: a fine baroque interior, with cherubs and gilded stucco everywhere. The sky-blue ceiling is particularly delightful. Legend has it that the black crucifix which gave the chapel its name was found floating in the sea by fishermen in 1428. The fishermen of Bastia still offer up the first catch of the season to Our Lord when this black "Christ des Miracles" is carried through the town every 3 May.

These are not all the processions in Bastia by any means: there is another one in honour of St Roch, too, and yet another in honour of a further Madonna. Their churches lie outside the citadel, in the Rue Napoléon, and can be visited on the way back to the Place Saint-Nicolas. The **Chapelle Saint-Roch** was built around 1604 as an act of gratitude after the dreadful plague epidemic of 1589 had come to an end. The interior is Florentine in style.

Next door to it, the **Chapelle de la Conception**, built in 1611 by the Confrérie de la Conception, was given its noble interior in the 18th century. The walls and pillars are hung with crimson damask and velvet, lending added intensity to the works of art inside the building. These include a copy of Murillo's *Immaculate Conception* above the main altar, an 18th-century Genoese crucifix, and the Statue of the Holy Virgin, which is given its annual airing on 8 December when it is carried to the church of Saint Jean-Baptiste. So grand is the interior of the chapel that it was used by Sir Gilbert Elliot for the first meeting of the Anglo-Corsican Parliament in February 1795.

Siesta time.

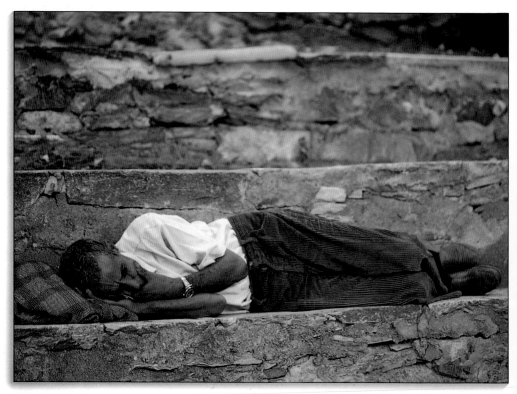

THE TRINIGHELLU

Bastia is one of the most important stations along the route of the *Trinighellu*, also known as "Fiery Elias". For more than a century the "Little Train", as the islanders affectionately call their narrow-gauge railway, has been a Corsican institution.

The railway was inaugurated on 1 February 1888. Experts tend to smile at the precision of the timetable. The nicknames testify to the main problems: the most common are TGV (Train à Grandes Vibrations – the "Big-Vibration Train") and TBV (Train à Basse Vitesse – the "Low-Speed Train"). "It often happens that the train has to stop to permit the removal of a cow which is unconcernedly grazing between the rails," reports Dumé, who studied in Corte and who became accustomed to the idiosyncrasies of the *Trinighellu*. She recounts a handful of experiences which make the journey seem even more folkloric: the frequent derailments, the stopping of the train by a FLNC commando unit which decides to distribute pamphlets to the travellers in the middle of nowhere; the engine, which breaks down before it is within eyesight of the next station, and has to be push-started to get it going again; the eternal waits at stations, which aren't proper stations at all; obstacles in the form of vehicles which have got stuck between the barriers at level crossings...

The route from Ajaccio to Bastia and Calvi runs through one of the loveliest regions on the island, much to the delight of the 800,000 passengers who embark each year. The journey from Ajaccio to Bastia takes three and a half hours – sometimes even four, although the distance is barely 110 km (68 miles). The slow pace, however, is more than compensated for by the magnificent views afforded during this trip across the island. The flocks grazing beside the line are blissfully unconcerned at the squeaking of the wheels on the rails, but for passengers the noise is somewhat disturbing when the train enters one of the 43 tunnels hewn in the solid rock, or chugs onto the impressive Vecchio Bridge after Vivario. The viaduct, designed by Gustave Eiffel, is 140 metres (448 ft) long and spans the mountain torrent at a height of some 100 metres (320 ft). Another significant engineering feat, the Vizzavona tunnel, is 4 km (2½ miles) long. When it was built it was the longest tunnel in Europe.

On the main stretch between Ajaccio and Bastia, the traveller passes through a cross-section of Corsican landscapes. After it has left Ajaccio, the *Trinighellu* enters the Gravona Valley and climbs up into the mountains, stopping several times at Bocognano, Vizzavona and Vivario, etc. Then it descends into the centre of the island, the area around Corte. Forest and *macchia* alternate until the train reaches the coast again at Bastia.

For some years the SNCF and the Corsican regional assembly have been tackling the modernization of the railway network. The five locomotives of the ABH Renault type, constructed in 1946, have been replaced by more modern, faster and more comfortable ones of the Soulé type. At the same time, work has commenced on the renovation of the stations; there is even talk of re-opening the section of line leading to the southern tip of the island. ∎

"Trinighellu" is a Corsican institution.

THE EAST COAST AND INLAND DETOURS

Along the 100-km (60-mile) stretch from Bastia to Solenzara, Corsica's eastern coastal plain is one long sandy beach, ideal for holidaymakers from spring to autumn. Tourists familiar with Corsica consider the region rather monotonous, however. This is hardly surprising when one considers how much tourism has flourished. The broad coastal plain is filled with incongruous-looking holiday villages, campsites and sometimes even high-rise hotels.

The N198 – the main road from Bastia to Bonifacio – runs in an absolutely straight line along much of its length. Being the only straight road on the island it is also the most dangerous, because the Corsicans take ample advantage of it to race their cars; even the speed traps set by the Gendarmerie don't seem to provide much of a deterrent. The villages along this road are devoid of character – the older settlements on the island were all moved up to the eastern mountain slopes centuries ago to provide protection against foreign invaders, mosquitoes and malaria.

The coastal plain itself, up to 15 km (9 miles) wide in places, is used predominantly for agricultural purposes, and (since the 1960s) mostly by French colonists from North Africa. Over 16,000 so-called *Pieds Noirs*, forced to leave the newly-independent countries of Morocco, Tunisia and Algeria, arrived on Corsica between 1962 and 1966. Their mentality is very different from that of the Corsicans, and integration here has not been without its share of friction. The former colonial landowners introduced winegrowing to the east coast on a large scale. More recently, citrus fruit has also been successfully cultivated here with the aid of irrigation.

But if you take the time to venture inland, the east coast also provides glimpses of the "real" Corsica. Heading along tiny side-roads, you'll discover traces of the island's past and encounter villages in which time seems to have stood still.

Bastia-Plage and La Canonica: Anyone arriving in Bastia by ferry who leaves the town and heads south will probably gain a rather poor initial impression of Corsica. The N193 – all four lanes of it – runs in a straight line through an incredibly ugly industrial area, which only comes to an end 20 km (12 miles) further on at **Casamozza**, where the N198 to Porto Vecchio and Bonifacio branches off to Corte and Ajaccio.

There is, however, a neat way of avoiding the ugly industrial sprawl of Bastia entirely: 5 km (3 miles) south of the town there is a side-road (D107) on the left, signposted to "Bastia-Plage". Follow this inconspicuous-looking sign and you'll soon find yourself in an entirely different world. The road runs past villas, hotels, campsites and sometimes just sand-dunes, along the tongue of land between the **Etang de Biguglia** and the sea. The lagoon is rich in fish and is particularly famous for its eels.

The beach behind the row of flat sand-dunes is easily accessible from just about everywhere and only tends to get rela-

Preceding pages: seaside fun for the kids. **Left,** waiting for the mender. **Right,** the East Coast is one long sandy beach.

tively full at weekends, when Bastia comes here to relax. Anyone planning to stay here for any length of time, though, should bear in mind that **Bastia-Poretta airport** is not far away.

The road comes to an end rather abruptly, at a crossroads. The left turn leads to the **Plage de Pinotto** and the right one takes you back to the N193. Before reaching it, however, the traveller will pass the **Church of La Canonica** standing at a bend in the road. Those in a hurry can also reach it directly from the N193: turn off towards Poretta airport in Lucciana and then turn right again immediately on to the D107. The church of La Canonica appears in the middle of the coastal plain and is visible for miles around.

It was here, 100 years before the birth of Christ, that the Roman general Gaius Marius founded the military colony of Mariana for war veterans who had remained loyal to him. The small town that soon arose on this site was a useful starting-point for the further colonisation of Corsica, and the Roman Emperor

Augustus had a harbour built here. Nevertheless, Mariana was never as prosperous as other Roman settlements. In the 4th century, the town received a basilica and a baptistry. Both were destroyed during raids by the Vandals and the Lombards in the 5th century, and then later covered by a layer of sediment when the Golo River flooded. The foundations of several brick houses at Mariana have been unearthed during excavations.

The remains of the Early Christian basilica and also the baptistry, each of them paved with mosaic floors, were also discovered. The church of La Canonica as we know it today was built in the 12th century on foundations dating back to the 5th century, and was consecrated by the Archbishop of Pisa in 1119. The sheer size of this church makes it clear how important it was in medieval times – it was the seat of the Bishop of Corsica. Despite suffering extensive damage in the 15th and 16th centuries, La Canonica remains one of the best-preserved examples of early

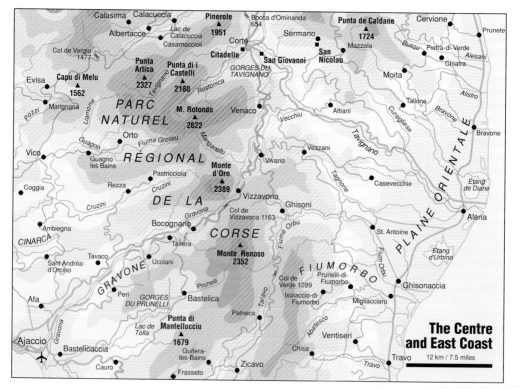

The Centre and East Coast

12 km / 7.5 miles

Pisan Romanesque architecture on the island. The building style of this period is characterised by simplicity of ornamentation and also alternating light and dark stripes in the stonework. A frieze with animal sculptures can be seen in the church's west facade, above the entrance.

A few hundred yards away to the south-west, stands the beautifully-proportioned church of **San Parteo**, surrounded by meadows. It is slightly older than La Canonica and is also early Pisan Romanesque in style. The fields have been excavated to reveal a cemetery, which was used from pagan right up to medieval times.

Those with time to spare can drive up to **Borgo** from the N193. Situated on a spur overlooking the plain, this village contains elegant old houses with beautifully carved doors and porches. It is to higher lying villages such as this one that people came to settle, fleeing from the marshy, malarial lowlands. From the village there is a splendid view of the Etang de Biguglia and the coastal plain.

The narrow little road here (the D7) leads on further inland along the northern slopes of the Golo Valley, through the villages of Vignale, Scolca, Volpajola, Campitello and Lento.

The last battle: But the main access to the Golo Valley is provided by the N193 as it turns inland from Casamozza. The road leads via Corte all the way over to the other side of the island, and is accompanied along much of its length by the *Trinighellu* railway (*see page 215*). Halfway up the valley is the village of **Ponte Nuovo**. Contrary to what the name might imply, the bridge here is in fact very old and dilapidated. It was built during the Genoese occupation of the island, and was the scene of the last great battle for Corsican independence. In the spring of 1769, the French army, which had been so crushingly defeated by Corsica one year previously near Borgo, marched once again against the Corsican troops under their leader Pasquale Paoli.

On 8 May 1769 Paoli had 2,000 of his men cross the Golo River and advance

Citrus fruit grows successfully with the aid of irrigation.

northwards. The attack was repulsed, and the Corsicans fled in the direction of the bridge, which had meanwhile been taken, however, by a group of German mercenaries. Trapped between the advancing French army and the banks of the Golo River, the Corsicans were completely wiped out. After this defeat, Paoli gave up the struggle and left Corsica. A memorial at the roadside stands as a reminder of these historic events.

Villages steeped in history: Returning to the coast and continuing southwards along the N198, **Moriani-Plage**, 20 km (12 miles) beyond Casamozza, is just one more of the faceless communities strung out along this main road: a handful of ugly, prefabricated modern hotels, several shoddy-looking buildings dotted along the roadside and – almost making up for it all – a magnificently broad sandy beach. Strange as it may seem, this place is also of historical significance: on the way to Paris from his exile on Elba, Napoleon Bonaparte landed here in February 1815. Only a short distance further inland, along the eastern flank of the mountains, several far less touristy villages can be found. They can be reached by taking the D34 from Moriani-Plage. The **Corniche de la Castigniccia** (D330) runs along the eastern slope of Monte Castello between the villages of **San Nicolao** and **Cervione**. It affords fine views far out to sea, all the way to Elba and Capraia. The road has been hewn out of the rock for part of the way: it runs through two short tunnels and crosses a noisy mountain stream.

Cervione is the largest village in the area. It even has its own 16th-century cathedral, built when the village was a bishopric for a brief period. King Theodore used the episcopal palace as his summer residence from April to November in the year 1736. Today it houses a folklore museum, allowing the visitor a glimpse of what everyday life in the region must have been like all those years ago.

Between Moriani-Plage and Aléria there are several large holiday villages situated between the main road and the **Cherries are also cultivated.**

sea. At the **Etang de Diane**, the seafood is excellent, especially the mussels and the trout.

The Roman town: Situated on a small rise, **Aléria** is an inconspicuous sort of place these days. In antiquity, though, it was one of the most important ports for seagoing traffic in the Western Mediterranean. The town was founded by the Phocaeans around 500 BC. They named it Alalia, and made use of it as a base for their fleet as well as a trading post. The Romans took Alalia in 250 BC, and it was from here that they began their colonisation of the island. After the Corsican population had been subdued, the town embarked on a long period of prosperity.

Alalia became one of the most important trading centres of the Western Mediterranean. The Roman Emperor Augustus had an amphitheatre, an aqueduct and several defensive walls built here. At that time the Etang de Diane served as a naval base, and the trading vessels would anchor in the Tavignano estuary. Alalia's prosperity ended, however, with the fall of the Roman Empire. In the 5th century, after it was sacked and burned by the Vandals, the town was abandoned once and for all. The entire area surrounding the Tavignano estuary then degenerated into swampland, and was an ideal breeding-ground for malaria mosquitoes until as recently as World War II. DDT put an end to the mosquito plague after 1945. The swamps were then successfully drained, the area newly populated and the land cultivated once more.

Excavations at the old Roman town of Alalia have revealed its former greatness once more. Only certain sections of it have been uncovered so far, including the Forum, a temple, the hot springs and also the Praetorium, official seat of the Roman governor of Corsica. Archaeological finds from the town's various periods of prosperity are on display in the **Musée Jérôme Carcopino**. These include magnificently painted earthenware goblets of Etruscan origin. The 2nd-century marble bust of Jupiter Ammon, found near the Forum, and the finely-worked Etruscan bronze statues

are also of particular interest. The museum is situated on the ground floor of the **Fort de Matra**, built by the Genoese in the 16th century.

There are several holiday villages along the wide sandy beaches around Aléria, and also a detention centre. The **Réserve de Chasse de Casabianda**, south of Aléria, is a conservation area containing several species of animal threatened with extinction.

Lonely valleys and ravines: Several valleys run inland between Aléria and Ghisonaccia, the largest and widest being the Tavignano Valley, which is practically devoid of human habitation all the way to Corte. The villages are situated on the ranges of hills on either side of the valley. Here, just a short distance away from the busy east coast, one can experience the remoteness and tranquillity of Corsican mountain villages. **Piedicorte-di-Gaggio**, on the northern side of the valley, awaits us, with its fantastic views and its 18th-century parish church. One of the most attractive villages on the south side of the valley is

A stroll through Roman Aleria.

Antisanti. The road that leads inland from the east coast to **Ghisoni**, though, is utterly different. It runs through two narrow ravines: the **Défilé de l'Inzecca** and the **Défilé des Strettes**. The rocky walls here, through which the river and the road wind their precarious way, are often no more than a few yards apart.

The **Fiumorbo** is a mountainous area, thickly overgrown with *macchia* and chestnut forests. All the roads that lead here are dead ends. Small hamlets and villages keep popping up quite unexpectedly, though. This region, still so remote even today, was a favourite hiding-place for bandits for a long time. Always allow plenty of time for any excursion into the Fiumorbo because of its narrow, winding roads.

Pietrapola-les-Bains has sulphur springs that have been in use since Roman times. People still come here to take the waters today. There is a fine view of the coastal plain and the mountains to be had from the terrace of the fortified church in **Prunelli-de-Fiumorbo**.

Mother-of-Pearl coast: In the course of the past 20 years, **Solenzara** has developed from a sleepy and dilapidated little coastal village into a full-blown beach resort. Hotels, campsites, discotheques, boutiques and a seemingly endless sandy beach stretching away to the north are all here to attract the tourists. The **Côte des Nacres** (Mother-of-Pearl Coast) begins south of Solenzara. The steep rocky coast, easily accessible from the main road which runs directly next to the sea, is a real diver's paradise, broken up now and then by romantic bays with fine sandy beaches. There are modest tourist facilities available in **Tarco** and **Fautea**.

In Solenzara, a turn off the N198 leads to one of the most varied mountain routes in all Corsica: the D628 up to the **Col de Bavella**. It starts off by following the course of the Solenzara River, then the very narrow road (no caravans) begins winding its way up pine-covered slopes to the **Col de Larone**. From up here there is a superb view of the Forêt de Bavella down in the valley basin below, and of the fantastic rocky landscape surrounding it. From the Col de Bavella (1,218 metres/4,000 ft) there is a particularly good view of the steep and jagged Aiguilles de Bavella, with massive Monte Incudine towering above them in the background. The road then continues on down the western side of the valley, through forests of chestnut and pine, until it reaches **Zonza**, a very pleasant place to spend one's summer holidays inland. Zonza is absolutely ideal as a starting-point for trips into the rugged landscape of the interior.

The route back from Zonza to the east coast in the direction of Porto Vecchio leads through the Forêt de l'Ospedale. This extensive wooded area consists mainly of oak and cork oak. Driving down from **Bocca d'Illarata** (991 metres/3,300 ft above sea-level) the visitor is greeted by a whole series of new and fascinating views of the Gulf of Porto Vecchio. The only hamlet along this stretch is **Ospedale**. From up here one can take in the entire south-eastern coastline of Corsica, and in clear weather, even the north coast of Sardinia.

Left, roof repairs in a mountain village. **Right**, Our Lady of the Snows on the Col de Bavella.

THE CASTAGNICCIA

The name "Castagniccia" means "small chestnut grove", but the region that bears this name is in reality a huge forest of sweet-chestnut trees, covering an area of more than 15,000 hectares (60 sq. miles). At one time the local inhabitants lived from the chestnuts: the fruits were ground to flouer and the wood was used for heating and building. But these days most of the groves are no longer tended; as a result of urban migrations only the older generations have remained behind in the villages.

Bubbling health springs: If you turn off the N198 on to the D506 at the village of Folleli and head west, the road begins by following the Fium'Alto river valley, and passes buildings that once belonged to the tannic acid factory of *Champlan*; today they house a pottery. The craftsmen here specialise in the production of local earthenware. A short while later the route passes the **Caldane Springs**, which were famous as far back as Roman times. Then the valley suddenly changes direction towards the south, and the road ascends steeply to the **Orezza Springs.**

Orezza means "refreshing shade", and the springs are indeed situated at the end of an avenue of shady plane trees, where the carbonated water (15°C/59°F) bubbles happily out of the rock. Once bottled, the refreshing *Eau d'Orezza* was sold all over the island. But in the middle of the nineties the exploration licence expired. A new contractor has yet to be found. The nearby hamlet of **Stazzona** provides modest accommodation for those taking the waters, and the ruins of the former Franciscan monastery of Orezza, once used as an assembly point by Corsican freedom fighters, can be seen on the opposite side of the valley.

Above the springs and the monastery, at an altitude of roughly 650 metres (2,100 ft) above sea level, numerous different villages form a semicircle at the end of the Fium'Alto valley: the **Conca d'Orezza**. They united in medi-eval times to form a so-called *pieve*, or cohesive political and economic unit, and it still survives today as a cantonal administration.

The main village in the canton of Orezza-Alesani is **Piedicroce**, which has around 200 full-time residents and is situated at the crossroads formed by the D71 and the D506, above the Fium'Alto. It's certainly worth taking a look at the baroque church of **Saint-Pierre et Saint-Paul** at this point. It dates from 1761, and has a magnificent interior which includes the oldest organ in Corsica, built in the 17th century and now wonderfully restored.

Regional specialities prepared from goat's cheese *(brocciu)* and roast sweet chestnuts *(fasgiole)* can be sampled at the hotel restaurant "La Refuge". Piedicroce is also a very good starting-point for an ascent of **Monte San Petrone**, the summit of which can be reached after a roughly three-hour-long walk along a mule path – highly recommended. The path leads past the hamlets of **Campodonico** and **Pastoreccia**, and

also the ruins of the 12th-century cathedral of Accia. From the 1,767-metre (5,800-foot) high peak one can enjoy a breathtaking view: the whole of the Cap Corse to the north; all the way to the mountains of the Fium Orbo to the south; eastwards, the entire coastal plain from Bastia to Solenzara; and to the west, Corsica's entire central range of mountains rising up from the Corte basin. It is truly a unique panorama. At your feet, like a green carpet, are the chestnut forests in the Fium'Alto and Alesani valleys, with all their tiny villages. This is definitely the place for an incredible, bird's-eye view of the whole of Eastern Corsica.

On the trail of Pasquale Paoli: If you follow the D71 from Piedicroce in a northwesterly direction, the road passes through **Campana**, with its picturesque *campanile*, and **Nocario**, where chestnut flour is still produced, before reaching **La Porta**. This village, with its population of roughly 500, lies at the bottom of a lateral valley of the Fium'Alto, and since 259 BC has served

as a centre of resistance against the Romans, the Vandals, the Byzantines, the Lombards, the Saracens, the Genoese and the French right up to the present day. The main attraction of La Porta, if not of the entire region here, is the richly-adorned **church of St John the Baptist**, designed by a Milanese architect and built in 1648. Its magnificent *campanile*, dating from (1702), is considered to be the finest baroque bell tower on the whole island. The church, with its polychromatic ceiling, contains a 17th-century figure of Christ painted on wood, an 18th-century painting of the Beheading of John the Baptist, and a very fine Italian organ. The latter was restored in 1963 by a Paris music teacher named Jacques Chailley, and it now plays an integral role in the concerts held here in the summertime.

The oil press, or *franghju*, at La Porta has also recently been restored as part of the government's attempt to stimulate a revival in olive production.

The D71 continues on to the 985-metre (3,200-ft) high **Prato Pass**. There

La Porta and its baroque campanile.

is a good view of the surrounding valleys to be had from the top of this pass, extending as far as **Morosaglia**, perched on a mountain slope 800 metres (2,600 ft) above sea level, which is one of the larger villages in the area.

There are several small hamlets up here, but only **Stretta** has become famous outside the region: it is synonymous with Pasquale Paoli, the Corsican national hero (*see page 61*) who was born here in 1725; his remains are also buried here, having been transferred to his native village from England in 1889, 82 years after his death.

The small museum in Stretta was closed for years, but has recently reopened as a Musée Departemental. For Corsicans, the little house is a national monument. Apart from a series of contemporary Corsican books and the first ever Corsican newspaper, the most striking sight here are two white silk flags displaying the mysterious moor's head, one with the symbols of slavery dating from the period before Paoli and the other with its headband pushed up and

no earrings, symbolising the liberation that Paoli brought.

Thanks to its superb location among its chestnut forests, and the many different walking and hiking possibilities provided by this green paradise, so unusual for the Mediterranean, Morosaglia today has acquired a good reputation as a mountain resort – a reputation that may be enhanced still further if a series of uninhabited buildings in the beautifully situated hamlet of **Rocca Soprana** are turned into holiday homes as part of a state-planned Paese Hotel project.

Clan settlements: The route now continues in a southerly direction along the D71 as far as the **Arcarotta Pass**, the watershed between the Fium'Alto and Alesani river systems. This area is where the famous green marble known as *Verde di Corsica* comes from; it was used in the construction of the Paris Opera and of the Medici chapels in Florence. In many ways, the history of the 22-km (14-mile) long Alesani Valley mirrors that of the whole island: it is one of invasion and resistance. The valley is

Saint-Pierre et Saint-Paul in Piedicroce.

also extremely beautiful; sharp contrasts in relief force the D71 up and down continually, and around a whole series of hairpins. The ruins of former watermills that once produced chestnut flour can be made out in several places on the main valley floor.

A garland of mountain villages clings to rocky outcrops, beneath dizzyingly steep rock-faces, in the mighty basin at the end of the Alesani Valley: **Piobetta, Tarrano, Felce, Pietricaggio, Perelli, Valle d'Alesani, Piazzali, Ortale** and **Novale**. An example of the settlement pattern typical of this region is provided by the municipality of **Felce**, with its hamlets **Poggiale, Piova, Volgheraccio** and **Milaria**.

This type of scattered settlement had its reasons, the main one being the inhabitants' need to protect themselves against enemies from outside, though continuous feuds between rival families also played a part. These often used to end in bloodshed. In the course of time this led to an isolated existence for many people inside clan settlements, where – in accordance with the code of honour of the *vendetta* – only members and relatives of a single large family were allowed to live.

The layout of the buildings within these clan settlements is almost fortress-like. The German geographer Friedrich Ratzel, who travelled through Corsica in the 19th century, gives us a telling description: "Clustered together, their grey backs turned towards us, they are reminiscent of a crowd of close friends who have a great deal to tell each other – and absolutely nothing to tell the outside world."

But there is still a lot that is picturesque about these communities, with their tall buildings, vaulted passageways, twisting staircases, white window-frames set into unplastered slate walls, and flower-filled niches. The surrounding forest is like something straight out of a fairy-tale, with its huge and ancient chestnut trees, many of them struck by lightning, its moss-covered rocks, bubbling springs and little stone houses overgrown with

The goatherd with his flock.

lianas – an idyll, that has been largely spared any outside interference.

A monastery steeped in history: The **Couvent d'Alesani**, a Franciscan monastery situated on the right-hand side of the valley below the hamlet of Casella, has long been the political and spiritual centre of this region. The monastery buildings have been passably restored. High on the wall of a side-chapel of the monastery church one can admire a 15th-century Virgin and Child painted on wood, known as the "Madonna with the Cherry". Since 1983 a copy has replaced the original which was painted by Sano di San Pietro, an artist from Siena, and is notable for its gentle use of colour and its Renaissance charm.

The monastery is more closely connected with the German baron Theodor von Neuhoff, a rogue and adventurer. At a gathering here in the year 1736, after he had brought weapons, money, grain and clothing to the rebels fighting the Genoese, he was appointed Corsica's first and only king. The spontaneous joy quickly evaporated into impatient anger two hundred days later. When the provisions were all used up it was clear that far too few replenishments were going to arrive. Disguised as a priest, von Neuhoff escaped from the island and died penniless in London in 1756.

The central area of the Alesani Valley is devoid of human habitation, because the mountain flanks are so close to each other at this point that the river has cut a ravine deep into the land. The Alesani River has been dammed up to form the Alesani Reservoir shortly before it enters the coastal plain, and the 11 million cubic metres of water here have been used to irrigate the lowland areas since 1970.

From Novale, the D 517 runs along the southern slope high above the reservoir, through the narrow section of the valley, passing through **Pietra-di-Verde** and the magnificently situated, almost Acropolis-like **Chiatra**. The view from here extends across the reservoir all the way to the coast.

Pietra-di-Verde and the Alesani Reservoir.

CORTE

Corte has been considered the "secret capital" of Corsica ever since Pasquale Paoli ruled his democratic island-republic from here. Unlike the fortress-towns along the coast it was not founded by the Genoese, and it lies right at the heart of the island at the confluence of two rivers – the Restonica and the Tavignano – and at the junction of several major traffic arteries, including the main road from Ajaccio to Bastia and the road from Aléria to Porto.

Corte is at its most imposing visually if you arrive from the direction of Ajaccio, via the Vizzavona Pass. Surrounded by barren mountains, the impressive citadel sits high up on a rocky outcrop, towering above the 400-metre (1,300-ft) high valley basin like the prow of an enormous ship. The older part of the town clings to this crag with its protective fortress, while the more modern sections are sprawled out at its feet.

The name "Corte" derives from the Cortinchi family, who ruled this valley in the early Middle Ages. In the 13th century, Corte fell into the hands of the Genoese, and in 1419 Vincentello d'Istria occupied it in the name of the King of Aragon, and began building the citadel. The town has been regularly fought over throughout Corsican history. The Genoese settled here once again, but the Corsicans managed to snatch the fortress away from them on several occasions: Sampiero Corso took it in 1553, and Gianpetro Gaffori stormed it in 1746. From 1755 Corte was the capital of independent Corsica for 14 years until the town was finally forced to surrender to the French.

An important event in the town's history was the foundation of a university here by Pasquale Paoli, who wanted to provide his people with access to higher education. Since 1981 Corte, with its population of around 6,200, has been a university town once more, and the students, of whom there are now about 3.500, have given the town a new lease of life. Alongside subjects such as law and economics, the Corsican language is also taught here, and *corsitude* is held in high regard. It really is no wonder that the island's students have become the predominant driving force behind its independence movement. But from spring until autumn, this small provincial town up in the mountains is also popular with tourists – it is a rendezvous point for hikers, climbers, anglers and canoeists.

Monuments and bullet-holes: The **Cours Paoli** in Corte is the equivalent of Ajaccio's Cours Napoléon: it is the main shopping street, albeit somewhat narrower and less cosmopolitan. Hunting and fishing supplies can be seen alongside the usual souvenirs in the shop-windows here, and rucksacks can be filled with provisions. Evening is the busiest time for the restaurants, cafés and bistros. The street ends at the **Place Paoli**, with its bronze statue of Corsica's most famous freedom-fighter. From here we mount the broad steps of the Rue Scoliscia and enter the labyrinthine Old Town.

In the **Place Gaffori** there is a statue of the famous general. His arm outstretched, he seems to be giving the command to storm the citadel – he did so despite the fact that the Genoese had taken his son hostage. Gaffori Junior survived the onslaught, however. There is also a memorial tablet on the statue's plinth to Gaffori's spirited wife, Faustina. A relief depicts her holding a lighted torch over an open barrel of gunpowder, recalling the occasion when she barricaded herself inside her own house during the Genoese siege of the town in 1750. The Genoese planned to kidnap Gaffori's wife in his absence, in order to blackmail him. Just as her friends and helpers were on the point of acceding to the Genoese demands, Faustina threatened to blow the entire house sky-high, thus managing to hold out until Gaffori came to her rescue. The **Gaffori house** was subjected to a hail of bullets, and the holes they made are still there to this day.

The town's **Eglise de l'Annonciation** also stands in this square; though it dates from 1450, it was given a new facade in the 17th century. The church contains a finely-carved pulpit, once the property of the town's former Franciscan monastery, plus a baroque crucifix.

The street climbs steeply to the **Place du Poilu**. House number 1 is the ancestral home of the Arrighi de Casanova family. Napoleon's parents lived here when Carlo Buonaparte was a supporter of Paoli. A plaque above the doorway announces that their first son Joseph, later to become king of Naples and Spain, was born here in 1768. To the left stands the **Palais National**, the seat of the independent Corsican government from 1755–69; today, fittingly enough, it houses the university's Institute of Corsican Studies.

The citadel, which was used as a barracks by the Foreign Legion, is also due to become a lively centre of Corsican culture now that the restoration work on it has been completed. Once referred to as "Corsica's Acropolis", it now houses the **Musée de la Corse** and the FRAC with contemporary art exhibitions.

Some shining examples of local handicraft.

Mountain torrents and glacial lakes: The best view of the 100-metre (300-ft) high rock with its citadel, and also of the slate and brick roofs of the Old Town, is definitely to be had from the appropriately-named **Belvédère**. To get there, follow the signs along the Rue Balthasar Arrighi. Below, the Restonica and Tavignano valleys emerge from their respective gorges, and in the distance rise the impressive peaks of the central highlands. Another view of the entire picturesque town panorama can be had if you drive out of town over the Restonica Bridge **(Pont-Neuf)** and then turn right towards the cinema (signposted *Cinéma*).

On the other side of the river, it is possible to drive a short distance up the **Gorges de la Restonica** along the narrow D623, but beware: there can be snow here as late as May. Almost immediately, the stylish and traditional "Auberge de la Restonica" comes temptingly into view. The trout here are, of course, fresh: they come straight from the mountain torrents nearby. Now the valley gets narrower; its steep rocky walls here are as popular with mountain climbers as they are with mountain goats, and the ravine is a favourite haunt of kayak and river-rafting enthusiasts. After winding its way across 17 km (10 miles) of pine forest, the small road finally comes to an end at the **Bergerie de Grotelle**. When you reach these stone huts belonging to the region's friendly shepherds you should definitely put your climbing shoes on and hike off to the two finest glacial lakes in all Corsica.

The **Lac de Melo**, at 1,710 metres (5,600 ft) above sea level, is about one hour away, and the **Lac de Capitello** (1,930 metres/6,300 ft above sea level), set into magnificent rocky scenery, is another hour's walk from there. When the bathing season is at its height in June down on the beaches there are still large chunks of ice floating around these mountain lakes.

The Restonica Valley is also a good starting-point for a fascinating day's hike across Corsica's second-highest peak, **Monte Rotondo** (2,622 metres/

Pasquale Paoli has not been forgotten, particularly in Corte.

8,600 ft). Whoever finds the difference in altitude of 1,622 metres (5,300 ft) too much to cope with should still go up as far as the **Lac d'Oriente** (2,061 metres/ 6,700 ft above sea level), with its green, grassy islands, where the Restonica River has its main source. "This incomparable source possesses such sharpness that it cleans iron as bright as a mirror in a very short space of time, and protects it from rust", wrote the historian Gregorovius, who undertook the walk across Monte Rotondo with a guide and a mule in the year 1852. During Paoli's time the Corsican fighters are said to have placed their rusty flintlocks in the waters of the Restonica in order to clean them.

The **Tavignano Valley**, upriver from Corte, is also a paradise for hikers. You don't need any great mountaineering talents to cover the marked route from Corte to **Refuge de Sega** and back, but plan for a six- to seven-hour-long hike. You leave Corte from the **Chapelle Sainte-Croix**, along the Rue Joseph. The swaying rope bridge over a section

of the Tavignano makes an ideal photograph. Here, and by the Sega *bergerie*, there are some fine river-beds for swimming. Instead of returning to Corte one can also continue on towards Calcuccia or the Lac de Nino.

Early Christian churches: One excursion definitely to be recommended is a car journey from Corte into the wild ravine of the **Scala di Santa Regina**, then on to the **Calacuccia Reservoir** and the **Col de Vergio**. On this route (the D18), only 10 km (6 miles) away from Corte, lies the picturesque village of **Castirla**. The cemetery here contains the pre-Romanesque chapel of **San Michele**. The apse contains some fine 15th-century frescoes, recently restored: one of them depicts Christ in majesty, surrounded by symbols of the Evangelists and Apostles. Next to it there is an Annunciation. Before proceeding up the path towards the chapel don't forget to ask for the key at the village hall.

At **Ponte Castirla**, stay on the D18 and avoid turning off into the Santa Regina ravine. The road will eventually branches off towards the mountain villages of **Castiglione** and **Poplasca**, both situated very picturesquely at the foot of the jagged red rocks known as the **Aiguilles de Popolasca**.

The ruins of two more Early Christian churches are located nearer to Corte. The twin apses of the **Eglise Santa Mariana** can be seen above the N193 roughly 2 km (1¼ miles) in the direction of Bastia. Although the church now stands in ruins, it is still possible to get an idea of its former glory. The same applies to the 9th-century church and baptistery of **San Giovanni Battista**, which can be reached by taking the N200 and following the fork to the right after 1.5 km (1 mile). Only the apse of the basilica remains, and pieces of Roman tile can be seen in its walls – an early example of recycling. Both the church and the adjacent baptistery may have been built on the site of a Roman village. 17 km (11 miles) from Corte, in the direction of Aléria, a well-preserved, simply-constructed, slate-roofed chapel can be seen next to the Tavignano Bridge, which was built by the Genoese.

Left, a ferocious roar on the Cours Paoli. Right, Gaffori's statue is outside his house.

THE NIOLU BASIN

Framed by the mightiest mountains on the island – the 2,710-metre (8,900-ft) high Monte Cinto and the Paglia Orba to the north, and the 2,622-metre (8,600-ft) high Monte Rotondo to the southeast – the mountain basin of **Niolu** can certainly be said to lie at the very heart of Corsica. This huge valley at the upper part of the Golo River, a massive granite basin roughly 900 metres (3,000 ft) above sea level, used to be one of the most remote districts of the island.

The only access to it is through the daunting ravine known as the Scala di Santa Regina to the east, or via the highest mountain pass in all Corsica, the 1,477-metre (4,800-ft) high Col de Vergio, to the west. The roads over the pass and through the ravine were only built towards the end of the 19th century. Before that time, the Niolu could only be reached along mountain paths, and during the wintertime was completely cut off from the outside world. In the autumn, herds of sheep and goats *en transhumance* were driven over the high passes into the milder coastal regions – through the Fango Valley, for instance, to the Gulf of Galeria, or through the Scala di Santa Regina to the east coast – and they only returned in springtime after the snows had melted.

The Niolu is full of mountains, valleys, meadows, forests and lakes. The region is very poor: the people here are usually simple shepherds, and their pastures lie around the Lac de Nino, on the upper reaches of the Golo River and beneath Monte Cinto. The local inhabitants have only very recently begun to reap some profit from tourism, especially from all those who come up here in the summer months to escape the heat of the beaches and enjoy the refreshing, cool mountain air.

The wild Scala di Santa Regina: If you approach the Niolu from either Ponte Leccia or Corte you will travel through one of the wildest pieces of landscape on Corsica: the Scala di Santa Regina. The barriers of red granite on the eastern side of the valley basin forced the Golo River to dig a huge trench for itself here, managing a drop of 555 metres (1,800 ft) within the space of just 21 km (13 miles). The road passes excitingly beneath rocky overhangs and over arch bridges. The old mule route can still be glimpsed now and then. It leads through the gorge like a staircase (*scala*) hewn out of the rock. At one point it is possible to walk right down into the ravine and join it, though the road is so narrow that there are not that many suitable stopping-places.

A good base for excursions in this area is the capital of the Niolu, **Calacuccia**. This village, with its 400 or so inhabitants, possesses a handful of hotels, restaurants and supermarkets, as well as a pharmacy and a post office. The **Calacuccia Reservoir**, completed in 1968, is a recent tourist attraction. It contains 25 million cubic metres of water, and the power station here provides the island with much of its electricity. Though the lake is picturesque it is almost impossible to swim in it because the water along the shore is covered by an unfortunate brown slick. The wooden crucifix hanging above the altar in the church in Calacuccia is a fine example of the Niolu woodcarving tradition, as is the statue of St Roch in Casamaccioli.

Only very few villages lie scattered across the Calacuccia basin. South of the reservoir is **Casamaccioli**, where an annual singing contest and fair take place between 8 and 10 September to mark the festival of *La Santa du Niolu*. The "young shepherds in good voice" here have become rather more elderly recently, but the tradition is still kept alive. The high point of the festivities is the procession on 8 September, when the statue of the *Santa du Niolu* is carried through the village (*see page 93*).

The village of **Albertacce**, to the south-west of Calacuccia, contains a small archaeological museum (Musée Archéologique Licinoi), with finds ranging from megalithic times to the Roman period. A menhir statue is on display here, as is a dolmen, and there are also various flints and ceramics. Photographs

Left, negotiating a bend in the Scala di Santa Regina.

display the settlement sites of the region's earlier inhabitants. A road and also a footpath lead from Albertacce to **Calasima**, the highest village in Corsica at 1,095 metres (3,600 ft). There is a fine hiking route from here that leads under the jagged peaks of the **Cinque Frati** ("Five Brothers") through the Viro Valley and then on to the **Refuge Ciottuli di i Mori**, beneath the peaks of the **Paglia Orba** and the **Capu Tafunatu**.

Corsica's highest peak: The village of **Lozzi**, 1,050 metres (3,400 ft) up, is the starting-point for any ascent of **Monte Cinto**. A track has been made here which almost reaches as far as the Bergerie d'Ercu, making the ascent of Corsica's highest mountain a lot shorter. Start the expedition by taking the D84 from Calacuccia in the direction of Albertacce and then take the turn-off to Lozzi. After passing through the main part of the village, the track then branches off towards Monte Cinto (7.2 km/4½ miles). A marked route then leads from the end of the track to the **Bergerie d'Ercu** (1,650 metres/5,400 ft above sea level).

The peak can be scaled in three hours, but be sure you start out early because the morning sun shines straight on to the mountain. In good weather the whole of Corsica is visible from the summit, and sometimes even Elba and Sardinia too. Visibility does tend to get hazy from midday onwards, though. The mountains of the central massif all around the peak, such as Paglia Orba, Capu Larghia and Monte Rotondo are all extremely impressive as well.

If you drive up the D84 to the Col de Vergio, you pass through the largest area of forest on the island, the **Forêt de Valdu Niellu**. This region comprises 4,638 hectares (11,460 acres) in total, and 70 percent of it consists of Corsican black pine, also known as Laricio pine, as well as deciduous trees such as beech and birch. Thin alder scrub can be seen along the tree line. The forest of Valdu Niellu possesses the finest stands of pine on Corsica: some of the trees are 500 years old and can grow to a height

Left, snow can fall until May on the Col de Vergio. Right, the Golo, still a mountain stream in the Niolu.

of about 40 metres (120 ft). In the centre of the forest, at an altitude of 1,076 metres (3,500 ft), lies the **Maison Forestière de Popaja**, the starting-point for hikes to the **Lac de Nino**.

The route, marked with yellow signs, first leads through tall pine trees and small forests of birch, and then alongside the small Colga River. An hour later one reaches the stone buildings of the **Bergerie Colga**, and it takes another hour to get to the **Bocca a Stazzona** (1,762 metres/5,800 ft) at the top of the pass leading to the grazing land by the Lac de Nino.

A devilish place: At the top of the pass there are several large and unusual-looking rocks strewn about, which, according to an old Niolu legend, are the petrified oxen of the devil. The Niolu is the scene of many stories concerning St Martin and the devil, some of which date right back to the dawn of Christianity. When the devil discovered that St Martin, in his role as a shepherd, was successfully converting a large number of people, he decided to disguise himself as a farmer and teach the local population a lesson. He created enormous valleys in the mountains with a huge ploughshare. St Martin coolly observed these attempts, and then made fun of the devil, wondering why his furrows were so full of bends and asking him why he was unable to plough in a straight line. In a sudden burst of anger, the offended devil threw his ploughshare away as far as he could. It flew straight through a rock, forming the huge hole that can still be seen today – **Capu Tafunatu**. According to the legend, the devil's oxen were then immediately turned to stone by St Martin to prevent any further mischief.

It takes a quarter of an hour to get from Stazzona Pass to the Lac de Nino. The landscape here is bathed in bright, clear light, cattle, horses and pigs graze away, and there is a marvellous tranquillity about the place. The marshy meadows with their meandering streams here are called *pozzines* (from *pozzi*, the Corsican word for spring), and are the remnants of lakes that were filled up

The reservoir at Calacuccia.

with sedimentation after the last Ice Age. The Lac de Nino, 1,743 metres (5,700 ft) above sea level, is the source of the Tavignano River. There is a wonderful eight-hour-long route back to Corte from here along its banks.

A good place for bathing: Another worthwhile walking tour to the **Bergeries de Gradule** and to the **Radule Falls** begins roughly 6 km (3½ miles) beyond the Popaja forest lodge, on the hairpin in the road called the **Fer-à-Cheval** (horseshoe), beneath the Col de Vergio. The GR20 trail with its red-and-white markers first runs through an idyllic forest filled with pine and birch.

The stone buildings of the Bergeries de Gradule, nestling in the middle of some unbelievably romantic rocky scenery, are reached in less than half an hour. Dangling copper pots and signs make it clear to visitors that freshly-prepared cheese can be purchased on the spot here. After leaving the the *bergeries* it is necessary to descend a scree slope in order to arrive at the Radule Falls, which are situated picturesquely at one end of

a ravine. If you continue following the red-and-white signs for the GR20 even further up the Golo River at this point, you will find plenty of rock-pools and little cascades in which to go bathing. From here it is still another two hours' hike to get to the *bergeries* called **Ciottuli di i Mori**, the starting-point for ascents of Paglia Orba and Capu Tafunatu.

On the **Col de Vergio**, 1,500 metres (4,900 ft) up, the snow can sometimes be as much as 1.5 metres (5 ft) deep, sometimes making access from Evisa quite impossible. A mountain hotel ("Castel de Vergio") and various ski-lifts cater for winter sports enthusiasts, though in summertime the installations and equipment tend to look rather forlorn. Roughly 200 metres (650 ft) below the pass there is a good view of the Calacuccia valley basin, and of the huge hole in the rock in Capu Tafunatu to the north. If you cross the pass here and go through the forests of **Aitone** you can then get back to **Evisa** and the **Gulf of Porto** on the West Coast.

A splash of springtime colour.

TWO SHEPHERDS

On a high plain, far from the bustle of the coastal cities, an encounter with two shepherds. The pattern of their lives is governed by the seasons and by transhumance, the seasonal migration of flocks. In summer, they live with their goats and sheep in the mountains, but before winter comes they lead them down to the coastal grazing lands. These shepherds, who are brothers, are following in their father's and grandfather's footsteps.

They look forward to their return to the coast, for in September they will stop at the Niolu annual fair. Here the men assemble for the "Festival of the Santa", joining together in the polyphonic songs handed down orally since the very dawn of time. They are songs which tell of love, of death and of the earth; songs which move the listener to tears. The shepherds softly hummed one of the beautiful melodies.

Then they suddenly burst out laughing as they saw a young goatherd chasing his animals. "Look," said the elder of the two gently, "That is a boy who went to school to learn how to be a shepherd. We have been tending our flocks since we were children. No teacher in the world can teach you how to become a shepherd." Working to the same harmonious rhythm, the two shepherds whittled away at an olive branch with their fine, sharp knives. It is a common occupation in the country, allowing concentration on intellectual matters.

They were reluctant to speak of their mother, whom like all Corsicans they revered. Pointing heavenwards, Paulo Andria said in a quiet voice full of emotion, "God rest her soul. We should leave her in peace. It is wrong to disturb the spirits." His words sounded like superstition, but did the pair also believe in God? The question surprised them. Their answer was, "We live in the *macchia*, but we're not savages. Look at the Holy Cross above the fireplace, and the branches of olive and palm trees which were blessed last year on Palm Sunday." Paulo Andria leapt to his feet and pointed to a brightly-coloured picture of the Virgin Mary, but not before he had carefully wiped it with his sleeve to remove the layer of dust. The two men crossed themselves, as if such a question might leave its evil mark on the stone walls of their hut.

Two rifles were also hung on the wall. "Don't think that they are there to protect us from bandits! Unfortunately we're the only ones left in the *macchia*. But have you ever seen a Corsican who wasn't armed?" Their grandfather taught them to shoot. "When he pulled the trigger of his old rifle, you had the feeling that the recoil might dislocate his shoulder," they recalled.

Did they regret their lonely lifestyle? "Never! Our father taught us to master our fear by taking us with him into the mountains. When we were only eight years old, transhumance was like a fascinating adventure. And we still enjoy it." A mist descending from the mountains brought our conversation to a close. Paulo Andria pulled the peak of his cap down over his face. The flocks on the mountainside felt the approaching storm as clearly as we did and retreated into their stall. Before we departed we all drank to each other, raising our glasses in a toast. They were filled with a remarkable schnapps, which smelled of the *macchia* and warmed both body and soul. ■

Shearing season.

FROM CORTE
TO SARTÈNE

The route from Corte to Sartène is one of the loneliest on the island. Its attraction lies in its mixture of what is still a primordial landscape with vast tracts of forest that seem to go on for ever.

Facilities for tourists along the way are few and far between. The only hotels are in Ghisoni, Zicavo and Aullène. Anyone travelling along this route in early spring or late autumn – when the trees are at their finest – may have trouble finding anything to eat at all: from Vivario all the way to Zicavo there are no restaurants open between the end of September and the middle of June, nor even any roadside snack bars. Tourists hungry for culture will find that there is even less on offer: the route contains no historically important monuments at all. Only at the very end of it – via a detour – is it possible to visit the prehistoric sites at Cucuruzzu.

The region is also relatively unhelpful where hikers are concerned: even though there are a few mountain walks along partially marked routes, most of the extensive forest areas here are scarcely touched on. The route should not pose too much of a problem for motorists who have managed to get used to Corsica's winding roads, although these are always a test for drivers taking part in the annual *Rallye Corse*. Since the verges have crumbled away in some places, drivers of larger vehicles such as motor-caravans should exercise particular caution when overtaking.

Observation point in the forest: From Corte as far as Vivario the road to follow

is the N193 in the direction of Ajaccio. On a right-hand bend you will suddenly see a turn-off: the D69 to Ghisoni. This road leads through attractive forest scenery up to the **Col de Sorba** (1,311 metres/4,300 ft). From the top of the pass on the west side, in clear weather, the view takes in Monte d'Oro and the Vecchio Valley and extends as far as the Corte basin. On the other side one can make out the Etang d'Urbino over on the east coast, glittering in the far distance and framed by the steep rock walls. From the Col de Sorba it takes a good hour to reach the 1,565-metre (5,100-ft) high **Punta Moro** to the northeast, via a stony forest path. There is an all-round panoramic view from the summit.

A local legend: The route from the Col de Sorba leads through tall forests down to **Ghisoni**. A large amount of forest was destroyed by fire in this region in 1985. Ghisoni lies at the foot of the massive towering rocks known as the **Punta Kyrie-Eleison** (1,535 metres/5,000 ft). In front of the main peak, in the middle distance, that particularly impressive jagged rock formation, the **Rocher Christe-Eleison**, can be seen towering steeply out of the valley. There is a legend attached to the names of these mountains: the last few supporters of the *Giovannali*, a reformist sect founded in 1530 in Carbini (near Levie), persecuted as heretics by the Inquisition, are meant to have fled to Ghisoni. They were captured here and, having been accused of communistic tendencies, indulging in superstitious sacrifi-

cial practices and nighttime debauchery in the church, were condemned to death. It is said that the *Giovannali* were burnt alive on a huge funeral pyre in the village, but the ash rising from the pyre then turned into a white dove. While the villagers were chanting the words of the requiem mass ("Kyrie Eleison... Christe Eleison..."), the dove slowly flew up towards the mighty rocks above. The sound of the chant is said to have re-echoed back from the mountains.

Ghisoni has another peculiarity too: above the village fountain there is a large statue of Neptune, killing a sea-monster with his trident. It reminds us of the proximity of the sea, and of the harbour at Aléria which was once the largest on Corsica.

Anyone who drives from Ghisoni to the east coast will pass through two of the finest ravines of the Fiumorbo, a region known for its turbulent history and the independent and recklessly brave nature of its people. The first one is the **Défilé des Strettes**. Then comes a small reservoir, and after a short tunnel one suddenly finds oneself in the steep, rocky gorge known as the **Défilé de l'Inzecca**. The road to **Col de Verde** (D69) runs southwards from Ghisoni through the huge **Forêt de Marmano**, and weaves its way uphill between mighty pine, oak and chestnut trees.

Hiking and winter sports: One turn off the road leads up to **Capanelle**, and it's definitely worth following it a short way. After a few kilometres the forests start to get brighter, and then there is a magnificent view of the Ghisoni valley basin and the mountains surrounding it. At the end of the road one reaches the **Bergerie de Capanelle**, where a large herd of sheep can be seen grazing in the summertime.

Capanelle is the favourite starting-point for ascents of **Monte Renoso**. The route, partly marked, leads past a small mountain lake, the **Lac de Bastiani**. After around three and a half hours' walk you will find yourself at the summit. On clear summer mornings Monte Renoso provides an utterly breathtaking view that takes in the entire southern part of the island. In wintertime the Bergerie de Capanelle is a favourite skiing destination, and there is a lift up to 1,960 metres (6,430 ft). People who come up here tend to favour long-distance cross-country skiing tours.

At Col de Verde (1,289 metres/4,200 ft), from which this route – the Route du Col de Verde – also gets its name, the D69 intersects with the GR20 long-distance hiking trail. *Verde* is the Corsican word for "green", and the landscape here certainly is. There are several footpaths on either side of the head of the pass leading off into lonely forest areas.

From Col de Verde, the road winds its way around countless bends, through the **Forêt de San-Pietro-di-Verde**, and then the **Forêt de St-Antoine**. A few kilometres past the head of the pass, the view suddenly opens out down into the thickly-wooded Taravo Valley. The first hamlet to be reached along here is **Cozzano**. In the large village square, the old men sit in the shade of the trees, waiting either for something to happen or for the weather to get cooler towards evening, which is the time when things

Forest fire above Corte.

really liven up: the men play *pétanque*, the southern French version of the beloved game of *boules*, while the women, ignoring the game, prattle away excitedly to each other.

The next village is **Zicavo**. Its inhabitants can look back proudly on an illustrious past: during the Corsican War of Independence, their ancestors were among the very last to surrender to the military might of the French troops. It is only when one drives down into the valley that one notices how the village houses cling tightly to the mountain slope. It's possible to make a short detour from Zacava to **Guitera-les-Bains**. The sulphur springs in this shallow valley basin have been famous since Roman times. A small hamlet has grown up around them, and some of the buildings – the Hôtel des Bains, for instance – have a melancholy charm, reminding us of the village's erstwhile ambitions as a spa town.

The sea-monsters of Aullène: Coming from Zicavo, the D69 first travels uphill gradually, through the beech forest of **Bosco di u Coscione**. A few kilometres further on, the landscape suddenly changes. Forest gives way to fern-covered slopes, allowing another view of the Taravo Valley and of the mountain ranges surrounding it. A detour can be made along this stretch, too: a bumpy forest road leads up to a small *Bergerie*. The D69 finally reaches the **Col de la Vaccia**. This lonely mountain pass lies in the middle of a broad, open stretch of landscape, the eastern part of which is extremely barren. The road makes another impressive loop through a valley basin very reminiscent of those in the Alps, below the **Punta d'Anola** (1,442 metres/4,700 ft).

Aullène is a tiny mountain village. Even though tourists have been part of everyday life here for quite some time, the nastier aspects of tourism have still not made themselves felt to any large extent. The simple village church of Aullène stands on the road to Zonza. The most remarkable thing about this church is its pulpit. A simple, chestnut-wood construction, it is supported by

View of Santo Pietro di Venaco.

four very finely-carved sea-monsters, who are supported in turn by a Moor's head fixed to the wall. The carvings remind us of the pirates from North Africa who raided Corsica right up until the 18th century; during their raids they often penetrated far into the island's interior, terrorising the population. Another interesting feature of this pulpit is the sculpture of a hand holding the Cross, projecting from its right-hand side. The church is usually closed, but if you stand in front of the entrance and look across to your left you will see a flight of steps with brown banisters roughly 100 yards away on the other side of the road. Ask there for the key.

Aullène is surrounded by a network of well-signposted hiking trails which penetrate deep inside the lonely forests. Those interested in cultural history should not drive on directly to Sartène at this point, but instead make a detour via **Quenza, Zonza** and **Levie** to visit the Torréen fortress known as the **Castello de Cucuruzzu** (see chapter entitled "The Sartenais"). Situated on a wooded hillside amidst orchards and vineyards, the beautiful village of **Sainte Lucie de Tallano** provides a wonderful finale to the trip as the road from Levie begins its descent into the valley of the Rizzanèse River. This was the domain of the great Corsican clan chief, Rinuccio della Rocca. He wasn't only a warlord who fought the Genoese, but also an avid fan of the Renaissance and a lover of art. He endowed a Franciscan monastery here in 1492, and both the monastery church and the parish church are still adorned with the works of art that he donated.

The Rizzanèse is spanned only a few kilometres further on towards Sartène by the famous old Genoese bridge of Spin'a Cavallu (horse's back). The two menhirs known as U Frate e a Suora (Brother and Sister) are also very close to here. Scholars are still in the dark as to the significance of these two weird-looking sculptures, standing right in the middle of their broad valley. Approached from this direction, Sartène, up on its hill high above the valley, looks particularly impressive.

The "horse's back" over the Rizzanèse.

A Fairy-Tale World

The enchanted mountain landscapes of Corsica and the close bond between the islanders and their natural environment provided just the right conditions for sagas, legends and fairy tales to flourish. The stories, which often served to expose human vices, were passed down by word of mouth from generation to generation.

At the beginning of the 1880s, J.B. Frédéric Ortoli researched this folk literature. He travelled to and fro across the island, noting down the stories he was told. The result was a collection of tales published in Paris in 1883. A notable feature is the realism, which often scorns the usual happy ending. The action only seldom took place in far-off imaginary lands; most stories are set in familiar places on Corsica itself. Here is an example of a fairy tale which transforms the Rizzanèse into a magical river landscape.

Once upon a time, a beautiful fairy lived in a grotto in the Rizzanèse. She could sometimes be seen in the morning, when she came out to do her laundry. A legend grew up that whoever managed to hold her fast by the hair would gain her for his wife.

One day a young man named Poli chanced to pass by just when the fairy had spread out her clothes to dry and was sitting resting on a stone. He crept up to her as quietly as he could, suddenly grabbed hold of her golden hair and cried out, "Now you are caught and belong to me!" The fairy beseeched him to let her go and promised Poli all the treasures in the world. But the young man remained steadfast and insisted that she become his wife. "You have won a victory over me, so I shall become your companion. But you must never try to see my naked shoulder, for if you do, I shall disappear from view in the very same instant," said the fairy. She allowed Poli to take her with him to Olmiccia, where a magnificent marriage took place.

The fairy was most unhappy at all this. She refused to eat, and she stopped smiling. She seldom left the house. When she went through the village, she hung her head as she walked. But she bore Poli three sons and three daughters, whom she loved dearly. One night, Poli asked his wife, "Why do you always refuse to take off your nightshirt? Why may I not see your shoulder? It is without doubt very beautiful." The fairy warned him, "If you look at it, I shall be dead for you."

This made the young man even more curious. "What is so remarkable about her shoulder?" he thought to himself. "She just wants to revenge herself on me for compelling her to marry me." And whilst she slept, he uncovered what he wanted to see. With a cry of despair the fairy woke up and, weeping, showed her husband a hole in her shoulder. "Look at that. It is the skeleton of our love, which you have just destroyed. Woe is you, O unhappy man! Woe is me! Why did you not heed my warning?" Poli begged her to forgive him, but the fairy explained to him, "In a few moments I shall disappear. We have six children. Tell me, which do you want to keep, the boys or the girls?" Poli asked for the sons, and she gave them to him. But the fairy warned him that henceforth his family would never have more than three children. And then she disappeared. Poli was in despair and often went to the grotto in the Rizzanèse, but he never saw his wife or daughters again. ■

An enchanted landscape.

255

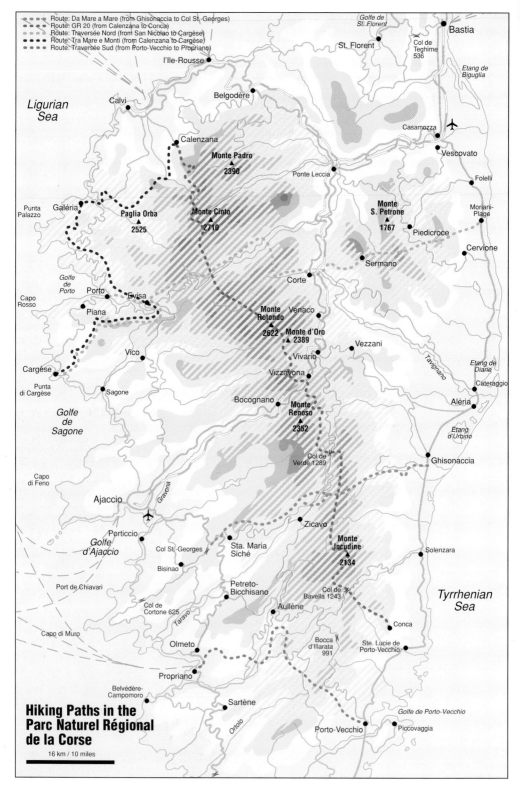

**Hiking Paths in the
Parc Naturel Régional
de la Corse**

16 km / 10 miles

Route: Da Mare a Mare (from Ghisonaccia to Col St.-Georges)
Route: GR 20 (from Calenzana to Conca)
Route: Traversée Nord (from San Nicolao to Cargèse)
Route: Tra Mare e Monti (from Calenzana to Cargèse)
Route: Traversée Sud (from Porto-Vecchio to Propriano)

*Ligurian
Sea*

Calvi

Belgodère

l'Ile-Rousse

Calenzana

Monte Padro
▲
2390

Ponte Leccia

*Golfe de
St. Florent*

St. Florent

Col de
Teghime
536

Bastia

*Etang de
Biguglia*

Casamozza

Vescovato

Folelli

**Monte
S. Petrone**
▲
1767

Moriani-
Plage

Punta
Palazzo

Galéria

Paglia Orba
▲
2525

Monte Cinto
▲
2710

Piedicroce

Cervione

Capo
Rosso

*Golfe
de
Porto*

Porto

Evisa

Piana

Sermano

Corte

**Monte
Rotondo**
▲
2622

Venaco

Monte d'Oro
▲ 2389

Vivario

Vezzani

Tavignano

*Etang de
Diane*

Cateraggio

Aléria

Vico

Vizzavona

Cargèse

Punta
di Cargèse

Sagone

*Golfe
de
Sagone*

Bocognano

**Monte
Renoso**
▲
2352

Col de
Verde 1289

*Etang
d'Urbino*

Ghisonaccia

Capo
di Feno

Ajaccio

Porticcio

*Golfe
d'Ajaccio*

Col St.-Georges

Bisinao

Sta. Maria
Siché

Zicavo

**Monte
Incudine**
▲
2134

Solenzara

Port de Chiavari

Petreto-
Bicchisano

Col de
Cortone 625

Gravona

Taravo

Col de
Bavella 1243

Conca

Ste. Lucie de
Porto-Vecchio

*Tyrrhenian
Sea*

Capo di Muro

Olmeto

Aullène

Bocca
d'Illarata
991

Propriano

Belvédère-
Campomoro

Sartène

Ortolo

Porto-Vecchio

Golfe de Porto-Vecchio

Piccovaggia

256

HIKING TRAILS

The Parc Naturel Régional de la Corse covers 354,000 hectares (875,000 acres), and is one of the finest nature conservation areas in all Europe. It incorporates the central Corsican mountain chain, which runs across the island from north-west to south-east. Planning work began on the project in 1963, and in 1969, just in time for Napoleon's 200th birthday, the park was established. The main aims were to create a harmonious balance between conservation, folkloric tradition and tourism.

On the conservation side, the most important task is to protect rare species of plant as well as to preserve the habitats of animals facing extinction. Instructing people about the dangers of forest fires is also especially important. In addition to its mountainous interior, part of Corsica's rocky coastline between Galéria and the Calanche has also been incorporated into the park. Old villages and traditional structures such as bridges, mills and shepherds' huts are being restored and preserved – and not just for the purposes of tourism. Tourists, however, have rekindled interest in Alpine dairy-farming and the sale of fresh cheese.

The GR20 hiking trail: When the Parc Naturel was still only in the planning stage, work had already begun on a long-distance Alpine hiking trail that has now become internationally famous and attracts thousands of walkers annually: the GR20. This is just one of the many long-distance paths in France – another is the equally famous GR10 in the Pyrennees – created and organised by Le Comité National des Sentiers de Grande Randonnée. Approximately 200 km (125 miles) in length, the GR20 is the very best way for hikers to get acquainted with the remoter parts of the island. Fitness and stamina are essential, though.

The trail starts at **Calenzana**, near Calvi, and ends 12 to 15 hiking days later at **Conca** on the Gulf of Porto Vecchio. Just as is the case with all the other French Grande Randonnées, the route is completely balisé (marked) in the distinctive stripes of white above red, painted on rock faces, boulders, walls, tree trunks and specially-erected posts and cairns when no other feature is available. These signs are usually no more than 50 metres (160 ft) apart. The "alpine variants" – the detours leading over more challenging territory – are usually coloured yellow.

The best season to tackle the GR20 is from the beginning of June to the end of September. Before then some stretches may still be snow-covered, and only passable with ice-picks and crampons. The section referred to as GR20 Nord, from Calenzana to Vizzavona, requires both firmness of foot and a head for heights in several places, while the GR20 Sud, from Vizzavona to Conca is easier going than its northern equivalent – and the landscape is just as impressive.

The main problem faced by hikers here is how heavy their rucksacks should be. Outside the main season, when the mountain pastures are still empty and

Right, the GR20 takes between 12 and 15 days.

the mountain hotels closed, extra provisions need to be packed. The total weight of equipment, clothing, food and water should not exceed 15 kilos (33 lb). The self-catering huts do contain stoves, but it's best to take along a medium-sized aluminium saucepan, a drinking flask, a bowl, cutlery, matches and a knife. Those not sleeping inside the huts (a fee is charged) can pitch their tents on the nearby campsites.

Right at the very start of the GR20, there's a 1,300-metre (4,300-ft) ascent, from Calenzana up to the **Réfuge di l'Ortu di u Piobbu**. If you survive the general rehearsal of the first day, you'll be more than rewarded on the second by the unforgettable view down into the **Bonifatu Basin**, before reaching the idyllically situated **Carrozzu** refuge the same afternoon.

The third day begins with a crossing of the Spasimata River – over a rope bridge – and then the trail leads on through a rocky region to the 1,985-metre (6,500-ft) high **Brèche de Stagnu** before descending again 563 metres

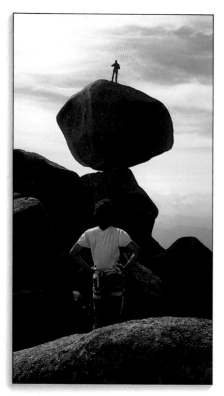

(1,800 ft) to the **Hotel Le Chalet** on the Plateau de Stagnu. This descent became necessary after the refuge at Altore was destroyed in a fire. The hotel is also a starting-point for climbers tackling the north side of Monte Cinto.

Not for the nervous: The next day, the route leads 600 metres (1,970 ft) up from the Plateau de Stagnu to the ruins of the Refuge d'Altore and then on to the 2,183-metre (7,200-ft) high **Col Perdu**. Now ropes and chains are needed as you descend into the **Solitude Basin**. Here, the hiker is confronted by fascinating rock formations – and firmness of foot and a good head for heights are essential. After scaling the **Bocca Minuta** (2,218 metres/7,200-ft) you then descend to the newly-refurbished huts at **Tighiettu**.

On the fifth day the trail leads round the base of **Paglia Orba** before reaching the refuges known as **Ciottuli di i Mori**, the starting point for ascending the 2,525-metre (8,300-ft) high peak. As you begin your ascent there is a good view of the huge hole in the rock over to the left – **Capu Tafunatu**. Anyone who decides against an ascent of the mountain can spend the day continuing their journey to **Col de Vergio** along the lovely banks of the Golo River.

The big attraction of the following day is the grassy countryside surrounding the **Lac de Nino**. The next section of the route takes us from the **Refuge de Manganu** up to the 2,225-metre (7,300-ft) high **Brèche de Capitello**. Beyond this wind gap comes one of the most delightful sections of the entire GR20. Along the length of the ridge leading to **Bocca a Soglia** there is an enchanting view of the **Lac de Capitello** and the **Lac de Melo** far below. The pleasant **Refuge de Petra Piana** at the end of this strenuous day's tour lies at the foot of **Monte Rotondo** (2,622 metres/8,600 ft), long believed to be the highest mountain in Corsica.

The next day provides enough time for a bit of dawdling, along the banks of the Manganello, though after the midday rest-stop in the idyllic **Bergerie Tolla**, the 500-metre (1,600-ft) ascent to the **Refuge d'Onda** can be really

The Uomo di Cagna is a prominent landmark.

tough going. After eight to ten days' hiking, with **Monte d'Oro** and the marvellous **Agnone Valley** behind us, we reach the summer mountain resort of **Vizzavona**. The island railway runs to Ajaccio and Corte from here.

Those wishing to continue along the GR20 will now be starting on its southern section. Over the next two days the route mostly runs through beech forests, beneath the **Monte Renoso** massif. After descending from **Col de Verde** to the **Refuge de Prati** you then proceed directly southwards along a long mountain ridge that provides you with your first views of the nearby east coast. The mountains gradually get lower now, with the last really big one, **Monte Incudine** (2,134 metres/7,000 ft), causing no problems, and then you suddenly plunge right back into the fascinating mountain world of Corsica as the rocky spires of the **Bavella** come into view.

Even after the **Bavella Pass**, the landscape, with its reddish rocks, is still as impressive as ever. Now the *macchia* starts to get more widespread as the

GR20 comes to an end near **Conca**. Anyone keen on spending a couple more days by the sea after the 170-km (105-mile) crossing of Corsica can relax very pleasantly at the beach at **Fautéa** or in the **Gulf of Pinarello**.

Tra Mare e Monti: For hikers who think they're going to find the mainly mountainous GR 20 too strenuous, the long-distance trail known as Tra Mare e Monti is definitely to be recommended. It takes eight to ten days, and runs from **Calenzana** to **Cargèse**. The well-marked route (signs are in orange) leads through the foothills along the central part of the west coast, and provides opportunities for a refreshing swim in the sea or a creek. The daily route takes between three and six and a half hours to cover, and at the end of each section there are so-called *Gîtes d'Etappe*, providing overnight accommodation. Luggage should be kept to an essential minimum on this route as well.

The Tra Mare e Monti gives us an entirely different impression of the natural scenery Corsica has to offer. The

One of the highlights of the GR20 – Lac de Nino.

hiker wanders here through typical coastal vegetation: *macchia*, with rockroses, strawberry trees and myrtle and juniper bushes. Villages and hamlets with ancient chestnut groves are strung out along the route. Remember, though, that the trail can get strenuous at times, and the height differences covered daily must not be underestimated.

Straight across the island: Alongside these two long-distance hiking trails which run vertically down the island, the park administration has laid out new trails in the past few years that run eastwest across the entire island, with overnight accommodation available on each leg of the journey. A large network of trails has thus been built up, and individual sections can, of course, be combined to form individual routes. The east-west trails run through various different regions of the island: the *macchia* landscape down by the coasts, the Corsican forests and also the mountains in the central range.

There are three hiking trails running from coast to coast, *da mare a mare*. All of them are signposted with orange markers. The **Traversée Nord** begins at the church of San Nicolao, just inland from the east-coast town of **Moriani-Plage** and takes you on a ten-day march to **Cargèse** on the west coast. The first two sections wend their way through the **Castagniccia** (between 200 and 1,090 metres/650–3,575 ft) over to its western side, the Boziu, at **Pianellu**. The next two days via **Sermano** to **Corte**, at altitudes of between 400 and 900 metres (1,300–3,000 ft), offer a splendid view up to the highest peaks such as the Monte Cintu (2,710 metres/8,900 feet).

On the fifth day the route gradually ascends the magnificent **Tavignano** valley, and then passes through a marvellous pine forest to reach the **Refuge de la Sega** (1,190 metres/3,900 ft). This is a good place for a swim in the river.

The Niolu is reached on the following day. The route ascends to the **Bocca a l'Arinella** (1,692 metres/5,550 ft) and then leads back down to **Calacuccia** and along the banks of the reservoir of

In the wilds...

the same name to **Albertacce**. The next section of the trip proceeds from here through the extensive area of Laricio pine forest known as the **Forêt de Valdu Niellu** up to the highest mountain pass crossed by a road in Corsica, the **Col de Vergio** (1,477 metres/4,800 ft).

On the next day the markers for the route begin next to a statue at the mountain hotel Castellu di Vergio and lead the hiker through the **Forêt d'Aitone**, then over the **Bocca a u Saltu** in the direction of Evisa. The nearby **Cascades d'Aitone** are a superb place for a bathe. The route then passes through a gorgeous chestnut forest on the way down to **Evisa**. From here it is still another two and a half hours' hiking before the *Gîte d'Etappe* in **Marignana**. The final stages of the journey then follow the route of the Tra Mare e Monti, finally ending up on the west coast at the town of **Cargèse**.

A nice strenuous route: The long-distance hiking trail which runs from **Ghisonaccia** to **Ajaccio**, takes six strenuous days to complete. It begins in

Abbazia, a few kilometres southwest of Ghisonaccia. From there it follows a road briefly as far as **Acquacitosa** (**Sualellu**). The first exhausting section up to **Catastaghiu** involves an ascent of 900 metres (2,900 ft) in five hours.

The second day is just as arduous: a six-hour-long slog that proceeds from an altitude of 523 metres (1,700 ft) above sea level right up to the **Col de Laparo** (1,525 metres/5,000 ft) and then down to **Cozzano** (727 metres/2,400 ft). The third stage leads via **Tasso** to **Guitera**, with its sulphur springs. If you like you can also reach Guitera by hiking from Cozzano via **Zicavo** – a very pleasant route through chestnut forests. The fourth stage of the journey ends in **Quasquara**, where a simple mountain hut provides refuge for the night. Day five sees you cross the last pass on this trail, the **Col St-Georges**, through which the N196 also passes. The destination, **Ajaccio**, is just a brief car ride from here – or, if you still feel like it, another seven gruelling hours on foot.

Another "sea to sea" route, this time

...one should be prepared for all sorts of encounters.

through Corsica's south, is the Traversée Sud, which leads from **Porto Vecchio** to **Propriano**. It starts at **Alzu di Gallina**, roughly 10 km (6 miles) from Porto Vecchio. The best way to get there is to take a cab from Porto Vecchio along the D159 to **Muratello**, and then walk northwards: the markings begin on the other side of the bridge across the Bola River. On the first section the route starts off steeply, rising to a height of 1,020 metres (3,300 ft) above sea level, and leads on to **Cartalavona** and **Ospedale**. One is well rewarded in **Ospedale**, however, with a breathtaking view of the entire Gulf of Porto Vecchio.

All the height gained on the first day gets lost on day two, however. The route descends via **Carbini** to an altitude of just 260 metres (850 ft), then ascends again to **Levie** (610 metres/2,000 ft). The third section leads through shady forests via **Zonza** to **Quenza**. This is a good place for planning a quick detour to the Torréen fortress at **Cucurruzzu**.

Now the landscape gets more barren. The fourth stage of the trip is mostly *macchia*, and takes us to **Serra di Scopamena**, where you can admire a renovated windmill. The fifth stage leads through oak and chestnut forests to **Sainte Lucie de Tallano**. And on the sixth day you'll finally end up in **Propriano**, on the Gulf of Valinco.

Attractive day excursions: Good starting points for rewarding hikes on Monte Cinto, Paglia Orba and down to the Lac de Nino are the **Calacuccia Basin** and the **Col de Vergio** (see Niolu chapter). The region around **Vizzavona** is also a very attractive hiking area. This mountain village, situated beneath the 2,389-metre (7,800-ft) high peak of **Monte d'Oro**, has three hotels and is surrounded by superb forests of beech and pine. It is a popular and refreshing destination in high summer, when the tourists are going bright pink down on the beaches.

There are 40 km (24 miles) of hiking trails in this area. The many rock-pools in the Agnone River, up above the **Cascades des Anglais**, are particularly inviting. To get there, follow the red-and-white markers of the GR20 Nord. This

The Refuge de Petra Piana beneath Monto d'Oro.

path also leads to the summit of Monte d'Oro, but just before you reach the **Bocca Muratello** you need to follow the yellow "Alpine variant" markers to the left. It is an hour's walk from Vizzavona to the Cascades des Anglais. The trip to the summit of Monte d'Oro and back takes a whole day.

On the **Col de Bavella** (1,218 metres/ 4,000 ft), nature has created a kind of rock garden with jagged needles and peaks that really do seem to glow independently when struck by the red light of the evening sun. These rocks, which are stable and easily manageable, and the brief ascents here combine to make the area an absolute paradise for climbers. It is thus not at all surprising that a large number of people make a detour from the beaches along the Gulf of Porto Vecchio to admire this fascinating mountain scenery. The Col de Bavella is also a good starting point for a number of very easy hikes.

One impressive tour takes you past Bavella Spires I and II and all the way to Spire III. The route begins to the left of the statue of Our Lady up on the Bavella Pass, and follows the red-and-white GR20 markers. Five minutes later the "alpine variant" of the GR20, marked with a double yellow line, branches off to the right. If you follow these markers for about two hours you will reach Spire III, which is easy to climb and gives you a good view back across the other two Bavella spires.

If you continue to follow the GR20 markers at this stage you will reach the **Réfuge d'Asinao**, the starting point for climbers with their eye on **Monte Incudine** (2,136 metres/7,006 ft). From here it takes approximately two hours to reach the summit.

You can also hike across the island's northern peninsula, the Cap Corse, although it hasn't been incorporated into the Parc Naturel yet and not all the routes are clearly marked. The ubiquitous *macchia* blooms here in springtime too, spreading its wonderful scent. Indeed, the early part of the year is definitely the best season for nature lovers to visit Corsica.

Back in civilisation.

INSIGHT GUIDES

Travel Tips

The World of Insight Guides

400 books in three complementary series cover every major destination in every continent.

CONTENTS

Getting Acquainted

The Place

- **Nationality:** French.
- **Location:** 41° north, 9° east.
- **Area:** 8,800 sq km (3,352 sq miles), the third largest island in the Mediterranean.
- **Distance from France:** 180 km (113 miles).
- **Distance from Italy:** 83 km (52 miles).
- **Distance from Sardinia:** 12 km (7ˇ miles) across the Straits of Bonifacio.
- **Length:** 183 km (115 miles), Cap Corse to Capo Pertusato.
- **Width:** 83 km (52 miles), Capo Rosso to Bravone.
- **General characteristics:** a mountain range rising from the sea. There is a coastal plain on the east side.
- **Coastline:** 1,000 km (625 miles).
- **Highest point:** Monte Cinto, 2,710 metres (8,891 ft).
- **Population:** 260,000.
- **Capital:** Ajaccio.
- **Départements:** Corse de Sud, Haute-Corse.
- **Official language:** French, though more than half speak Corsican, a Romance dialect.
- **Religion:** Roman Catholic.
- **Currency:** French franc.
- **Time zone:** Greenwich Mean Time + 1 hour, Eastern Standard Time + 7 hours. In summer the time is advanced by one hour.
- **Dialling code:** International access (00) + France (33) + Corsica (495). From elsewhere in France: 0495.

The People

Forty-two percent of the island's population resides in the two principal towns of Ajaccio and Bastia.

Members of established Corsican families, who have lived on the island for centuries, still make up the majority of the residents, despite the emigrations. Ever since the Genoese first arrived, many young Corsicans have gone to the mainland. These emigrants often return after retirement to spend the twilight of their lives on their native island soil.

The Corsicans are an island folk whose history has left an indelible mark on the present. The result of continual settlement by other peoples is a deeply-rooted distrust of just about everything that comes from across the sea.

Corsica also has a tradition of immigration: 200 years ago Greek Orthodox refugees finally settled in Cargèse. After the last war Italians came as agricultural workers and they adapted fairly quickly to life on the island. The settlement of about 17,000 French colonists from North Africa, so-called *pieds-noirs*, in 1962–66, caused political conflicts and finally led to the formation of different "nationalist" and even underground movements.

Today thousands of manual labourers from Morocco are employed in agriculture and construction.

Death and Vendettas

The rejection of foreign influences and the seclusion of entire valley regions have at least partially contributed to the preservation of ancient island customs, including an intensive **cult of the dead**. The dead are commemorated by large burial chapels that are sometimes not even located in cemeteries, but on private property. The cult of the dead was once expressed in song. Following the death of a family member female relatives began singing *lamenti* (lamentations) while a violent death of a family member required passionate *voceri* which urged family heads to take revenge.

The **blood feud**, or vendetta, is another deeply-rooted element of Corsican tradition which in its most direct form rarely occurs today. A vendetta, or the duty to carry out a blood feud, originated when the honour of the family was in some way besmirched and may last for generations. It can not be bribed away or paid off.

Family Life

Family life in Corsica centres on the traditional clan which holds together through thick or thin. The head of the family has great importance. Familial structure is still strictly patriarchal, especially in isolated valleys. Personal connections are important, particularly in the more rural areas. People who do business with Corsicans or who are simply looking for a hotel room for one night during the peak tourist season will be surprised to find out how the acquaintance with a certain *patron* can make the impossible possible.

As a result of the rapid development of tourism, especially in areas near the coast, Corsican hospitality has taken quite a beating. However even today in the island's interior, visitors can count on finding a friendly reception.

Economy

A good third of the gainfully employed population in Corsica is occupied in some sort of agricultural pursuit. Nevertheless, the agricultural products which are imported from the mainland are on the whole cheaper to buy than those produced on the island itself. As a result, more and more small farming businesses are having to cease operations. In order to try to halt this development existing structures are being changed to

Climate

- **Summer:** long, hot, reaching 36°C/96°F on the coast.
- **Winter:** wet and moderately cool.
- **Average annual temperature:** 12°C (54°F).
- **Rainfall:** 95 days a year, mostly falling between November and May.

Climatic conditions vary greatly from region to region, depending upon elevation. For instance it may well be possible to bask in the sunshine on the coast in April while there is still snow in the mountains, which may remain into June. During the summer the temperature in the high mountains is pleasant. **Storms** are more likely to occur on the west coast and in the mountains than anywhere else. The prevailing **winds** are from the southwest. The *Scirocco* is a hot southeasterly wind which may blow sand from the Sahara Desert onto the island. The cold *Mistral* from the northwest can also reach Corsica. The *Libecciu* blows in from the west to southwest, often in conjunction with the *Mistral*, and is characterised by gusts and large fluctuations in temperature. The *Libecciu* blows particularly strongly on the east coast of Cap Corse, where it can quite suddenly sweep over the coast road with hurricane-like force.

May 1981, the Region Corse received a statute of autonomy, granting – at least on paper – extensive authority to the 61-member regional government. In the wake of the outbreaks of violence and strikes in 1991 and subsequent elections in 1992, another even more extensive statute of autonomy was established. Subsequent discussions about allowing the island the state of a "Territoire d'Outre-Mer" (TOM) like French Polynesia and New Caledonia have been rejected.

make home produce more competitive. Farms are becoming larger and different methods of production and cultivation are being introduced. The cultivation of fruit is increasing in importance. Particularly in the east, there are large orchards of apples, cherries and plums. Large-scale irrigation has enabled the cultivation of citrus fruits. Olives and chestnuts are cultivated for local consumption. In the area around Porto Vecchio, cork production from cork oaks is also significant.

Various regions on the island are involved in wine-growing. High-quality Corsican wines are above all produced on Cap Corse (Rogliano) in the Nebbio (Patrimonio) and in the areas around Ajaccio, Sartène and Figari. The vineyards along the east coast – some of which have now been abandoned – were laid out in the 1970s by the new French-Algerian arrivals.

Livestock breeders in Corsica raise cattle, sheep, goats and pigs. The latter are generally allowed to run about freely and root for food in the forests. Bee-keeping is also of some significance on the island. Coastal fishing does not contribute markedly to the economy.

Tourism is Corsica's second most important industry but a large portion of tourist-related businesses are operated by French from the mainland or Algerian-French. With the exception of a few medium-sized businesses in greater Ajaccio and Bastia, there is hardly any industry to speak of in Corsica.

Government

Corsicans have never liked the idea of being governed from Paris and since the 1960s a regional movement has been increasingly involved in combating the central French power. The movement's radical wing, above all the FLNC (Front de Libération Nationale Corse) demands self-determination and is not afraid of using violent means when the interests of the Corsican people are thought to be under threat.

In 1975 Corsica's administration was divided into two *départements*: the Corse du Sud (Ajaccio Prefecture) and the Haute-Corse (Bastia Prefecture). Taken together these two *départements* make up the Region Corse (with its headquarters located in Ajaccio), which has been given a certain amount of authority in making governmental decisions. Following the election of the Socialist Francois Mitterand to presidency in

Planning the Trip

Visas & Passports

Citizens of countries belonging to the European Union, or from the rest of western Europe, Canada, the US and New Zealand do not need a visa to visit France. All other nationals should contact the visa section of their local French embassy or consulate. Children under the age of 16 must be in possession of their own passport, or must be included in the passport of one of their parents.

Extended stays: Visitors wishing to stay longer than three months in France are no longer considered tourists and are obliged to apply for a *carte de sejours* (residence permit). Further information regarding extended visits can be obtained from the residence permit authorities responsible for the district you wish to remain in. These officials are also responsible for processing applications.

Customs

Tourists arriving directly from the French mainland, whether by boat or by plane, are free to set off in any direction immediately after reaching the island.

Since the Schengen-Convention between members of the European Community has been adopted, there is no more customs and passport control when arriving from Italy. But there may be spot checks by customs officers; even carrying small portions of hashish can cause a lot of trouble.

Health

Reciprocal medical protection agreements exist between the different European Union countries. But even EU visitors may want to take out additional cover. Most doctors can speak at least a little English.

Money Matters

The unit of currency used in Corsica is the French franc. Food, drinks and other services purchased aboard Italian ferries may be paid for in French francs as well.

It is a good idea to bring some French francs with you. There are banks in all the bigger holiday resorts and they are open for business from Monday to Friday on all mornings and most afternoons.

Eurocheques are more and more reluctantly accepted at banks. For these you will need your passport, and the highest amount you can cash per cheque is 1,400 FF.

There are **cash dispensers** (*distributeurs de billets*) outside most banks and major post offices. Your normal PIN number should work: check with your own bank before leaving.

Festival Calendar

Most festivals which take place in Corsica are of religious origin and are celebrated with an intensity founded on deeply-rooted faith.

Holy Week is without a doubt the climax of the Corsican festival calendar. The festivities begin with the procession of *Canistrelli* in Calvi on **Maundy Thursday**.

On **Good Friday** a number of processions take place at various places. The best-known of these is probably the *Catenacciu* in Sartène, where the Grand Penitent, barefoot and in chains, drags a heavy wooden cross through the candlelit streets and alleyways of the town centre. Only the priest of Sartène knows the identity of this man whose face is covered by a red hood. In times past, bandits who hoped to atone for their misdeeds took on the role. Today, the waiting list of men wanting to act the Grand Penitent is still a long one.

In the towns of Calvi and Corte penitential processions are also held on the evening of Good Friday. In Erbalunga there are two parades on Good Friday. In the morning the procession *La Cerca* (the Search) wends a more than 7-km (4-mile) path from one church to another. In the evening torchlit procession, cowled penitents enact here and in Calvi the *granitula* (snail), which possibly has its roots in a pre-Christian fertility ceremony. The column coils up, unrolls and coils up again in a visual allegory of life from its origins until death and the resurrection.

Traditional cantatas are sung during the Good Friday procession in Bonifacio. In contrast to this, in the Greek Church in Cargèse, Good Friday is celebrated in accordance with Orthodox rites. The lamentations sung in the completely darkened church on the evening of Good Friday and the lighting of the candles at midnight on Easter Saturday are especially impressive.

There are a number of other local religious festivals observed at many different places. In Ajaccio on 18 March the festival of **Nôtre Dame de la Miséricorde**, the patron saint of the city, is celebrated. The city of Bastia commemorates its own holy patron **Saint Jean Baptiste** on 24 June, and on 8 September the **Santa Festival** takes place in Casamaccioli (Niolu).

Shrove Tuesday is celebrated everywhere. The carnival parades and masquerade balls in Corte are especially well-known.

There are also a number of **local festivals**, particularly in the summer. Tourist information centres can provide further information.

See also Events on page 282.

It is advisable to take **traveller's cheques** instead of cash. For a small fee these cheques can be insured and in most cases involving their loss or theft will be rapidly replaced. Traveller's cheques can be cashed at most banks hotel receptions, camp grounds and holiday villages for a certain commission. If you do exchange money at any of these places, the commission can be noticeable.

International **credit cards** are now accepted by most hotels, supermarkets and service stations.

Value Added Tax

In France a value added tax *(TVA = Taxe Valeur Ajoutée)* of 20.6 percent is added to most articles. For certain services it may not be necessary to pay the value added tax. It is possible to apply for a reimbursement of the value added tax on larger purchases which are intended for export.

Getting There

How you get to Corsica really depends on the kind of holiday you are intending to have. For visitors wishing to tour the island with their own car, there are ferry services leaving from various ports in France and Italy. Those headed for the beach will probably have booked a charter flight. But there are also scheduled flights to Corsica.

BY AIR
Scheduled Flights
From France: Direct scheduled flights from elsewhere in France depart from Paris, Marseille and Nice. There are also a few flights operating from Lyon. Planes destined for Corsica land daily at either Ajaccio (Campo dell'Oro airport), Bastia (Poretta Airport) or, less frequently, Calvi (Sainte-Cathérine Airport).

All coast-to-coast-connections between Corsica and the French mainland (Nice or Marseille) are serviced by the regional Compagnie Corse Méditerranée (CCM).

From the UK: If you're flying from the UK, both British Airways and Air France operate daily scheduled flights from London Heathrow to Ajaccio via Nice and Marseille.

From Italy: During the peak season there is also a regular service offered from Rome to Bastia.

For details of internal flights see page 273.

For Air France enquiries:
Canada: 151 Bloor Street West, Suite 600, Toronto, Ontario. Tel: 922-3344.
Ireland: 29–30 Dawson Street, Dublin 2. Tel: 77-8272 (reservations: tel: 77-8899).
UK: Colet Court, Hammersmith Road, London W6. Tel: 0181-742-6600.
US: 142 West 57th Street, New York, NY10019-3300. Tel: 212-830-4000; (ticket office and reservations: tel: 800-232-2746).

Charter Flights
Charter airlines offer direct flights from all over Europe. These flights usually land in Ajaccio, Bastia or Calvi. There are also direct charter flights to Propriano and Figari, near Porto Vecchio. Most charter flights are part of a complete holiday package including accommodation. Those leaving the UK generally depart from Gatwick; TAT operates a service from Stansted to Calvi and Figari.

Book Early

Those wishing to visit Corsica during the peak tourist season (the middle of June until the end of August) should try to make their travel arrangements as early as possible. Ferries as well as flights are frequently booked solid during this time of year. Locally-bought tickets may save you money but they invariably lead to seemingly endless waiting in the often rather unattractive harbour areas.

Airport Transfer
Buses run between the Campo dell'Oro Airport and Ajaccio as well as Poretta Airport and Bastia. There

Public Holidays

- **1 January** New Year's Day
- **March/April** Easter Monday
- **1 May**
- **Ascension Day**
- **Whit Monday**
- **14 July** National holiday
- **1 November** All Saints
- **11 November** 1918 Armistice
- **25 December** Christmas

is no shuttle bus between Calvi and the Sainte Cathérine Airport; so you need a taxi. Visitors arriving either at Campo dell'Oro or Poretta airports who do not wish to go directly into the town have to take the same option. It's best to agree on the price of the journey with the driver before setting out.

Taxis are usually ready and waiting at the other airports in Corsica at the time of scheduled flight arrivals. However, if there doesn't seem to be any cabs available, it is possible to order a local one by phone.

BY SEA
There are regular ferry services to Ajaccio, Bastia, Calvi, Propriano, Ile-Rousse and Porto-Vecchio from the Italian ports of Genoa, and Livorno, and the French ports of Nice, Marseille and Toulon. There are a total of four companies running these services, and it really pays to compare prices as rates differ depending on departure dates and the total duration of the journey. On the busiest days of the year you can expect to pay the highest prices. However these peak travel days are not always the same for vessels leaving France and Italy. When comparing rates don't forget to take into account the price of getting to the port of embarkation (motorway tolls and total distance) as well as the quality of the boat service offered.

On Arrival
All ferries to Corsica are of the "roll-on-roll-off" variety. Car passengers should arrive at the harbour at least an hour prior to the scheduled

departure time. The Italian shipping companies (Corsica Ferries and Moby Lines) require that your ticket be stamped at a check-in counter. The SNCM (Société Nationale Corse Méditerranée) controls tickets for cars and their passengers at a checkpoint as you enter into the harbour compound. Precise information regarding ferry schedules, prices and reservations are available at travel agencies or directly from ferry company representatives.

Choosing a Ferry Terminal

It is important to consider the length of the journey involved in getting to the ferry terminal of your choice. All ports of departure can be reached directly via motorway. Note that for the Italian ports you'll need to take into account the extra time required for getting through the traffic jams that have become the rule rather than the exception during peak holidays, especially for visitors coming over the major Alpine passes (the Brenner, San Bernadino and Gotthard). But the main routes to the South of France can also be pretty busy during the high season; the first weekend in August and the public holiday on the 15th are usually the worst times to travel, so try to avoid these dates if at all possible.

Crossing from France

Until 1995 boat connections leaving the French mainland and arriving in Corsica were operated by SNCM and the CMN (Compagnie Méridionale de Navigation). Now that this monopoloy has ended, there is some competition.

Since 1996, the two companies SNCM and Corsica Ferries have extended their services by two speedboats each, running mainly on the shortest distances between Nice and Calvi (Ile Rousse) and Nice and Bastia at least twice a day from Easter to the end of October. The boats have cut crossing times in half to 2hr 45 min and 3hr 30 min respectively. In season SNCM even serves Ajaccio in four hours from Nice. These boats have a comparable capacity of about 500 passengers and 150 cars.

From the year 2000 Corsica Ferries will replace some of its other ships by four more speedboats,and SNCM has ordered a super-speedboat. At the same time ordinary ferry traffic continues with the big SNCM boats *Napoléon Bonaparte*, *Danielle Casanova* and *Ile de Beauté*.

These ships offer lounges, sun decks, self-service cafeterias, restaurant and cinema. For night-time crossing you have a whole range of accommodation from (free) lounge chairs and couchette-compartments with two or four berths up to luxury cabins.

The big SNCM cargo boats (*navires mixtes*) such as *Paglia Orba* and *Monte d'Oro* are an execellent, year-round alternative for overnight travelling.

Embarkation ports are Marseille, Nice (Nizza) and less often, Toulon. Time of crossing can be very different, between five hours during the day and up to 12 hours by night

Crossing from Italy

Three shipping companies operate between Corsica and Italy: The Corsica Ferries fleet consists of four medium-large vessels which travel regularly to the island. Moby Lines maintains a total of 12 medium-large boats and Corsica Maritima runs a number of SNCM boats (*see above*) between Bastia and Livorno. There are duty-free shops on most boats sailing between Italy and Corsica.

Passengers who have booked an early morning crossing to Corsica are often permitted to spend the preceding night (along with their cars) on board the ferry. The total time of the crossing differs considerably from company to company depending on the route, and can be anywhere between three hours (Livorno–Bastia) and six hours (Savona-Ile Rousse).

Crossing from Sardinia

There are ferries operating between Santa Teresa-di-Galliura on the Italian island of Sardinia and

Nude bathing

Corsica's east coast in particular is known as a haven for those who prefer to sunbathe in the nude. But sunbathing *sans* swim-suit is prohibited on all beaches not expressly allowing it. Since all beaches in France, and therefore in Corsica too, are public, nude bathing aficionados do not have the right to exclusive use of any particular beach. The most popular nudist holiday villages and campgrounds, most of which are located directly on the beach, are as follows:

- **Riva Bella** F20270 Aleria
- **La Bagheera** F20231 San Nicalau.
- **Tropica** F20230 San Nicalao
- **U'Furu** F20137 Porto Vecchio (on a stream, 8 km/5 miles from the beach)
- **Villata** C10144 Ste-Lucie-de-Porto Vecchio

Bonifacio. This passage takes an hour. In the peak tourist season (June–August) ferries cross several times a day; at other times of the year they run at least once a day.

Motorail

As an alternative to driving your own car to the ferry terminal there are several SNCF motorail services that you might want to consider, not only those departing from Paris, but also the direct overnight connections between Calais and Nice. Putting your car on the train is much more relaxing and also saves you time; it might also save you money when you consider the cost of the extra overnight stays otherwise involved. French motorail schedules are partially synchronised with ferry departure times. Both information and reservations for all the above services are available from:

French Railways Ltd, French Railways House, 179 Piccadilly, London W1V 0BA. Tel: (0171) 499 2153.

Rail Europe Inc., 226–230 Westchester Avenue, White Plains, NY

10604, tel: (914) 682 2999.

Frenchrail Inc., 1500 Stanley Street, Suite 436 Montreal, Quebec H3A IR3. Tel: (514) 288 8255.

In Australia and New Zealand details are available from **Thomas Cook** offices.

SNCF has a central reservation office in Paris, tel: 08 36353535 (they speak English).

Maps

All maps of France are based on the surveys of the Institut Géographique National (IGN). The IGN also publishes its own maps in a variety of scales. Good maps for drivers are the IGN map Nr. 116 (scale 1:230 000) and the Michelin map Nr. 90 (scale 1:200 000).

More detailed are the IGN maps Nr. 73 and 74 (scale 1:100 000). Recommended for hiking and climbing are the IGN maps in the scale of 1:50 000 or 1:25 000, of which there are several sheets.

Children

Corsica is a great place to take the kids on holiday. The water at most of the island's sandy beaches is relatively shallow and the breakers are small. However, it is best to avoid the beaches along the rugged part of the west coast, where the water often becomes deep quite suddenly and the undertow can be dangerous.

There are few recreational or entertainment facilities specifically for very young visitors to Corsica, although there is a Go-Cart track located in Sarrola (near Ajaccio) for people over 12 years of age and the Aqua Cyurne Gliss in Porticcio.

Practical Tips

Security & Crime

Tourists are the targets of thieves the world over, and Corsica is no exception. In the busy towns pick-pockets and purse-snatchers are often at work but theft also occurs in more rural areas as well as on nearly empty beaches.

Emergency Numbers

- **Ambulance** 15
- **Police** 17
- **Fire brigade** 18
- **Sea rescue** 9520 1363

You should deposit money and valuables in the safe at your hotel reception or campground. Apart from the fact that camping wherever you feel like it (including in a caravan or trailer) is strictly prohibited, doing so only increases the risk of a possible theft.

Car drivers should realise that their vehicles are not safes; car boots are frequently broken into. Car radios or other items of value, such as cameras present relatively easy targets for the experienced car thieves.

Medical Services

SAMU is the organisation which deals with medical emergency service in general and their emergency phone number is 15
Ajaccio: SAMU.
Tel: 215050.
Bastia: Centre Hospitalier Paese Nuovo.
Tel: 331515
Calvi: SAMU Antenne Médicale.
Tel: 651122.
Corte: Hôpital Civil.

Tel: 450500.
Sartäne: Hôpital Cacciabello.
Tel: 779500.
In case of poisoning: Centre Anti-Poison, Marseille,
Tel: 0491 752525.

The addresses of chemists' open for emergency service nights and weekends (*Pharmacie d'urgence*) are posted in chemist shop windows. You can also find out the address of the chemist's nearest you which is open by calling telephone information (tel: 12), or the police.

Some chemists' in Ajaccio Bastia remain open until 8pm each day during the summer tourist season.

Business Hours

Business hours in France are fairly flexible. **Shops** in Corsican cities and small towns are generally open from 9am–noon and again from 3–7pm including Saturdays.
Supermarkets open at 8.30am and close at 7pm. In peak season they remain open even during lunch time. Many shops located in **tourist areas** are also open on Sunday, at least until noon. Fashion boutiques often stay open until midnight.
Banks normally conduct business from 8.45 to 11.45am and from 2 to 5pm Monday to Friday.

Tipping

A service charge is usually included in hotel and restaurant prices (*Service compris*). It is customary for satisfied guests to leave an additional tip amounting to about 10 percent of the total bill. Taxi drivers and tourist guides also expect tips of around 10 percent.

Religion

Although Corsicans are mostly Catholic, pre-Christian elements surface in local customs and celebrations. Christian festivals are often lavishly celebrated. In Cargèse, where the descendants of 17th-century Greek immigrants live, the congregation is Greek Orthodox.

Media

PRINT

There are two daily papers in Corsica: the *Corse Matin* and *La Corse*. Both are Corsican editions of newspapers published on the French mainland (*Nice Matin* and *Le Provençal*, respectively). There are purely Corsican weekly and monthly magazines, too. All of them, dailies and periodicals, have some articles written in Corsican.

RADIO

In addition to the national French stations there are several local and regional ones. However, these can only usually be received in the areas around Ajaccio and Bastia. They are for the most part music programmes punctuated by often interminably long chat shows, as are common in France.

TELEVISION

The six French television networks are part privately and part publicly operated. FR3 is a regional programme for Corsica. On the east coast Italian television stations can be received and if you have a satellite dish in your baggage, you can count on good reception for broadcasts directed towards southern Europe and north Africa.

Postal Services

Post offices in villages close at noon. Those in cities and beach-resorts remain open from 9am–6pm. Postcards and letters weighing up to 20 grams destined for other EU countries are treated as domestic mail. Stamps may be purchased in the *Bureaux de Tabac* as well as in post offices.

Telecoms

The French telephone network is extremely modern and since a ten-digit code has been introduced there are no longer connection problems between the island and the mainland or other countries. All numbers start with 0 when calling from within France.

Calling from abroad: First dial the international code (00 from the UK), followed by 33 for France and then, skipping the 0, start with 495 for Corsica, and the remaining digits.

From within France: For telephone connections within France start with the dialling code 0495.

On the island: There are a large number of telephone booths on the island, some even in small mountain villages. But only a few accept coins (50 centimes, 1, 2 or 5 francs). If you don't have a Télécard which you can buy in post offices and tobacco shops, there are telephones in bars and other public places under the sign of 'Point Phone', which still take coins.

Calling abroad: First dial the international access code 00, then the national code (44 for the UK, 61 for Australia, 1 for the US and Canada).

Call collect: Dial 0 800 99 (free of charge) and then the national code to get in touch with an operator:
UK: 0044 (BT)
Canada: 0016
United States: 0011 (ATT).
   In most kiosks you can also receive a call; you will find the number of that particular telephone posted on the information board inside the kiosk.

Fax: There are public telefax machines (*Publifax*) for sending faxes at all larger post offices.

Tourist Offices

Information on Corsica can be obtained at the French tourist information offices outside France, at the Agence du Tourisme de la Corse (ATC) in Ajaccio and at local tourist information centres situated throughout the island.

● **Corsica**
Agence du Tourisme de la Corse: Tel: 517777.
Ajaccio: Place du Marché, Tel: 515303.
Bastia: Tel: 0495 559696.
Bonifacio: Place de l'Europe, Tel: 731188.
Calvi: Tel: 651667.
Saint-Florent: Tel: 370604.

● **Outside Corsica**
UK: Maison de la France, Tel: 0142 967000.
London: French Government Tourist Office, 178 Piccadilly, London W1V 9DB. Tel: 0891 244123.
Eire: Dublin: French Tourist Office,

c/o CIE Tours International, 35 Lower Abbey Road, Dublin, Eire. Tel: 1-703 4046.
USA: (Maison de la France/French Government Tourist Office):
New York: 610 Fifth Avenue, Suite 222, New York, NY 10020-2452. Tel: (212) 757 1125;
Los Angeles: 9454 Wiltshire Boulevard, Beverley Hills, Los Angeles, CA 90212-2967. Tel: (213) 272 2661;
Chicago: 645 North Michigan Avenue, Suite 630, Chicago, IL 60611-2836. Tel: 337 6301;
Dallas: Cedar Maple Plaza, 2305 Cedar Springs Road, Suite 205, Dallas, Texas 75201. Tel: (214) 720 4010.
Canada: Montreal: 1981 McGill College, Tour Esso, Suite 490, Montreal H3A 2W9, Quebec. Tel: (514) 288 4264;
Toronto: Suite 2405, 1 Dundas Street West, Toronto M5G IZ3 Ontario. Tel: (416) 593 4723.

Embassies & Consulates

The nearest consular services are in Paris.
Australian Embassy
Tel: 0140 593300 (information)
Tel: 0140 593306 (visa).
British Embassy
Tel: 0144 513100/01
Canadian Embassy
Tel: 0144 432900
Irish Embassy
12 Avenue Foch, 75116 Paris
Tel: (16) 4059 3310
US Embassy
Tel: 0143 122347 (information)
Tel: 0836 701488 (visa)

Getting Around

Public Transport

FLIGHTS WITHIN CORSICA

There are five airports on the island. Ajaccio (Campo dell'Oro), Bastia (Poretta), Calvi (Sainte Catherine) are the larger ones, and there are also airports at Figari and Propriano. The airlines operating regular flights from these airports are as follows:

Air France and **Compagnie Corse Méditerranée,** central reservations, Tel 0 802 802 802.
Compagnie Corse Air International (Nouvelles Frontières), Tel 0 803 333 333
Kyrnair, serving Ajaccio and Bastia from Toulon, Tel: 0495 235685,
Air Littoral connecting Bordeaux/Nantes via Montpellier with Ajaccio and Bastia, Tel: 0 803 834 834.

Airline offices in Corsica:
Air France
3, Boulevard Roi Jérome, 20 000 Ajaccio and 6, Avenue Emile Sari, 20 200 Bastia
(use central number, 0 802 802 802).
Compagnie Aérienne Corse Méditerranée (CCM)
Aéroport Campo dell'Oro, Ajaccio Tel: 290500.
Nouvelles Frontières
12, Place Foch, 20 000 Ajaccio Tel: 215555, and
33 bis, rue César Campinchi, 20 200 Bastia
Tel: 320515.

BY BUS
With the exception of those operating along a few major traffic routes, bus connections in Corsica are not particularly good. For the most part there are several buses a day which travel along the major roads between the larger settlements and Ajaccio, Bastia and Corte. Buses destined for smaller towns and the more remote valleys run just once a day or even only a few times a week. Frequently they don't return to town until the following day.

Bus excursions are offered from all holiday centres in Corsica. Visitors who come to the island without their cars can discover some of the most beautiful scenery in Corsica by joining up with one or more of these relatively inexpensive bus tours.

Flight Information

- **Ajaccio** Tel: 235656
- **Bastia** Tel: 545454
- **Calvi** Tel: 658888
- **Figari** Tel: 711010
- **Propriano** Tel: 763115

BY TAXI
In addition to the cabs in the main towns there are also taxis in many smaller towns. For passengers wanting to hire a taxi for a longer journey or excursion, it's best to agree on the price with the driver beforehand.

BY RENTAL CAR
In addition to the large car rental agencies such as Hertz, Avis, Europcar and Interrent, there are local rental companies in many places. During the summer it's a good idea to reserve a car well in advance. It is possible to do this even prior to your expected arrival in Corsica. Local tourist offices can supply you with details. Agencies usually require that you present a credit card as security when renting a car. The minimum age to hire a car is 21.

ON THE ROAD
Despite the fact that some of the major roads in Corsica are relatively new and well maintained, most of the island's roads are narrow and have an abundance of sharp bends. Pot-holes are no rare occurrence either and you should be aware that honking before driving into a blind curve is mandatory. It is quite possible that the road you're on suddenly becomes blocked by a herd of cows or pigs.

When organising a longer journey, plan on a maximum average speed of about 40 kph (25 mph). Filling stations can only be found in larger towns and unleaded petrol (*sans plomb*) is not available everywhere. Drivers of large caravans and trailers should be well-practised in manoeuvring their vehicles in the mountains. Passing places are few and far between.

BY RAILWAY
The Corsican Railway is not only a means of transport but also an experience in itself. The narrow-gauge railway between **Ajaccio** and

Walking Holidays

The fragrance of the *macchia* and the tranquillity of the scenery make hiking in Corsica a truly memorable experience. There are several marked hiking trails on the island (*see* the chapter on the *Hiking Trails* and the accompanying map).

For high mountain tours, such as those to Monte Cinto, mountaineering equipment and a guide are necessary. It's not advisable to set off bushwhacking through the *macchia*. Hikes through the mountains in Corsica lasting from one to several days are offered by various organisations such as **Muntagnoli Corsi**. They can be reached at either 11 blvd Sampiero, F-20188 Ajaccio, tel: 9574 6228; or F-20122 Quenza, tel: 9578 6405.
- **For more information:**
Parc Naturel Régional de la Corse, 4 rue Général Fiorella, BP 417, F-20184 Ajaccio. Tel: 9521 5654.

Bastia with a branch veering off to **Calvi** was built at the end of the last century. The track makes its way straight through Corsica's mountainous region, in part over extremely impressive viaducts. There are several trains a day operating between Ajaccio and Bastia with a connection to Calvi in **Ponte Leccia**. In addition to a few carriages dating back to the 1950s, modern units are also in service.

According to the official railway time-table the trip from Ajaccio to Bastia takes three hours. The track between Calvi and **L'Ile Rousse** runs directly along the beach.

During the summer season there are 30 rail buses travelling this particular stretch. These *Tramway de la Balagne* serve as beach shuttle buses.

Railway Stations

- **Ajaccio** Tel: 231103
- **Bastia** Tel: 328061
- **Calvi** Tel: 650061
- **Corte** Tel: 460097

BOAT TOURS & EXCURSIONS

For those visitors wishing to get to know Corsica by boat, but who do not own their own ocean-going vessel, tour agencies offer a number of opportunities in the form of organised cruises or yacht voyages. Boat excursions present a relatively inexpensive means by which to explore the Corsican coastline. The following trips are possible:

Ajaccio to the Iles Sanguinaires.
Bonifacio to the Grotte du Sdragonato and other caves in the sea cliffs as well as to the islands of Lavezzi, Baïnzo and Cavallo.
Calvi to Girolata and Ajaccio.
Porto to the Calanche of Piana.

BY BICYCLE

Riding a bicycle in Corsica requires above all that you be in good physical shape. Lengthy and steep ascents are no rarity and the tenacious rider will be rewarded with fantastic views and, of course,

a painless descent. Cyclists can experience the varied landscape and vegetation contained in a small area more intensely than car passengers. Traffic is especially light along minor roads in the island's interior. A good map is indispensable for bike touring.

Rental: It is also possible to rent bicycles in Corsica, by the hour, day or week. There are rental agencies for example in Bastia, Porticcio and Saint-Florent.

Where to Stay

Accommodation on the island is limited. During the summertime it is absolutely imperative that you reserve a hotel room or site at a campground in advance. If you decide that you would like to remain in your hotel room or at your campsite longer than originally planned, be sure to tell the reception as early as possible. In the larger tourist centres during the peak season it is practically impossible to extend the length of your stay at short notice. In the tourist areas there are a number of modern and higher-class hotels, whereas small family-run hotels are a more common feature in the interior.

Seasonal opening: There are only a handful of hotels that are open all year round; most are closed from October until April or May. Therefore, if you are planning to visit the island out of season, bear in mind the limited accommodation.

Rates: The rate applies only to the hotel room and does not include breakfast.

Prices: There is no pricing policy for any of the hotels in Corsica, and often the tourist offices themselves do not know what the hotels are charging. In the high season some hotels may charge up to double their low season rates. Others will remain at the same price throughout the year.

Classifications: The *Ministère du Tourisme* classifies the hotels in France using a star system (shown below). Information about the level of comfort that can be expected is posted on a hexagonal board at the entrance to the hotel. Bear in mind that the official classification is largely based on the staff/guest ratio and facilities such as air-con, television, garage, car park or swimming-pool, and does not always correspond to the price range.

Hotels

Ajaccio
Campo dell'Oro ☆☆☆☆
Plage du Ricanto
Tel: 223241
Fax 206021
130 rooms.
Albion ☆☆☆
15, Avenue du Général Leclerc
Tel 216670
Fax: 211755
Characterful, quiet, with a tradition of British customers. Close to the big Napoleon monument at Casone, a few minutes from the town centre.
Fesch ☆☆☆
7 rue du Cardinal Fesch
Tel: 516262
Fax: 218336
Traditional Corsican hotel with old furniture and modern ceramics behind a dull facade in a pedestrianised precinct close to the harbour and market.
Spunta di Mare ☆☆
Quartier Saint Joseph
Tel: 237440
Fax: 208002
61 rooms.

Albertacce
Castel de Vergio ☆
Station de Vergio
Tel: 480001
Fax: 607951
40 rooms.

Algajola
Beau Rivage ☆☆
Tel: 607951
36 rooms.

Asco
Le Chalet ☆
Haut Asco
Tel: 478108
22 rooms.

Aullène
De la Poste ☆
Fax: 786121
20 rooms.

Bastelica
U Castegnettu ☆☆
Tel: 2870721
15 rooms.

Bastia
L'Alivi ☆☆☆
Route du Cap, Palagaccio
Tel: 316185
Fax: 310395
A few minutes north of the town towards Cap Corse. All rooms have a balcony directly overlooking the shore. Open all year.
Ostella ☆☆☆
RN 193 Sud
Tel: 335105
Fax: 331170
30 rooms.
Bonaparte ☆☆
45 Boulevard du Général Graziani
Tel: 340710
Fax: 323562
A few steps from the ferry in the town centre. Open all year.
Posta Vecchia ☆☆
3 rue Posta Vecchia/Quai des Martyrs de la Libération
Tel: 323228
Fax: 321405
The only hotel on the promenade. View of the Tuscan archipelago and close to restaurants. Open all year.

Belgodere
Niobel ☆☆
Tel: 613400
Fax: 613585
12 rooms.

Bonifacio
Genovese ☆☆☆
Quartier de la Citadelle
Tel: 731234
Fax: 730903
Ancient governor's residence high above the harbour. The very best hotel in town. Open all year.
La Caravelle ☆☆☆
Quartier de la Citadelle
Tel: 730003
Fax: 730041
14 rooms.
Roy d'Aragon ☆☆☆
13 Quai Comparetti
Tel: 730399
Fax: 730794
Renovated old house by the yacht harbour. Open all year.

Solemare ☆☆☆
Port de Plaisance
Tel: 730106
55 rooms.
Des Etrangers ☆
Avenue Sylvère-Bohn
Tel: 730109
Fax: 731697
Simple accommodation, under the white cliffs at the entrance to the town. Open April to November.

Calacuccia
Les Touristes ☆☆
Tel: 480004
50 rooms.

Calcatoggia
Castel d'Orcino ☆☆☆
Tel/Fax: 522238
35 rooms.
Le Grand Bleu ☆☆
Tel: 522035
Fax: 522539
212 rooms.
Les Sables de la Liscia ☆☆
Route de Sagione
Tel: 525150
Fax: 522612
40 rooms.

Calvi
La Villa ☆☆☆☆
Chemin de Notre-Dame-de-la-Serra
Tel: 651010
Fax: 651050
On the hillside overlooking Calvi and its gulf. One of the best addresses on the island. Swimming pool. Open April to October.
Balanea ☆☆☆
6, rue Clémenceau.
Tel: 659494.
Fax: 652971.
On the port, overlooking the citadel, beach and mountains. Open all year.
La Caravelle ☆☆
La Plage
Tel: 650121
34 rooms.
Saint-François ☆☆
Pointe St-François
Tel: 650361
Fax: 653320
This residence-hotel with mini apartments is situated on a rock opposite the citadel. Swimming pool. Open April to October.

Cargèse

Bel Mare ☆
Tel: 26401
Fax: 264824
Old-time charm with a restaurant on street level and a fantastic view over the coast. The simple rooms are on the cliff underneath the terrace. Open March to November.
La Spelunca ☆☆
Tel: 264012
20 rooms.
Helios ☆☆
Route de Sagone
Tel: 264124
Fax: 264719
A few hundred metres outside the village, hidden in the greenery. Small apartment-like rooms. Good atmosphere. Pool. Open all year.

Centuri-Port

Le Centuri ☆
Tel: 356170
Fax: 356420
Not the cosiest hotel in this picturesque fishing village but the best place for a wide view of it. Open Easter to October.

Hotel Prices

☆ The star rating applied to hotels here reflects their category and not their price. Hotel prices vary enormously, and often even the tourist offices don't know what hotels are charging.
  Some hotels have markedly different prices between high and low season. Others keep their prices the same.

Corte

Auberge de la Restonica ☆☆
Route de la Restonica
Tel: 460958
Fax: 610391
Only a minute by car from the centre of town but already you find yourself in the wilderness of the Restonica valley. Typical Corsican ambience. Open all year.
Sampiero Corso ☆☆
Avenue Président Pierucci
Tel: 460976
31 rooms.

Evisa

L'Altone ☆☆
Rue Principale
Tel: 962004
32 rooms.

Ferayola

Auberge de Ferayola ☆☆
Tel: 652525
10 rooms.

Galeria

Cinque Arcate ☆☆
Tel: 620254
25 rooms.

Ghisoni

Kyrie ☆
Tel: 576033
30 rooms.

L'Ile Rousse

La Pietra ☆☆☆
Le Port
Tel: 600145
Fax: 601592
On the narrow isthmus between the beach resort and the red rocks with a lighthouse and a Genoan tower. Great view. Open April to October.
L'Amiral ☆☆
Boulevard de la Mer
Tel: 602805
Fax: 603121
Modern building on the beach close to cafes. Open April to September.
Le Vieux Moulin ☆☆
Route de Monticello
Tel: 601689
37 rooms.

Macinaggio

U Libecciu ☆☆
Tel: 354322
33 rooms.

Moriani-Plage

Le Corsica ☆☆
Tel: 385143
14 rooms.
Monte Cristo ☆
Tel: 385143
90 rooms.

Patrimonio

L'Albinu ☆☆
Embranchement du Cap Corse
Tel: 370769
9 rooms.

Piana

Capo Rosso ☆☆☆☆
Tel: 278240
Fax: 278000
57 rooms.
Les Calanches ☆☆
Tel: 278208
17 rooms.
Les Roches Rouges ☆☆
Tel: 278181
Fax: 278319
One of the first hotels ever built on the west coast. It has all the charm of the beginning of the century and the most splendid view on the Gulf of Porto and the famous *calanche*. April to October.

Piedicroce

Le Refuge ☆
Tel: 358265
Fax: 358442
20 rooms.

Pietrapola-les-Bains

Les Thermes ☆☆
Tel: 567003
Fax: 567520
35 rooms.

Pinarellu

La Tour Génoise ☆☆☆
Road from Santa-Lucia-di-Porto-Vecchio
Tel: 714439
A beach hotel situated on the intimate Gulf of Pinarellu, lying opposite an island which has an old watch tower. Open from June to September.

Ponte Leccia

Les Touristes ☆
Tel: 476111
This hotel lies at the crossroads between Bastioa, Calvi and Ajaccio and is a good stop if it is getting late. Quiet terrace. Open April to October.

Porticcio

Le Maquis ☆☆☆☆
Tel: 250555
Fax: 251170
30 rooms.
Agosta Plage ☆☆
Tel: 254026
30 rooms.

Les Flots Bleus ☆☆
Les Marines d'Agosta
Tel: 254957
Fax: 255457
33 rooms.

Porto
Les Flots Bleus ☆☆
Tel: 2611126
Fax: 261264
In the marina with a view of the coast and the famous Genoan tower. Open April to September.
Kallisté ☆☆☆
Tel: 261030
Fax: 261275
53 rooms.
Cala di Sole ☆☆
Tel: 261244
18 rooms.
Corsica ☆☆
Tel: 261089
Fax: 261388
Lying in the valley of the Porto river among eucalyptus trees, this is a quiet spot. Open May to October.
Idéal ☆☆
Tel: 261007
22 rooms.

Porto Pollo
Les Eucalyptus ☆☆
Tel: 740152
Fax: 740656

Porto-Vecchio
Belvédère ☆☆☆
Route de Palombaggia
Tel: 705413
Fax: 704263
Like a Pacific island village on the southern shore of the Gulf. with its own private beach. Open from April to October.
Cala Verde ☆☆☆
Route de Marina di Fiori
Tel: 701155
40 rooms.
Grand Hotel Cala Rossa ☆☆☆
Tel: 717878
Fax: 716011
Luxury in a very Mediterranean way, with a private beach, at the northern shore of the Gulf of Porto-Vecchio. The restaurant is by far the best on the island. Open April to October.
Holzer ☆☆
Tel: 0495 700593

My House is Your House
Under the name 'Casa Toia', which is the Corsican for 'Your house', a dozen typical country hotels offer more than a good value stay. Included in the itinerary are various organised activities such as hiking, biking, riding, fishing, hunting, skiing, para-gliding and canoeing. They send customers on their own *route des auberges* around the island, recommending other hotels, restaurants, farm-bistros and wine-cellars which they know personally. There are hotel members in Martino-di-Lota, Belgodère, Monticello, Pioggiola, Corte, Serriera, Evisa, Bastelica, Alata, Quenza and Sant'Amanza.

● **Information, reservations:**
Auberge d'Aghjola, Joseph Albertini, F-20259 Pioggiola.
Tel: 619048.
Fax: 619299.

Fax: 704782
27 rooms.
Le Mistral ☆☆
Tel: 700853
Fax: 705160
21 rooms.
La Rivière ☆☆
Route de Muratellu
Tel: 701021
Fax: 705613
An oasis in the near hinterland, between rocks, palm trees and cork oaks. In early summer there are lotts of nightingales. Swimming pool, tennis. Open April to October.

Propriano
Grand Hotel Miramar ☆☆☆☆
Route de la Corniche
Tel: 760613
Fax: 761314
On the hillside overlooking the Gulf. Another 'Grand' with a southern touch. Excellent restaurant close to the swiming pool. Open May to October.
Roc e Mare ☆☆☆
Tel: 760485
Fax: 761755
62 rooms.
Arena Bianca ☆☆
Chemin des Plages
Tel: 760601
Fax: 761212
Le Lido Beach ☆☆
Tel: 761774
Fax: 760654
17 rooms.
Loft Hotel ☆☆
3, rue Jean-Paul Pandolifi
Tel: 761748
Fax: 762204
A wine store transformed into a

cool, functional hotel, in US-roadside style. Close to the harbour. Quiet, Open all year.

Quenza
Sole e Monti ☆☆
Tel: 786253
Fax: 786388
20 rooms.

Sagone
Cyrnos ☆☆☆
Tel: 280001
24 rooms.
U Libbiu ☆☆☆
Riniccio
Tel: 280606
Fax: 280623
22 rooms.
A Rena d'Oro ☆☆
Esigna
Tel: 280009
Fax: 280702
60 rooms.

Saint-Florent
Bellevue ☆☆☆
Route de Patrimonio
Tel: 370006
Fax: 371483
A hotel that lives up to its name – the view over the Gulf and Cap Corse is beautiful. There are blue-white accents from the facade to the bedrooms. Very good restaurant. Mostly Parisian *chic* clientèle. Open April to October.
Auberge Europe ☆☆
Tel: 370033
Fax: 371736
Old Corsican house near the port and the *boule* games. Open all year.

Santa Maria ☆☆
Cisternino
Tel: 370444
34 rooms.

Saint-Pierre-de-Venaco
Le Petit Bosquet ☆
Tel: 470011
Fax: 470642
40 rooms.

San-Martino-di-Lota
De la Corniche ☆☆
Tel: 314098
Fax: 323769
16 rooms.

Hotel Prices

☆ The star rating applied to hotels here reflects their category and not their price. Hotel prices vary enormously, and often even the tourist offices don't know what hotels are charging.

Some hotels have markedly different prices between high and low season. Others keep their prices the same.

Santa-Reparata-di-Balagna
La Santa ☆☆
Tel: 600473
Fax: 604947
16 rooms.

Sartène
La Roches ☆☆
Tel: 770761
71 rooms.
Villa Piana ☆☆
Route de Propriano
Tel:770704
Fax: 734565
Not in the most Corsican of towns, but it nevertheless looks very beautiful. Open April to September.

Serriera
L'Aiglon ☆☆
Plage de Bussaglia
Tel: 261065
Fax: 261477
18 rooms.

Sisco
U Pozzu ☆☆
Marine de Sisco
Tel: 352117
14 rooms.

Soccia
U Paese ☆☆
Tel: 283192
33 rooms.

Solenzara
Maquis et Mer ☆☆☆
Tel: 574237
46 rooms.
La Solrenzara ☆☆
Tel 574218
Fax: 574684
A sort of country manor between the road and the sea. Open all year.

Sotta
Mondolino ☆☆
Tel: 712098
Fax: 712285
22 rooms.

Speloncato
A Spelunca ☆☆
Tel: 615038
In an ancient cardinal's palace in one of the most beautiful hilltop villages. Swallows nest above the windows. Open June to September.

Tiuccia
Cinarca ☆☆☆
Tel: 522139
46 rooms.
Roc e Mare ☆☆
Tel: 522386
24 rooms.

Venaco
Paesotel E Caselle ☆☆☆
La Vallon
Tel: 470201
Fax: 470665
A whole village built out of large pebbles from the nearby mountain river. Open May to October.

Vezzani
U Sambucco ☆
Tel: 440338
11 rooms.

Vico
U Paradisu ☆
Tel: 266162
Fax: 266701
21 rooms.

Vizzavona
Monte d'Oro ☆
Col de Vizzavona.
Tel: 472106
Fax: 472205
59 rooms.

Zicavo
Du Tourisme ☆
Tel: 244006
15 rooms.

Zonza
L'Incudine ☆☆
Tel: 786771
Traditionally built out of square stones, in a mountain village close to the rock needles of Bavella. Open Easter to October.

Campsites

Ajaccio: Barbicaja.
Tel: 520117.
Adumbratu: Caravan and Mobile Home Rental
Tel: 528839.
Aleria: Marina d'Aleria
Tel: 570142.
Algajola: De la Plage
Tel: 607176;
Cala di Sole
Tel: 607398.
Appietto: Apietto: De Lava
Tel: 100484.
Argentella: La Morsetta
Tel: 652528.
Asco: Monte Cinto
Tel:478448.
Bastia: San Damiano
Tel: 336802.
Les Sables Rouges:
Tel: 333608.
Biguglia: San Damiano
Tel: 336802.
Borgo: Esperanza
Tel: 361509.
Bonifacio: U Farniente
Tel: 730547;
Des Iles
Tel: 731189;
Campo di Liccia
Tel: 730309.

Calcatoggio: La Liscia
Tel: 522065.
Calvi: Bella Vista
Tel: 651176;
Clos du Mouflon
Tel: 650353;
Paduella
Tel: 650616.
Cargèse: Torracia
Tel: 264239.
Corbara: Le Bodri
Tel: 601086.
Corte: Tuani
Tel: 461165.
Coti-Chiavari: La Vallée
Tel: 254466.
Evisa: L'Acciola
Tel: 262301.
Galeria: Les deux Torrents
Tel: 620067.
Ghisoaccia: Arinella Bianca
Tel: 560478.
L'Ile ousse: L'Orniccio
Tel: 601732.
Lecci-de-Porto-Vecchio: Mura
dell'Onda
Tel: 716164.
Lopigna: De Truggia
Tel: 289479.
Lozari: Clos des Chênes
Tel: 601513.
Lozzi: U Monte Cintu
Tel: 480445.
Lumio: Monte Ortu
Tel: 607393.
Macinaggio: De la Plage
Tel: 354376.
Moltifa: A Tizzarella
Tel: 478392.
Moriani-Plage: Merendella
Tel: 385347.
Morsiglia: L'Isulottu
Tel: 356281.
Oletta: La Pinède

Tel: 370726.
Imeto-Plage: L'Esplanade
Tel: 76503;
Vigna Maiore
Tel: 760207.
Osani: E Gradelle
Tel: 273201.
Palasca: L'Ostriconi
Tel: 601005.
Patrimonio: A Stella
Tel: 301437.
Pietrosella: De l'Europe
Tel: 251930.
Ponte Leccia: De Griggione
Tel: 476525.
Porticcio: Mare e Macchia
Tel: 251058.
Porto: Les Oliviers
Tel: 261449;
Sole e vista
Tel: 261571.
Porto Pollo: U Caseddu
Tel: 740180.
Porto Vecchio: U Stabiaccu
Tel: 703717;
La Matonara
Tel: 703705.
Propriano: Colomba
Tel: 760642;
Tikiti
Tel: 760832.
Pruno Casetta: Les Cascades
Tel: 369191.
Quenza: I Muntagnoli Corsi
Tel: 786405.
Sagone: U Mintrastettu
Tel: 280415.
Saint-Florent: Kalliste
Tel: 370308;
Acqua Dolce
Tel: 370863.
Ste-Lucie-de Moriani: U Ponticchiu
Tel: 385779.
Ste-Lucie-de-Porto Vecchio:

Bon'Anno
Tel: 732135;
California
Tel: 714924.
Santo-Pietro-di-Tenda: U Paradisu
Tel: 378251.
Serriera: Le Bussaglia
Tel: 261572.
Sisco: A Casaiola
Tel: 352150.
Solaro: Les Eucalyptus
Tel: 577743.
Solenzara: Des Nacres
Tel: 574065.
Trinité-de-Porto-Vecchio: Golfo di
Sogno
Tel: 700898;
Les Ilots d'Or
Tel: 700130.
Ucciani: Les Eaux Vives
Tel: 528109.
Vico: La Sposata
Tel: 266155.

Camping Guide

There are 116 campsites in Corsica and they are subject to similar classification as hotels. All of them have to meet certain minimum standards. Campground facilities can be classified in general from satisfactory to good. Towards the end of the season, however, signs of exhaustion in the campsite personnel can sometimes be detected. With a few exceptions, campsites are situated on the coast, frequently even directly on the beach. Because they are even more dependent on the season than the hotels are, most are only open from May until the end of September.

Campers must stay only on camp grounds. Wild camping is prohibited and the law is vigilantly enforced.

Where to Eat

The fine art of French cooking has not been able to make many inroads into the typically hearty Corsican cuisine. Regional specialities show similarities with Italian cuisine and there are also North African influences. Along the coast you will find many seafood restaurants, whereas in the interior pork and game are more likely to appear on the menu.

Native Corsicans rarely visit the big restaurants in tourist centres. Instead, they prefer the smaller, frequently inconspicuous restaurants where the regional dishes are authentic.

Most restaurants offer several multi-course set menus for various prices at both lunch and dinner. Such a meal usually consists of at least three or four courses with a choice of main course, and can be an economical way of eating.

Restaurants

You're most likely to find good regional cuisine at pleasant prices in the small, inconspicuous eateries where the restaurant owners themselves do the cooking and serving. Restaurants in tourist areas often have mixed fortunes from one year to another, depending on the chef who has been hired for the season. While the culinary disaster of the preceding year may turn out to be a fantastic tip the following season, the exact opposite is also just as possible. The following restaurants are perennially popular:

Ajaccio
L'Amore Piattu, 8 Place Général de Gaulle. Corsican and international cuisine, a lovely terrace.

Da Mamma, Rue Fesch/ Passage de la Guingettea. A cosy, friendly local restaurant with lots of atmosphere.
France, 59 Rue Fesch. Corsican and international cuisine.
Petit St Germain, 10 Rue Maréchal d'Ornano. International and French cuisine.

Bastelicaccia
Auberge Seta. Typical Corsican dishes, especially game.

Bastelica
Chez Paul. Corsican dishes are served up in a homely atmosphere.

Bastia
La Brocherie, Vieux Port. Fish specialities. The restaurant is done out to look like an old ship inside.
La Citadelle, 6 Rue Dragon. French cuisine and tasty fish specialities.

Bonifacio
Le Voilier, marina. Fish specialities.

Calvi
L'Abri Cotier and **Comme Chez Soi** are both located at the harbour, so it is not surprising that they serve delicious fish specialities.
Cesario, Maison Bertoni. Corsican and international cuisine; the fish dishes are particularly good.

Cauro
Napoléon. Corsican specialities.

What to Drink

Water: Corsican spring water, such as Aqua Corsa, St-Georges and Zilia, has quite a pleasant taste. It is also an ingredient in a number of bottled soft drinks.
Beer: Pietra is a tasty Corsican beer based on chestnuts. French brands come from northern France and Alsace. Beers from Belgium, Holland and Denmark are popular, and German beer can also frequently be found at tourist centres.
Wine: Corsicans themselves primarily drink wine. Red, rosé and white wines are produced on the

Col de Bavella
Auberge du Col de Bavella. Game specialities and Corsican regional cooking; beautiful view of the Bavella peaks from the terrace.

Corte
A Scudella, Cours Paoli/near the Paoli monument. Homey decor. Grilled dishes are prepared at an open fireplace.

L'Ile Rousse
Le Laetitia, at the harbour. Fish specialities.

Reading the Menu

To decipher what's on the menu, turn to Eating Out in the Language section on page 284–8

Patrimonio
Osteria di San Martino. Corsican and Italian specialities.

Petreto-Bicchisano
France. Corsican and international cuisine.

Porto
Le Romantique. Fish specialities and Corsican game dishes.

Porto Vecchio
Roches Blanches, at the marina.
Lucullus, Rue Général de Gaulle. French and Corsican specialities.

island as well as natural sweet Muscat and Rappo. There are eight high-quality districts. Dry and sweet whites are a speciality of Cap Corse; around Patrimonio you will find excellent white, rosé, red and Muscat wines; the wine from the Ajaccio region is mostly red and rather powerful; from the Sartenais in the southern part of the island (Figari, Pianottoli) there are pleasant white, red and rosé wines. Good wine is made along the east coast where some of the grapes are mechanically harvested.

Propriano
Lido, at the harbour. Fish specialities.
La Rascasse, Rue Pêcheurs. Excellent fish dishes.

Saint-Florent
A Lumaga, at the harbour. Above all, delicious fish dishes.

Sartène
La Chaumière, 39 Rue Capitaine Benedetti. Rustic decor, Corsican cuisine.

Vero-La Vignole
Auberge Mamy. Regional Corsican cuisine, game dishes.

Attractions

Museums

Museums in Corsica mainly have collections of archaeology (early history) and regional history, culture and ethnography.

There are two collections of paintings, Fesa in Ajaccio and FRAC in Corte.

Ajaccio
Musée Napoléonien
The Napoleon Museum, dedicated to the island's most famous son, is in the city hall at Place Foch.
Maison Bonaparte
Rue Saint-Charles.
The house where Napoleon was born.
Musée Fesch
Rue Fesch, next to the Chapelle Impériale.
Painting collection.
Musée du Capitellu
18 bd D. Casanova
Private collection of 18th- and 19th-century paintings, sculpture and furniture from Ajaccio.
Musée a Bandera
1 Rue Général Levie.
Corsican military history.
Les Minelli
Country residence of the Bonaparte family; crafts museum, exhibitions. Take the D6 from Ajaccio and follow the signs.

Aleria
Musée Jerôme Carcopino
in Fort Matra.
Etruscan, Greek and Roman excavations.

Bastia
Musée D'Ethnographie Corse
in the governor's palace on the citadel.
Corsican cultural and military history.

Cervione
Musée de Cervione
Ethnography, religious art.

Filitosa
Musée archeologique
Archeological museum.

Morosaglia
Musée departemental
The house where Pasquale Paoli was born and is buried.

Levie
Musée departemental
Archeological museum.

Sartène
Musée de préhistoire corse et sites archéologiques
Archeological museum in the former prison.

Concerts

During the month of August organ concerts are regularly scheduled and performed in the parish church at La Porta.

Cinema

There are cinemas in Ajaccio, Bastia, Calvi, Corte, Ghisonaccia, L'Ile Rousse, Porticcio, Porto Vecchio and Prunelli-di-Fiumorbo. However, only the cinemas in Ajaccio and Bastia offer a sophisticated programme. The films are usually dubbed in French.

Nightlife

Corsica is not exactly a night owl's paradise. Nightlife at holiday resort areas is modest and consists mainly of a few loud and expensive discos which only run at full power in the peak tourist season. In Ajaccio and Bastia nightlife options are more promising and correspond to what you would find in a French provincial town.

Pubs in which you can listen to folk guitar music are called *Cabaret Corse*. One is the Son des Guitares in the Rue du Roi-de-Rome, Ajaccio. Corsica's only gambling **casino** is also in Ajaccio.

Traditional Music

Various groups keep the tradition of Corsican music alive. But there is a difference between the folkloric guitar music presented in 'Cabarets Corses' and the soul-stirring recitals of plain '*lamenti*' or the '*paghjelle*' for several voices. This purely vocal music seemed forgotten at the end of the seventies but it has had a renaissance since becoming part of the 'Corsitude', the awareness of a Corsican identity.

The most famous groups are A Filetta, Canta, Caramusa, E Voce di u Cumune, I Chiami Aghjalese, I Muvrini, Les Nouvelles Polyphonies Corses, Orizonte and Estudiantina Ajaccina. The most outstanding singers are Antoine Ciosi, Petru Guelfucci, Jacky Micaelli, Jean Paul Poletti, Patricia Gattaceca and Patricia Poli.

Events

The most important events in Corsica are part of the Christian calendar, and local events often have a religious character, too. But there are many other entertainments to look out for.

The 'Merendella in Castagniccia', the first of a number of **agricultural fairs**, takes place at Easter in the village of Piedicroce. Two more take place in May, at Ucciani in the Gravona valley, and in Venaco where the Fiera di u Casgiu specialises in Corsican cheese. A **wine fair** takes place at the beginning of June at Luri on the Cap Corse.

Musical events are more recently introduced entertainments. International singers are invited to 'Festivoce' in the Balagne village of Pigna in the first half of June. In the second half of the month a jazz festival is held between the citadel and the sea in Calvi. At the same time noted musicians perform at the 'Nights of the guitar' in Patrimonio. Midsummer is celebrated with fireworks at several places, and Bastia holds the 'Allegria of St-Jean' with street-

theatre and concerts. 'Settembrinu di Tavagna' is a music festival which unites five villages of the Castagniccia in September, around the same time that the citadel of Calvi becomes the scene of 'Les Rencontres Polyphoniques', a meeting of international *a-capella* groups. At the end of October Bastia presents the 'Musicales', with concerts and ballets

There are also a number of **historical pageants** and events. On the second Saturday of June Bastia commemorates the arrival of the Genoese Governor in an historical spectacle. On the first weekend in August the 'Fetes Napoléoniennes' in Ajaccio celebrate the birthday of the emperor with parades, spectacles and ceremonies

Contemporary art is on show in June in the village of Oletta under the motto of 'Parcours du regard'.

Other colourful fairs to look out for are 'Foire di a Bocca di u Pratu' at the Castagniccia pass on the first weekend in August, and the illumination of the village of Nonza at Cap Corse in the middle of August when various cultural events take place. A **Mediterranean Film Festival** is held in Bastia at the ends of November.

Shopping

What to Buy

Most items are more expensive due to transport costs, and the selection in boutiques and other shops is neither especially original nor exclusive. There are duty-free shops on ferries sailing from Italy where you can stock up primarily on cigarettes, drink and perfume.

Corsican products: typical locally made items include ceramic items, baskets, wood carvings, jewellery and woven goods such as table-cloths. Modern Corsican arts and crafts are clearly showing a renaissance of traditional, local patterns. Because of this development, products often have a rather local character. Corsican artists and craftspeople are united in CORSICADA. This organisation operates a number of its own shops called Case di l'Artigiani. In these stores you are guaranteed the products are truly Corsican. **Case di l'Artigiani** can be found in Ajaccio, Bastia, Bonifacio, Cargèse, Corte, Evisa, Murato, Pigna, Sartène and Zonza. Independent craftspeople have their own shops at work on the island.

Wine: Before buying Corsican wine to bring back home with you, consider the fact that even the high-quality wines bearing the phrase *Appelation d'Origine Controlée* (AOC) generally don't take very well to travelling.

Sport

Golf

There is an attractive 18-hole golf course laid out amidst the *macchia* near Bonifacio (Golf Spèrone). There are nine-hole golf courses at Lucciana near Busha, and at Spanu near Lumio and in the Regino valley near Mounticello (both of which are in the Balagne).

Horse Riding

Corsica offers excellent opportunities for a real riding holiday. Horseback riding fans can join up with guided several-day trips straight through virgin island landscapes. There are riding centres in Ajaccio, Bastia, Borgo, Bravone, Calvi, La Porta, L'Ile Rousse, Moriani, Oletta, Porticcio, Porto Vecchio, Propriano, Sagone, Sartène, Venaco and Viggianello.

Sporting Events

With the exception of soccer matches there are few organised sporting events held on the island.

The following annual events can be worth watching:
- **April** The Canoe-Kayak rendezvous with white-water competitions. The Tours de Corse Automobile, with contestants roaring all over the island.
- **May** The big sailing regattas off the island are: Virée Corse in Calvi and the Troffeo Vela d'Oro in Bastia. The boats competing in the Mediterranean Trophy put into Corsica as well as into Sardinia.

Mountain Climbing

Those wanting to attack Corsican peaks with ropes and pitons can either consult pertinent travel guide literature published in their own country or obtain information from: Comité Départemental Randonnée Montagne de Corse du Sud, Mr. Paul Borelli, lieu-dit Colombina, 20129 Bastelicaccia, Tel: 200043, and Comité Départemental de Haute Corse, Mr. Acquaviva, Route de Cuccia, 20224 Calacuccia. Tel: 480522.

Tennis

There are public tennis courts in Ajaccio, Bastelicaccia, Bonifacio, Borgo, Calvi, Porticcio, Propriano, Sagone, and Solaro. Nearly all the larger hotels as well as the more modern campgrounds and holiday villages have their own tennis courts.

Watersports

You can participate in nearly all watersport activities in Corsica. There are several well-developed marinas with good facilities around the island, a number of smaller harbours and, of course, secluded bays with romantic spots to anchor in. You'll find sailing schools at all larger bathing areas.

The rugged west coast is above all popular with scuba divers. There are diving schools and refill services for oxygen tanks at almost all larger bathing beaches. Corsican rivers present the opportunity to go white-water canoeing as well as river-rafting (the latter in the springtime when the winter snows thaw).

Fishing is permitted in all the island's lakes and rivers, provided that you have a valid fishing licence. Licences can be obtained from local fishing associations.

Hang-gliding

Hang-gliding and paragliding are popular. Courses are offered by about a dozen organisations.

Information from:
Ligue Corse de Vol Libre
lieu-dit A Pianella
20224 Calacuccia
Tel: 480443
Altore
Route de la Cathédrale
20217 Saint-Florent
Tel: 371930.

Language

The official language on the island is French but Corsicans also speak their own native tongue, which is both a spoken and written language in its own right. It is a blend of Latin with some Italian and a little bit of French thrown in. Other ancient, scarcely traceable sources include Iberian. Corsican is similar to Latin with Tuscan influences in the north, a touch of Ligurian and Sardinian in the south and a few loanwords from French all over the island. In the 16th century the first attempt to write the language was made by an Italian monk who thought it should be treated as an Italian dialect. This error is the cause of much difficulty in the continuing attempt to preserve the language. A number of spellings have had to be translated back from Italian into Corsican.

Until recently the language was transmitted only orally in a variety of local dialects. Now there is a universally valid French-Corsican dictionary, elaborated by courses at the university in Corte. A whole post-war generation was not allowed to speak Corsican in school, but now there are lessons on an optional basis. A number of Italian spellings have been re-translated into Corsican. Signposts have double names: Ajaccio/Aiacciu, Corte/Corti, Monticello/Munticellu, Sartène/Sartè and Cargèse/Carghjese.

Visitors will find French, which all the islanders speak, more useful. A list of helpful French terms follows.

Words & Phrases

How much is it? *C'est combien?*
What is your name?
Comment vous appelez-vous?
My name is... *Je m'appelle...*

Do you speak English? *Parlez-vous anglais?*
I am English/American *Je suis anglais/américain*
I don't understand *Je ne comprends pas*
Please speak more slowly *Parlez plus lentement, s'il vous plaît*
Can you help me? *Pouvez-vous m'aider?*
I'm looking for... *e cherche*
Where is...? *Où est...?*
I'm sorry *Excusez-moi/ Pardon*
I don't know *Je ne sais pas*
No problem *Pas de problème*
Have a good day! *Bonne journée!*
That's it *C'est ça*
Here it is *Voici*
There it is *Voilà*
Let's go *On y va. Allons-y*
See you tomorrow *A demain*
See you soon *A bientôt*
Show me the word in the book *Montrez-moi le mot dans le livre*
please *s'il vous plaît*
thank you *merci*
(very much) *(beaucoup)*
you're welcome *de rien*
excuse me *excusez-moi*
hello *bonjour*
OK *d'accord*
goodbye *au revoir*
good evening *bonsoir*
here *ici*
there *là*
today *aujourd'hui*
yesterday *hier*
tomorrow *demain*
now *maintenant*
later *plus tard*
this morning *ce matin*
this afternoon *cet après-midi*
this evening *ce soir*

On Arrival

I want to get off at... *Je voudrais descendre à...*
Is there a bus to the Louvre? *Est-ce qui'il ya un bus pour le Louvre?*
What street is this? *A quelle rue sommes-nous?*
Which line do I take for...? *Quelle ligne dois-je prendre pour...?*
How far is...? *A quelle distance se trouve...?*

Validate your ticket *Compostez votre billet*

airport *l'aéroport*
la douane *customs*
train station *la gare*
bus station *la gare routière*
bus *l'autobus, le car*
bus stop *l'arrêt*
platform *le quai*
ticket *le billet*
return ticket *aller-retour*
hitchhiking *l'autostop*
toilets *les toilettes*
This is the hotel address *C'est l'adresse de l'hôtel*
I'd like a (single/double) room... *Je voudrais une chambre (pour une/deux personnes)...*
...with shower *avec douche*
...with a bath *avec salle de bain*
...with a view *avec vue*
Does that include breakfast? *Le prix comprend-il le petit déjeuner?*
May I see the room? *Je peux voir la chambre?*
washbasin *le lavabo*
bed *le lit*
key *la cléf*
elevator *l'ascenseur*
air conditioned *climatisé*

On the Road

Where is the spare wheel? *Où est la roue de secours?*
Where is the nearest garage? *Où est le garage le plus proche?*
Our car has broken down *Notre voiture est en panne*
I want to have my car repaired *Je veux faire réparer ma voiture*
It's not your right of way *Vous n'avez pas la priorité*
I think I must have put diesel in the car by mistake *Je crois que j'ai mis du gasoil dans la voiture par erreur*
the road to... *la route pour...*
left *gauche*
right *droite*
straight on *tout droit*

Time

At what time? *A quelle heure?*
When? *Quand?*
What time is it? *Quelle heure est-il?*
● *Note that the French generally use the 24-hour clock.*

far *loin*
near *près d'ici*
opposite *en face*
beside *à côté de*
car park *parking*
over there *là-bas*
at the end *au bout*
on foot *à pied*
by car *en voiture*
town map *le plan*
road map *la carte*
street *la rue*
square *la place*
give way *céder le passage*
dead end *impasse*
no parking *stationnement interdit*
motorway *l'autoroute*
toll *le péage*
speed limit *la limitation de vitesse*
petrol *l'essence*
unleaded *sans plomb*
diesel *le gasoil*
water/oil *l'eau/l'huile*
puncture *un pneu de crevé*
bulb *l'ampoule*
wipers *les essuies-glace*

Shopping

Where is the nearest bank (post office)? *Où est la banque/Poste/PTT la plus proche?*
I'd like to buy *Je voudrais acheter*
How much is it? *C'est combien?*
Do you take credit cards? *Est-ce que vous acceptez les cartes de crédit?*
I'm just looking *Je regarde seulement*
Have you got...? *Avez-vous...?*
I'll take it *Je le prends*
I'll take this one/that one *Je prends celui-ci/celui-là*
What size is it? *C'est de quelle taille?*
Anything else? *Avec ça?*
size (clothes) *la taille*
size (shoes) *la pointure*
cheap *bon marché*
expensive *cher*
enough *assez*
too much *trop*
a piece *un morceau de*
each *la pièce (eg ananas, 15F la pièce)*
bill *la note*
chemist *la pharmacie*
bakery *la boulangerie*
bookshop *la librairie*

library *la bibliothèque*
department store *le grand magasin*
delicatessen *la charcuterie/le traiteur*
fishmonger's *la poissonerie*
grocery *l'alimentation/l'épicerie*
tobacconist *tabac (can also sell stamps and newspapers)*
markets *le marché*
supermarket *le supermarché*
junk shop *la brocante*

Sightseeing

town *la ville*
old town *la vieille ville*
abbey *l'abbaye*
cathedral *la cathédrale*
church *l'église*
keep *le donjon*
mansion *l'hôtel*
hospital *l'hôpital*
town hall *l'hôtel de ville/la mairie*
nave *la nef*
stained glass *le vitrail*
staircase *l'escalier*
tower *la tour (La Tour Eiffel)*
walk *le tour*
country house/castle *le château*
Gothic *gothique*
Roman *romain*
Romanesque *roman*
museum *la musée*
art gallery *la galerie*
exhibition *l'exposition*
tourist information office *l'office de tourisme/le syndicat d'initiative*
free *gratuit*
open *ouvert*
closed *fermé*
every day *tous les jours*
all year *toute l'année*
all day *toute la journée*
swimming pool *la piscine*
to book *réserver*

Dining Out

Table d'hôte (the "host's table") is one set menu served at a set price. **Prix fixe** is a fixed price menu. **A la carte** means dishes from the menu are charged separately.

I am a vegetarian *Je suis végétarien*
I am on a diet *Je suis au régime*

False Friends

False friends are words that look like English words but mean something different.
le car motorcoach, also railway carriage
le conducteur bus driver
la monnaie change (coins)
l'argent money/silver
ça marche can sometimes mean walk, but is usually used to mean working (the TV, the car etc.) or going well
actuel "present time" *(la situation actuelle* the present situation)
rester to stay
location hiring/renting
personne person or nobody, according to context
le médecin doctor

What do you recommend? *Que'est-ce que vous recommandez?*
Do you have local specialities? *Avez-vous des spécialités locales?*
I'd like to order *Je voudrais commander*
That is not what I ordered *Ce n'est pas ce que j'ai commandé*
Is service included? *Est-ce que le service est compris?*
May I have more wine? *Encore du vin, s'il vous plaît?*
Enjoy your meal *Bon appétit!*

breakfast *le petit déjeuner*
lunch *le déjeuner*
dinner *le dîner*
meal *le repas*
first course *l'entrée/les hors d'oeuvre*
main course *le plat principal*
made to order *sur commande*
drink included *boisson compris*
wine list *la carte des vins*
the bill *l'addition*
fork *la fourchette*
knife *le couteau*
spoon *la cuillère*
plate *l'assiette*
glass *le verre*
napkin *la serviette*
ashtray *le cendrier*

Breakfast and Snacks
baguette **long thin loaf**

The Alphabet

Learning the pronunciation of the French alphabet is a good idea. In particular, learn how to spell out your name.

a=ah, b=bay, c=say, d=day e=er, f=ef, g=zhay, h=ash. i=ee, j=zhee, k=ka, l=el, m=em, n =en, o=oh, p=pay, q=kew, r=ehr, s=ess, t=tay, u=ew, v=vay, w=dooblah vay, x-=eex, y ee grek, z=zed

pain **bread**
petits pains **rolls**
beurre **butter**
poivre **pepper**
sel **salt**
sucre **sugar**
confiture **jam**
oeufs **eggs**
...à la coque **boiled eggs**
...au bacon **bacon and eggs**
...au jambon **ham and eggs**
...sur le plat **fried eggs**
...brouillés **scrambled eggs**
tartine **bread with butter**
yaourt **yoghurt**
crêpe **pancake**
croque-monsieur **ham and cheese toasted sandwich**
croque-madame **with a fried egg on top**
galette **type of pancake**
pan bagna **bread roll stuffed with salad Niçoise**
quiche **tart of eggs and cream with various fillings**
quiche lorraine **quiche with bacon**

First course

An amuse-bouche, amuse-gueule or appetizer is something to "amuse the mouth", served before the first course
anchoiade **sauce of olive oil, anchovies and garlic, served with raw vegetables**
assiette anglaise **cold meats**
potage **soup**
rillettes **rich fatty paste of shredded duck, rabbit or pork**
tapenade **spread of olives and anchovies**
pissaladière **Provençal pizza with onions, olives and anchovies**

Meat and Fish

La Viande **Meat**
bleu **rare**
à point **medium**
bien cuit **well done**
grillé **grilled**
agneau **lamb**
andouille/andouillette **tripe sausage**
bifteck **steak**
boudin **sausage**
boudin noir **black pudding**
boudin blanc **white pudding (chicken or veal)**
blanquette **stew of veal, lamb or chicken with a creamy egg sauce**
boeuf à la mode **beef in red wine with carrots, mushroom and onions**
à la bordelaise **beef with red wine and shallots**
à la **cooked in red**
Bourguignonne **wine, onions and mushrooms**
brochette **kebab**
caille **quail**
canard **duck**
carbonnade **casserole of beef, beer and onions**
carré d'agneau **rack of lamb**
cassoulet **stew of beans, sausages, pork and duck, from southwest France**
cervelle **brains (food)**
chateaubriand **thick steak**
choucroute **Alsace dish of sauerkraut, bacon and sausages**
confit **duck or goose preserved in its own fat**
contre-filet **cut of sirloin steak**
coq au vin **chicken in red wine**
côte d'agneau **lamb chop**
daube **beef stew with red wine, onions and tomatoes**
dinde **turkey**
entrecôte **beef rib steak**
escargot **snail**
faisan **pheasant**
farci **stuffed**
faux-filet **sirloin**
feuilleté **puff pastry**
foie **liver**
foie de veau **calf's liver**
foie gras **goose or duck liver pâté**
gardiane **rich beef stew with olives and garlic, from the Camargue**
cuisses de grenouille **frog's legs**
grillade **grilled meat**
hachis **minced meat**
jambon **ham**

lapin **rabbit**
lardon **small pieces of bacon, often added to salads**
magret de canard **breast of duck**
médaillon **round meat**
moelle **beef bone marrow**
mouton navarin **stew of lamb with onions, carrots and turnips**
oie **goose**
perdrix **partridge**
petit-gris **small snail**
pieds de cochon **pig's trotters**
pintade **guinea fowl**
Pipérade **Basque dish of eggs, ham, peppers, onion**
porc **pork**
pot-au-feu **casserole of beef and vegetables**
poulet **chicken**
poussin **young chicken**
rognons **kidneys**
rôti **roast**
sanglier **wild boar**
saucisse **fresh sausage**
saucisson **salami**
veau **veal**

Poissons Fish

Armoricaine **made with white wine, tomatoes, butter and cognac**
anchois **anchovies**
anguille **eel**
bar (or loup) **sea bass**
barbue **brill**
belon **Brittany oyster**
bigorneau **sea snail**
Bercy **sauce of fish stock, butter,**

Emergencies

Help! Au secours!
Stop! Arrêtez!
Call a doctor
Appelez un médecin
Call an ambulance Appelez une ambulance
Call the police Appelez la police
Call the fire brigade
Appelez les pompiers
Where is the nearest telephone?
Où est le téléphone le plus proche?
Where is the nearest hospital?
Où est l'hôpital le plus proche?
I am sick Je suis malade
I have lost my passport/purse
J'ai perdu mon passeport/porte-monnaie

Basic Rules

Even if you speak no French at all, it is worth trying to master a few simple phrases. The fact that you have made an effort is likely to get you a better response. More and more French people like practising their English on visitors, especially waiters in the cafés and restaurants and the younger generation. Pronunciation is the key; they really will not understand if you get it very wrong. Remember to **emphasise each syllable**, but not to pronounce the last consonant of a word as a rule (this includes the plural "s") and

always to drop your "h"s. Whether to use **"vous"** or **"tu"** is a vexed question; increasingly the familiar form of "tu" is used by many people. However it is better to be too formal, and use "vous" if in doubt. It is very important to be polite; always address people as **Madame** or **Monsieur**, and address them by their surnames until you are confident first names are acceptable. When entering a shop always say, "Bonjour Monsieur/ Madame," and "Merci, au revoir," when leaving.

white wine and shallots
bouillabaisse **fish soup, served with grated cheese, garlic croutons and** *rouille,* **a spicy sauce**
brandade **salt cod purée**
cabillaud **cod**
calmars **squid**
colin **hake**
coquillage **shellfish**
coquilles Saint-Jacques **scallops**
crevette **shrimp**
daurade **sea bream**
flétan **halibut**
fruits de mer **seafood**
hareng **herring**
homard **lobster**
huître **oyster**
langoustine **large prawn**
limande **lemon sole**
lotte **monkfish**
morue **salt cod**
moule **mussel**
moules **mussels in white marinières wine and onions**
oursin **sea urchin**
raie **skate**
saumon **salmon**
thon **tuna**
truite **trout**

Légumes Vegetables
ail **garlic**
artichaut **artichoke**
asperge **asparagus**
aubergine **eggplant**
avocat **avocado**
bolets **boletus mushrooms**
céleri **grated celery**
rémoulade **with mayonnaise**

champignon **mushroom**
cèpes **boletus mushroom**
chanterelle **wild mushroom**
cornichon **gherkin**
courgette **zucchini**
chips **potato crisps**
chou **cabbage**
chou-fleur **cauliflower**
concombre **cucumber**
cru **raw**
crudités **raw vegetables**
épinard **spinach**
frites **chips, French fries**
gratin dauphinois **sliced potatoes baked with cream**
haricot **dried bean**
haricots verts **green beans**
lentilles **lentils**
maïs **corn**
mange-tout **snow pea**
mesclun **mixed leaf salad**
navet **turnip**
noix **nut, walnut**
noisette **hazelnut**

oignon **onion**
panais **parsnip**
persil **parsley**
pignon **pine nut**
poireau **leek**
pois **pea**
poivron **bell pepper**
pomme de terre **potato**
radis **radis**
roquette **arugula, rocket**
ratatouille **Provençal vegetable stew of aubergines, courgettes, tomatoes, peppers and olive oil**
riz **rice**
salade Niçoise **egg, tuna, olives, onions and tomato salad**
salade verte **green salad**
truffe **truffle**

Fruits Fruit
ananas **pineapple**
cavaillon **fragrant sweet melon**
cerise **cherry**
citron **lemon**
citron vert **lime**
figue **fig**
fraise **strawberry**
framboise **raspberry**
groseille **redcurrant**
mangue **mango**
mirabelle **yellow plum**
pamplemousse **grapefruit**
pêche **peach**
poire **pear**
pomme **apple**
raisin **grape**
prune **plum**

Sauces Sauces
aioli **garlic mayonnaise**
béarnaise **sauce of egg, butter, wine and herbs**
forestière **with mushrooms and bacon**

Numbers

0 *zéro*	11 *onze*	30 *trente*
1 *un, une*	12 *douze*	40 *quarante*
2 *deux*	13 *treize*	50 *cinquante*
3 *trois*	14 *quatorze*	60 *soixante*
4 *quatre*	15 *quinze*	70 *soixante-dix*
5 *cinq*	16 *seize*	80 *quatre-vingts*
6 *six*	17 *dix-sept*	90 *quatre-vingt-dix*
7 *sept*	18 *dix-huit*	100 *cent*
8 *huit*	19 *dix-neuf*	1000 *mille*
9 *neuf*	20 *vingt*	1,000,000 *un million*
10 *dix*	21 *vingt-et-un*	

● The number 1 is often written like an upside down V, and the number 7 is crossed.

hollandaise **egg, butter and lemon sauce**
lyonnaise **with onions**
meunière **fried fish with butter, lemon and parsley sauce**
meurette **red wine sauce**
Mornay **sauce of cream, egg and cheese**
Parmentier **served with potatoes...**
paysan **rustic style**
pistou **Provençal sauce of basil, garlic and olive oil; vegetable soup with the sauce.**
provençale **sauce of tomatoes, garlic and olive oil.**
papillotte **cooked in paper**

Puddings Dessert
Belle Hélène **fruit with ice cream and chocolate sauce**
clafoutis **baked pudding of batter and cherries**
coulis **purée of fruit or vegetables**
gâteau **cake**
île flottante **whisked egg whites in custard sauce**
crème anglaise **custard**
pêche melba **peaches with ice cream and raspberry sauce**
tarte tatin **upside down tart of caramelised apples**
crème caramel **caramelised egg**

On the Telephone

How do I make an outside call?
Comment est-ce que je peux téléphoner à l'exterieur?
I want to make an international (local) call
Je voudrais une communication pour l'étranger (une communication locale)
What is the dialling code? *Quel est l'indicatif?*
I'd like an alarm call for 8 tomorrow morning.
Je voudrais être réveillé à huit heures demain martin
Who's calling?
C'est qui à l'appareil?
Hold on, please
Ne quittez pas s'il vous plaît
The line is busy
La ligne est occupée
I must have dialled the wrong number
J'ai dû faire un faux numéro

Non, Non, Garçon

Garçon is the word for waiter but is never used directly; say *Monsieur* or *Madame* to attract his attention.

custard
crème Chantilly **whipped cream**
fromage **cheese**
chèvre **goat's cheese**

In the Café

If you sit at the bar (*le zinc*), drinks will be somewhat cheaper than if you sit at a table. Settle the bill when you leave; the waiter may leave a slip of paper on the table to keep track of the bill. A tip of 10 percent is customary. The French enjoy bittersweet aperitifs, which are often diluted with ice and fizzy water.

drinks *les boissons*
coffee *café*
...with milk or cream *...au lait or crème*
...decaffeinated *déca/décaféiné*
...black/espresso *express/noir*
...American filtered coffee *filtre*
tea *thé*
...herb infusion *tisane*
...camomile *verveine*
hot chocolate *chocolat chaud*
milk *lait*
mineral water *eau minérale*
fizzy *gazeux*
non-fizzy *non-gazeux*
fizzy lemonade *limonade*
fresh lemon juice served with sugar *citron pressé*
fresh squeezed orange juice *orange pressé*
full (eg full cream milk) *entier*
fresh or cold *frais, fraîche*
beer *bière*
...bottled *en bouteille*
...on tap *à la pression*
pre-dinner drink *apéritif*
white wine with cassis, black-currant liqueur *kir*
***kir* with champagne** *kir royale*
with ice *avec des glaçons*
neat *sec*
red *rouge*
white *blanc*
rose *rosé*

dry *brut*
sweet *doux*
sparkling wine *crémant*
house wine *vin de maison*
local wine *vin de pays*
Where is this *De quelle région*
wine from? *vient ce vin?*
pitcher *carafe/pichet*
...of water/wine *...d'eau/de vin*
half litre *demi-carafe*
quarter litre *quart*
mixed *panaché*
after dinner drink *digestif*
brandy from Armagnac region of France *Armagnac*
Normandy apple brandy *calvados*

cheers! *santé!*
hangover *gueule de bois*

Days and Months

Days of the week, seasons and months are not capitalised in French.

● **Days of the week**
  Monday *lundi*
  Tuesday *mardi*
  Wednesday *mercredi*
  Thursday *jeudi*
  Friday *vendredi*
  Saturday *samedi*
  Sunday *dimanche*
● **Seasons**
  spring *le printemps*
  summer *l'été*
  autumn *l'automne*
  winter *l'hiver*
● **Months**
  January *janvier*
  February *février*
  March *mars*
  April *avril*
  May *mai*
  June *juin*
  July *juillet*
  August *août*
  September *septembre*
  October *octobre*
  November *novembre*
  December *décembre*
● **Saying the date**
  20th October 1999, *le vingt octobre, dix-neuf cent quatre-vingt-dix-neuf*

Further Reading

General

An Account of Corsica, by James Boswell (contained in *Boswell on the Grand Tour*). Yale Editions, New York and Londo288n, 1955. Descriptions of his journey around the island and visit to Pasquale Paoli.

Columba, by Prosper Mérimée. Paris 1840. Based on the story of the *vendetta* that took place in the village of Fozzano in the Sartenais in 1833.

Corse Romane, by Geneviève Moracchini-Mazel. Paris 1972. Includes English translation to text describing this illustrated guide to the island's romanesque churches.

Corsica: Columbus's Isle, by Joseph Chiari. London 1960. Delves into the possibilities of Columbus actually having been born in Calvi.

The Dream-Hunters of Corsica, by Dorothy Carrington. Weidenfeld and Nicholson, London, 1995. An excellent study of the folk customs of the island by one of the island's distinguished residents.

Granite Island: a Portrait of Corsica, by Dorothy Carrington. Penguin paperback, New York and London, 1984.

Journal of a Landscape Painter in Corsica, by Edward Lear. London 1870. Through both his engravings and his writings, Lear was one of the first to portray the splendours of Corsica to the outside world.

The Life and Letters of Sir Gilbert Elliot, by Emma Eleanor Elliot. London 1874. Compiled by the grand-daughter of this aristocratic Scot, who as the Viceroy from 1794–96 acquired a genuine love of the island.

His Majesty of Corsica, by Valerie Pirie. London 1939). Biography of Theodor von Neuhof (King Theodore).

Napoleon and his Parents on the Threshold of History, by Dorothy Carrington. London, 1987.

Pasquale Paoli: an Enlightened Hero, by Peter Adam Thresher. London 1970. The most authoritative work on the island's greatest hero.

The Summer King, by Aylmer Vallance. London 1956. Another account of the fortunes of the Westphalian nobleman who wanted to rule Corsica.

The Scented Isle: a parallel between Corsica and the Scottish Highlands, by Joseph Chiari. Glasgow 1945. Comparing Corsica with his native country.

Other Insight Guides

The Insight Guide series covers nearly 200 destinations. These are among the titles on Mediterranean hot spots.

Insight Guide: France. Europe's most diverse nation is captured in 408 full-colour pages. And it's further explored in the Insight Guides to **Alsace, Brittany, Burgundy, The French Riviera, Normandy, Paris, Provence** and **The Loire Valley**.

Insight Guide: Sardinia is another of Insight's island guides. Other Mediterranean island titles cover **Crete, The Greek Islands, Cyprus, Malta** and **Sicily**.

In Insight's companion *Compact Guide* series, handy-sized books designed as mini-encyclopedias for instant on-the-spot reference, current titles include **Malta, The Greek Islands, Tuscany, Paris** and **Rome**.

The *Insight Pocket Guide* series is written by local hosts. The books, many with full-size fold-out maps, take you on specially worked-out tours which help to make the most of a visit when time is limited. Current titles include **The Aegean Islands, Corsica, Ibiza, Mallorca, Malta, Rhodes, Sardinia** and **Sicily**.

ART & PHOTO CREDITS

INSIGHT GUIDE CORSICA

Cartographic Editor **Zoë Goodwin**
Production **Stuart A Everitt**
Design Consultants
Carlotta Junger, Graham Mitchener
Picture Research **Hilary Genin**

Index